Mississippi River Improvement Convention

Official Report of the Proceedings of the Mississippi River Improvement Convention

Held in Saint Louis, Missouri, on October 26th, 27th and 28th, 1881

Mississippi River Improvement Convention

Official Report of the Proceedings of the Mississippi River Improvement Convention
Held in Saint Louis, Missouri, on October 26th, 27th and 28th, 1881

ISBN/EAN: 9783744716512

Printed in Europe, USA, Canada, Australia, Japan

Cover: Foto ©ninafisch / pixelio.de

More available books at **www.hansebooks.com**

OFFICIAL REPORT

OF THE

PROCEEDINGS

OF THE

Mississippi River Improvement Convention

HELD IN

SAINT LOUIS, MISSOURI,

ON

OCTOBER 26TH, 27TH AND 28TH, 1881,

INCLUDING

LETTERS FROM DISTINGUISHED MEN THROUGHOUT THE COUNTRY, AND PRESS COMMENTS.

TOGETHER WITH A

MEMORIAL TO CONGRESS

PREPARED BY THE COMMITTEE OF TWENTY-ONE, AS AUTHORIZED BY THE CONVENTION.

SAINT LOUIS:
GREAT WESTERN PRINTING COMPANY,
1881.

PREFACE.

There is presented in this little book a record of the most important River Convention ever held in the Mississippi Valley — a Convention composed of delegates from nearly every section of the Union, who represented every variety of industrial interests, and fairly reflected the matured opinions of the people upon the important question of river improvement as the chief adjunct to cheap transportation. The Convention met to carry out a well-defined purpose, as set forth in the "Official Call," and the unanimity of its action, as expressed in the resolutions unanimously adopted, after a full and free discussion, was a marked feature of its deliberations. Representatives of twenty States and three Territories declared, "as with one voice," that the imperative duty of our National Legislature was to bestow such aid for the improvement of the Mississippi, and its navigable tributaries, as the demands of an ever-increasing commerce required, according to the judgment and plans of the River Commission, and United States Engineers, in charge of the works. The attempt has been made to record accurately what was said and done at the meetings. In a few instances, the names of delegates addressing the Chairman have necessarily been omitted. The request was distinctly made, that persons on rising should first give their names; but, in some cases, this request was not heeded, and in place of the name, the compiler has been forced to use the word "delegate." The speeches have been carefully revised, in order to give the exact words of those addressing the Convention; and it is hoped and believed that the compilation will be adopted as, in the main, full and accurate in detail.

REPORT OF THE PROCEEDINGS

OF THE

Mississippi River Improvement Convention.

SECTION 1—FIRST DAY.

St. Louis, October 26, 1881.

The Convention was called to order by Mr. Michael McEnnis, President of the Merchants' Exchange, who said:

"GENTLEMEN: With your permission, I will ask Mr. George L. Wright to read the official call under which we have met here to-day."

Mr. George L. Wright then read the official call, as follows:

"The Merchants' Exchange of St. Louis, through the undersigned, its Executive Committee, duly appointed, hereby issues a call to the people of the Mississippi Valley for the selection of delegates to a Convention to be held in their city on the 26th day of October, 1881, to deliberate on the question of improving the great Mississippi river and its navigable tributaries. The call is made in pursuance of a general desire, communicated through the press, emanating from various commercial bodies recognizing the importance of united and intelligent action on a subject of the most vital importance, and fixing upon St. Louis, the central city of the Valley, as the proper place for holding the Convention.

"The rapid growth and settlement of the Mississippi Valley, and with it the development and enlargement of the export trade,—a trade made up in largely controlling proportions of its products,—has forced upon the thought of the country the question of cheap transportation. All the later commercial and trade experiences have demonstrated that only by the cheap water route can this question be so placed, as in its resultant influences to represent and embrace fair profit to the farmer, the manufacturer and merchant, the classes through which all others become participants in the profits of industry.

"The necessity of improving these navigable streams, and the correlative duty of the General Government to give its aid as to a great national work, is derived from a consideration of their functions in the commerce and trade of the country. Within the area of States and Territories drained by the Mississippi and its navigable tributaries are produced 90 per cent. of the corn, 73 per cent. of the wheat, 83 per cent. of the oats, 64 per cent. of the tobacco, 77 per cent. of the cotton, and 66 per cent. of the value of the live hogs of the whole country. In addition to the vast supply of food and textile products, the abundance of coal, iron and timber mark it as the seat of manufacturing industries, the great and unquestioned source of American production and national revenue.

"Even in the present imperfect condition of navigation one-seventh of the amount of this vast production which enters into the export trade of the country goes to the ocean by way of the Mississippi river at a cost of less than one-third at which it can be carried by any other route.

"When it is remembered that this region has in the later years furnished to the markets of the world the products which have changed the balances of trade in our favor and made us among kindred commercial races the creditor instead of the debtor nation, the necessity for united and intelligent work on the part of its people, and of liberal and comprehensive action on the part of the national legislature in the improvement of these water-ways, becomes too apparent for argument.

"With channels made equal to the demands of trade, from the highest point of navigation in these great national arteries to the Gulf, maintained throughout the year in successful competition with the trunk lines of railroad, the question of cheap transportation—the supreme question of the hour, the foundation to all future prosperity—is settled, and the country will enter upon a new career of progress.

"We may regard with some satisfaction what has been accomplished in reducing the cost of transportation, yet what has been witnessed is but a tithe of what may be anticipated in the future, when the river system, under wise method and liberal appropriations, is placed as its matchless value deserves, as its power of development demands.

"With even more satisfaction may we regard the advanced thought which now requires that the improvement of the great river shall stand as a national work, on its own merits, and unconnected with any other subject or object of appropriation. [Loud applause.]

"In view of the magnitude of the interests involved and the results to be obtained, we cordially and earnestly invite the various boards of trade of the Valley so largely interested in these results, as well as those from communities outside the Valley who appreciate the scope of the Convention, to send delegates fully penetrated with the necessity of action, and with ability to represent the great interests at stake.

"The Convention will be composed of delegates from the States and Territories in the Mississippi Valley, Governors being hereby authorized and requested to appoint ten from each State and five from each Territory.

"From each board of trade or cotton exchange two delegates for each 100 members, said bodies to be entitled to at least two delegates.

"From corporate cities of the Mississippi Valley where no

boards or exchanges exist, two delegates from each, to be appointed by the mayor of each city.

"The President and Vice-President of the United States, members of the Cabinet, Senators and Representatives in Congress, and Governors of States and Territories, will be invited as guests of the Convention and assigned seats on the floor during its deliberations.

"[Signed] MICHAEL McENNIS, *President*.
" JOHN JACKSON, E. O. STANARD,
" JOHN A. SCUDDER, H. C. HAARSTICK,
" FRANK GAIENNIE, E. W. GOULD,
" HENRY HITCHCOCK, JOHN T. DAVIS,
" HENRY LOUREY, NATHAN COLE,
" C. F. ORTHWEIN, R. J. LACKLAND,
" CHARLES PARSONS, E. C. SIMMONS,
" A. H. SMITH.

"FRANK GAIENNIE,
"*Secretary*.
" GEORGE L. WRIGHT,
"*Corresponding Secretary*."

At the conclusion of the reading of the call Mr. McEnnis then addressed the Convention as follows:

GENTLEMEN: As chairman of the Executive Committee, appointed by the Merchants' Exchange of St. Louis, under whose authority this call has been issued, it devolves upon me to call this Convention to order.

The language of the call sufficiently explains the objects and aims of the Convention. It is strange that at this late day there should be a necessity for calling the people of this valley together to urge upon Congress its duty and obligation to enact measures for the improvement of the Mississippi and its navigable tributaries. The people of the United States are famous for their public spirit and enterprise. Every subject involving the interest or happiness of the people has received due attention, except alone the question that has brought us together. I mean the improvement of our great waterways. What causes this indifference to a question so vital to the prosperity of the people? Are we ignorant of their value, or can we dispense with them? No; we have frittered away much time and money over small schemes and purely local questions. It is time we stopped and altered our course. This valley of ours includes eighteen States and three Territories.

It is capable of producing sufficient to feed, clothe and house the world. It now contains one-half the population of the United States, and could sustain ten times as many. It now yields a surplus of production that has turned the balance of trade in our favor and made us the creditor instead of the debtor nation. Its products will soon enable us to control the financial destiny of the world, and we will reap the rich harvest always within the grasp of a people so highly favored. But we must do our duty. This duty is plain and imperative. We must go before Congress with such overwhelming proofs of the necessity of improving these rivers, by deepening their channels, removing obstructions, and giving us a free outlet to the sea, that our petitions (I would rather say demands) will meet with immediate and favorable consideration. The Government engineers have completed their surveys. Their recommendations have been approved and adopted by Congress and the War Department. A commission has been appointed and is now at work within the scanty limits of the appropriations,—and doing good work. The time has now arrived when we, the people of the Mississippi Valley, must unite and insist that these improvements shall be pushed forward with vigor, and that sufficient money shall be appropriated to permit work to be inaugurated at all necessary points at one and the same time. [Applause.] We should not tolerate any more ten or twenty-year delays. We want a systematic, far-seeing, statesmanlike management of this great work. The labor and cost of properly improving these streams would not be one-fourth that necessary for the building of the railroad to the Pacific. Look at the difference from the standpoint of national advantage. The one was a private enterprise, upheld by the credit of the Government, the other is a great public undertaking, designed for the good of all, and destined to repay every cent of the cost in a few years in the increasing revenues to the Government and in the enhanced value of the products that would float down on the waters to the sea. Have these watery highways improved and this vast valley will sing with the song of happy millions bound together by a common bond of interest.

We purpose, with your help, gentlemen, to make this Convention the dawn of a new era in the commercial history of this valley. We do not intend to permit the actions of this Convention to be pigeon-holed or buried in a committee at Washington. [Loud applause.] We will compile and print the correspondence, discussions and acts of this Convention, with statistical information that will sustain and justify an agitation that shall not cease until justice is done this valley [renewed applause] and our local representatives are brought to a vivid realization of the fact that they must protect the interests of their constituents or go back to that private life which men lacking the ability or the foresight to discern and execute the will of their constituents deserve.

These are my individual sentiments, and in them I think the sentiments of the Merchants' Exchange are reflected.

To you, gentlemen, we surrender the further consideration of this subject. You bring to its elucidation the lessons of political economy and experience. May your deliberations be guided by wisdom and crowned by success. [Loud applause.]

At the conclusion of the above address Mr. McEnnis said:

"Gentlemen, the Executive Committee has requested Hon. Henry Hitchcock to deliver the address of welcome. Mr. Hitchcock will now address you."

Mr. Hitchcock then came forward amid applause and addressed the Convention as follows:

GENTLEMEN OF THE CONVENTION: In behalf of the Merchants' Exchange of St. Louis, at whose call you have assembled, I am requested to greet you upon the threshold of your deliberations.

In their behalf, as the organized representatives of the mercantile interests of this city, itself the commercial and manufacturing center of this great valley, I have the honor and the great happiness to offer a cordial welcome to you who come accredited to represent the productive industry and the commercial enterprise of the millions who inhabit it. And I beg to assure you, gentlemen, that however earnest that welcome, it must be an inadequate expression alike of the heartfelt good-will with which all classes of their fellow-citizens welcome your advent, and of the deep interest which they feel in the vitally important subject you have assembled to consider.

That subject, gentlemen, has already been announced in the call just read in your hearing, and in response to which this large and distinguished assemblage has met. In a word, it is the question of improving the Mississippi river and its navigable tributaries. It is the question of cheap transportation,—to us Western men, as that call so well and earnestly declares, "the supreme question of the hour." [Applause.]

It is not needful, if it were indeed appropriate at this moment, that I detain you by dwelling in detail upon the wonderful resources and the still more marvelous possibilities of this imperial valley. Its star of empire already shines brightly far above the horizon. Already the wise men of the East have turned towards it their inquiring and not unanxious gaze. [Loud applause.] And if, with the modesty characteristic of Americans, and, above all, of Western men [laughter], we concede that this new empire is yet in its infancy, we are reminded, if I may use the well-worn figure, of the infancy of Hercules, who smilingly strangled in his cradle the Python who came to destroy him.

These, gentlemen, are figures of speech. More prosaic, but far more eloquent, are those figures of the statistician, some of which are given in the call for this assemblage. You were reminded by those figures of the enormous contributions of this valley to the sustenance not only of this nation, but of the civilized world. It tells you what percentage of the vast product of this nation, in grain, in tobacco and in cotton came from the teeming fields of the Mississippi Valley. But the percentage is only one factor in that great sum. May I ask your attention for a moment to the other factor, which discloses the significance of that percentage? When we are told from official data that within the area of States and Territories drained by the Mississippi and its navigable tributaries has been harvested ninety per cent. of the corn produced by the whole country in one year,—that means, gentlemen, ninety per cent. of one billion five hundred and forty-seven million (1,547,901,000) of bushels of Indian corn, which is the official statement of the total production of that grain in the United States for 1879. When we are told that this valley has produced seventy-three per cent. of the wheat of the whole country,—it is that proportion of four hundred and forty-eight millions (448,000,000) of bushels, produced in 1879. Eighty-three per cent. of the oat crop of the country means eighty-three per cent. of three hundred and sixty-three millions (363,761,000) of bushels. Seventy-seven per cent. of the cotton means seventy-seven per cent. of 2,367,540,900 pounds, —say 4,700,000 bales,—and so for the rest. These figures relate to nineteen States which are drained by the rivers of this valley. The percentage is but little less if it be confined to the fourteen States, which are the "Valley States" proper. Enormous as are these results, they cease to be surprising when we consider or attempt to consider and realize what the area of that valley is. Referring again to official statistics, and particularly a tabular statement compiled, I believe, by Professor Von Steinwehr, in connection with the census of 1870, it appears that the whole country may be properly divided, with reference to the distribution of its water-courses, into four great drainage systems. These were styled respectively the Atlantic Coast System, the Pacific Coast System, the Northern Lake System, and the Mississippi Valley System, and the area of the district included in each system was carefully compiled. That of the Atlantic Coast System is 204,538 square miles; that of the Pacific Coast System, 834,314 square miles; of the Northern Lake System, 185,337 square miles,—these three systems together aggregating something over 1,344,000 square miles of area. But the area of the Mississippi Valley System is 1,683,303 square miles [applause], the excess alone of the last-named system, over all the rest combined, being 338,000 square miles; and that excess itself being many thousand square miles greater than the entire area of the Atlantic Coast System, and nearly double the area of the one designated as the Northern Lake System.

But, gentlemen, after all these figures are stated, who does, who can, in truth, realize their significance? The astronomers used to tell us,—at least I was so taught when I was a boy,—that the sun was 96,000,000 of miles distant from the earth. Of late years, I believe, their calculations have been revised and the distance is now stated at ninety-seven and a half or ninety-eight millions. But mathematicians also tell us that for practical purposes it makes no great difference which is correct; for, it is said, the human being does not live who has ever been able to form a really correct conception of *one million* of anything. Gentlemen, the significance of these figures is not found merely in piling up these statistics, however large they sound or however striking an impression they produce, unless we look behind them at what they truly mean. I shall not detain you by enlarging upon that meaning. You do not need from me even the suggestion that these millions upon millions of bushels of the staple products which sustain human life, harvested in a single year upon more than a million and a half of square miles, not yet densely populated by twenty-five millions of people, mean human prosperity, human comfort, human freedom. They signify and demonstrate the welfare of thousands, of hundreds of thousands of peaceful and happy families. They mean that faithful and intelligent labor is reaping its just reward, under equal institutions; that more and more are being thrown off the burdens which have weighed down humanity in the ages that are past, and the nobler energies of the soul set free from the sordid cares and anxieties which attend merely physical wants, to pursue a still higher flight in its immortal career. [Loud applause.]

May I ask your attention, however, gentlemen, for a few moments to some thoughts connected more immediately with the objects of this Convention. May I ask you to consider with me, retrospectively, the growth of the public sentiment which finds its latest expression in this large and important Convention,—the largest and most representative, and, as we have every reason to hope, likely to be the most influential, of the many that have assembled.

I need not remind you that this is by no means the first inter-State convention which has assembled to consider this great subject. For more than a generation past such bodies have met at various points in the great Valley, and during the last few years with increasing frequency, and, if possible, more and more pronounced earnestness of purpose. Along the whole length of the great river, from St. Paul on the north, to New Orleans on the south, such assemblies have met from time to time, representing alike the productive and the commercial and manufacturing interests of the Valley, to take into consideration this same question of the improvement of its river navigation and cheaper transportation to be gained thereby, and to urge upon Congress the prosecution of these public works, which have been, and which are, and which will continue to be rightfully demanded, until due and regular and permanent provision shall have been made for their complete execution and their permanent maintenance. [Applause.]

There was recently republished in this city the record of the first convention of this character—the first inter-State convention, so far as I know, and I think there is no doubt that it was such—which to any extent considered this great question. It met in the city of Memphis as long ago as 1845. It assembled first in July of that year, six States being represented, and after organizing and doing a certain amount of business, it adjourned to the following November. On its re-assembling in that month, twelve States were represented by some five hundred delegates. The president of that convention was no less distinguished a man than John C. Calhoun, of South Carolina. It embraced, among others, thirty-five delegates from Missouri; and we have the pleasure of knowing that one of those delegates from Missouri, and who was the member from this State of the committee on nominations appointed by that convention, sits with us to-day as an honored member of the delegation from the St. Louis Merchants' Exchange.

That convention, however, was not called exclusively, or even chiefly, with reference to the improvement of the Mississippi river. It considered many subjects, and finally adopted eighteen or twenty resolutions, sixteen of which referred to various matters of public importance; some of them to railroads, some to arsenals, some to docks, some to coast defenses, and four of them to questions relating to the river itself. That convention is memorable, as it seems to me, for two things. Its utterances were, so far as we know, the first expression publicly made with reference to subjects of this character, by a delegated body, including men of national reputation from the various States of the South and Southwest. And it is further memorable from the fact that that distinguished man and eminent statesman, John C. Calhoun, whose opinions are a part of the history of this country, distinctly declared before that body that the political views which he entertained, as we all know, concerning the functions of the General Government, did not interfere in his opinion with the right of those there assembled to call upon that Government to contribute to and take charge of the improvement of what he felicitously styled our "Inland Sea." [Loud applause.]

Two years later another convention assembled, also famous in its day,— the great river and harbor convention held in Chicago in July, 1847. At this convention were also present many men who were then, or afterwards became, of national reputation. Abraham Lincoln and Charles Hempstead, of Illinois; Thomas Corwin and Robert C. Schenck, of Ohio; Horace Greeley, David Dudley Field and John C. Spencer, of New York; Andrew Stewart, of Pennsylvania; and Thomas Butler King, of Georgia,—these men were among the members of that convention; and among the letters received favoring its objects—objects indicated by the name bestowed upon it—were letters from Henry Clay and Silas Wright. May I be permitted to add that that convention had for its presiding officer one whose spotless life as well as his silvery eloquence is still remembered with affection and honor in this State. It is said that of all the eloquent words spoken there none created greater enthusiasm than the brilliant closing address of its president, Edward Bates, of Missouri. [Loud applause.]

Four years later,—and I shall refer particularly to only two other conventions, for reasons which I shall mention presently,—four years later, thirty years ago this month, it was my privilege, as one of the youngest members of a numerous delegation from this city, to attend a very large convention held at Burlington, Iowa, which was called for the special purpose of advocating the improvement by the General Government of what were then and are still known as the Rock Island, or Upper, and the Des Moines, or Lower, Rapids of the Mississippi River. Many States were represented there also, and resolutions were passed earnestly calling Congress to make this important improvement. Up to that time nothing had been done with reference to them except that up to 1837 those Rapids had been more than once surveyed under the orders of the War Department, and one of those surveys was made by Lieutenant Robert E. Lee, of the engineer corps. Fifteen years passed before anything more was done with reference to that subject.

In 1866 another convention assembled at Dubuque, also held for the special purpose of considering the improvement of the Upper and Lower Rapids of the Mississippi. The City of St. Louis was represented in that Convention also. Five hundred delegates were there in attendance, including a large number of the members of the Iowa Legislature; and the chairman of our St. Louis delegation to-day—who is a veteran in this service—was called to preside over its deliberations. Strong resolutions were passed by that body urging Congress to make the improvements in question. In 1867 another convention was held in the City of St. Louis, also with special reference to the improvement of these same Rapids. At that convention twelve States were represented, over four hundred delegates being in attendance; and there were passed not only resolutions in favor of the particular improvement in question, but other resolutions also, by which was invoked earnest and immediate action by Congress for the improvement of the Mississippi river from the Balize to St. Paul, and of the Ohio river, and the works at the Falls of the Ohio; the resolutions also commending to the earnest and favorable action of Congress the improvement of the other great affluents of the Mississippi river.

I have particularly alluded to these conventions, for two reasons: first, because it is pleasant for us to remember that from the beginning the merchants of St. Louis and the citizens of Missouri have not been backward in their earnest efforts to promote improvements of this kind,—not only those which they themselves desired, but those also which were or might be beneficial to their brethren in whatever part of the Valley; and secondly, because as a result no doubt a part of these strong expressions of public sentiment,— certainly as a result in part of the holding of the later conventions which I have mentioned,—we know now that not only the improvement of the Lower Rapids by a canal which is in constant and successful use during the period of navigation, but also the deepening of the Upper Rapids, at an expense for them both of several millions of dollars to the General Government, have passed into the region of accomplished facts. Certainly we have reason to look with satisfaction upon these natural and legitimate results of such expressions of public opinion on the part of the people for whose immediate benefit these works were planned,—the people who pay so large a part of the taxes which furnish the means of constructing them, and who have the right to demand that they shall be constructed. [Loud applause.]

The list of similar conventions held since the date last given, I shall briefly glance at, and simply in order to recall to our minds that this assemblage does not spring from a new or crude public opinion. The fact that many such conventions have been held is familiar to us all; but I doubt whether we all realize, unless we stop to think of it, what a steady and powerful and constantly increasing current of public sentiment they represent. And of this let them take heed whom it concerns.

In Keokuk, in 1867, another convention was held, also having special reference to the improvement of the Upper and Lower Rapids. Other conventions have been held with reference to the same general subject, as many of you know, and in which many of you have taken active part,—for I am merely reminding men of larger experience and far more practical knowledge than myself of these facts,—in New Orleans in 1869, in 1875, in 1876, in 1879, and 1880; at St. Louis in 1872, and again in 1873, when there was a very important conference of Congressmen held here pursuant to an invitation issued by the St. Louis Merchants' Exchange to all the then members of Congress. That assemblage was a conference rather than a convention, and was intended especially to furnish information to the gentlemen thus invited, and impress upon them the importance of the subject. Its proceedings were published by the St. Louis Merchants' Exchange, and contain a great mass of valuable information.

There was also a similar convention held at Vicksburg in 1875, another at St. Paul in 1877,—possibly that was in 1878,—another at Quincy in 1879, and another at Davenport in 1881. Some of these conventions were called with special reference to improvements of what may be termed a local character, but in every one of them the idea of the improvement of the Mississippi river was necessarily the key-note of their action, for the great value of these local improvements depends upon the existence of that greatest of all water-ways.

I say nothing of other conventions which have been held at other points in the Valley of the Mississippi, whose composition and whose purposes were not, strictly speaking, of an inter-State character. They have been numerous and influential, and if I omit to mention them here, it is not in the least that I undervalue their importance, but because they do not belong to the class of inter-State conventions of which I speak.

As the result of these successive conventions, representing, if, you please, the stream of public sentiment continually growing,—and you will observe the coincidence of their dates with the assembling of successive Congresses,—besides these, and, as it were, like the growth of shrubbery, herbage and trees on the banks of the mighty stream itself, there has been growing up quite as steadily as those trees, grass and shrubbery have grown up, a literature relating to the improvement of the rivers, which is itself exceedingly interesting and of great importance,—for in that literature are recorded the successive steps of the growth of this great valley.

Another and important result of these conventions has been the appointment, as many of you know, within two or three years past, of an " Inter-State Commission " of which Judge Underwood, of Louisville, was made the President. An address issued by this body to the Governors of the various States interested in its objects, was responded to by the Governors of fourteen of those States, who appointed in all thirty-six members of that Commission; and the address issued by that Commission is another of these documents full of interesting facts and statistics, and weighty arguments based upon them.

Now, during the last fifteen years other important events have also contributed to the growth of this public sentiment in favor of the improvement of our great rivers by the General Government. Especially since the close of the civil war, thousands of miles of railway have been built, not only trans-continental, but within and connecting the various Western States; and to the building of these railways the General Government has made enormous contributions in money and in land. We do not complain of this; but we do call attention to the fact that the Government aid thus given in land and bonds and money actually advanced, running up into hundreds of millions of dollars, has far exceeded all that has ever been asked for the improvement of the Mississippi river and its tributaries.

The result of this railroad building, and one of the conditions of the development of the West, was the constant extension westward of the frontier line of settlement and civilization. From year to year that line has moved towards the setting sun as the shadow moves on the face of a dial, hour by hour,—only that instead of recording the hours it recorded degrees of longitude, and instead of noting the passage of time, it has marked the reclamation of the wilderness, the redemption of a new empire from barbarism by civilization. But what was the result of this sublime movement, this ever-advancing wave of civilization? It differed from the onward march of Attila's hosts as the rush of a tidal wave differs from the inundation of the Nile,—the one submerging to destroy; the other peacefully overflowing that it may fertilize.

One result of this extension of the cultivated area of the West was that it pushed further from the river, further from a market, the area of cheap cultivation,—not only of lands entered at a dollar and a quarter an acre, but of homesteads occupied and settlements rapidly springing up without any cost except for the labor which made them habitable. There was attracted to these new lands a large part not only of the yearly immigration from foreign shores, but also of that restless and most valuable element of the young blood of our own country, which is constantly pushing forward in advance of the older members of civilization and society, subduing the wilderness and preparing the desert and the prairie to blossom like the rose. [Loud applause.]

The inevitable result was that the ever new settlers constantly found themselves farther and farther from the markets of the world. Another result was that the very development of these new lands actually added to the burden of which the dwellers on the river complained, for the production thus increased could not be accommodated with transportation. Undoubtedly the railroads have endeavored to meet with adequate facilities this new burden. But it is not in the nature of things for railroads to supply for the staple products of an agricultural country, destined to distant markets, the cheap transportation which their profitable production demands. And thus it is—as the call for this Convention truly asserts—that the question of cheap transportation, the question of the rate of freight for agricultural products, is a vital one. If I had the time, or it were appropriate for me to go into it, there are facts and figures at hand of the highest interest, relating to this question. But I shall not weary you at this moment with any details on that subject. I only ask you to consider the cardinal facts at different and successive periods in regard to this question of comparative freights.

In the proceedings of the Congressional Conference held at St. Louis in 1873, already mentioned, I find a statement made by the late Hon. Henry T. Blow—formerly a member of Congress from this city, and whose energy and public spirit are well remembered here—to the effect that the cost of transportation by rail at that time was thirteen mills per ton per mile, while by river it was three and a half mills per ton per mile. That single comparison throws a flood of light on the question of the wants of this ever-increasing area of cultivation, and the comparative value to its inhabitants of rail and river transportation for their staple products.

It is interesting to compare still later statements of the rates of freight, and see how the increasing demands of commerce, even with only crippled rivers to respond to them, have pressed down the freight rates since then. In a valuable pamphlet issued by the Board of Trade of Cincinnati for the year ending in March last, the statement is made, in a very able Report on Internal Commerce and Navigation, that the cost of transportation on rivers is now only one mill per ton per mile, and that this is but one-tenth of the cost of the tonnage movement by rail west of the Mississippi river. Thus in eight years, according to this statement, based on official data, the rate of freight has fallen from three and a half mills to one mill per ton per mile for the river, and from thirteen mills to ten mills, or one cent per ton per mile, for railroads. I am informed by those familiar with the subject, that the rate per ton per mile by rail, under circumstances favoring the shipper, has been reduced to eight mills or even to seven.

Now, gentlemen, if that downward movement of freight has thus already been going on and can be accelerated by the improvement of the river, both in respect of freight rates on the river itself, and rates on the railroads under competition of the river,—as we well know that it can be, and that is why you are here to-day,—it would be a simple matter to make a calculation on the figures already before us, which should show in dollars and cents the ultimate benefit of such improvements, not only to the people of the Mississippi Valley, but to the nation at large—yes, to the consumers of the world. The official statistics already referred to show that the production of Indian corn by the fourteen Valley States in 1879 was more than twelve hundred and fifty million (1,250,000,000) bushels; that their production of wheat in the same year was very nearly three hundred million (300,000,000) bushels, and of oats, not less than two hundred and twenty million (220,000,000) bushels,—say eighteen hundred million (1,800,000,000) bushels in these three staples. Now, if by removing from the Mississippi river and its great tributaries the existing impediments to navigation,—sand-bars, snags, treacherous banks and the like,—it is made practicable and profitable, now that the Jetties have opened the port of New Orleans to the largest steamships, to send only one-half of that eighteen hundred million

(1,800,000,000) bushels to the markets of the world by way of the river instead of by rail, with the consequent reduction in the actual cost of transportation which is represented by the difference between river transportation and transportation by rail per ton per mile, already mentioned,—how many millions of dollars would represent the actual gain, by means of this cheaper transportation, to the producer and the consumer both? You can figure it out for yourselves.

And yet, gentlemen, we are to-day holding this Convention for the purpose of imploring—no, of demanding—of Congress that these improvements shall be made. Although the stream of public sentiment began to flow in this channel more than a generation ago; although the numerous conventions already mentioned show that its volume has been increasing from year to year throughout the whole length of this valley; although the demands of the farmer, of the manufacturer, and of the carrier by river, have become more and more pressing from year to year,—yet to-day we are holding one of the largest and probably the most important Convention ever yet held with reference to this subject, and the people of this whole valley are to-day feeling a deeper and stronger anxiety for the success of this effort than ever before. Why should this state of facts exist? Why should we be still endeavoring to concentrate our forces to bring about that result?

There seem to have existed, during all these years, perhaps three chief obstacles in the way of the rapid development of cheap transportation on the Western rivers. One may be said to have been the imperfection of the means of transportation themselves,—I mean the steamboats and their machinery, which were in vogue many years ago. Another, obviously, is found in the condition of the rivers themselves,—in the difficulties and impediments to navigation which we are asking the Government to remove. The third—and I beg leave to say that it seems to me to be the one to which the attention of this Convention needs to be most seriously directed—has been the failure on the part of the people of the West, at least until within the last two or three years, to so direct and wisely concentrate their efforts as to secure the results to which, as members of this great nation, they are justly entitled.

As to the first of these difficulties—the early imperfections of steamboats and their machinery—the characteristic ingenuity and energy of our people have steadily lessened them. May I give one illustration of this? It was in 1815, I believe, that the first steamboat began to navigate the Mississippi river. In 1819, as we learn from a very interesting address read last year by Mr. Overstolz, late mayor of this city, before the Missouri Immigration Society, the first through steamboat came from New Orleans to St. Louis, carrying 130 tons of cargo, and puffing its weary way through these same tortuous and difficult channels during a period of *twenty-seven days*. To-day our splendid steamers of 2,000 tons burden ply between New Orleans and St. Louis in six and seven days. And when we remember that in 1837 the first ocean steamers, the Great Western and Sirius, carrying 1,500 tons, crossed the Atlantic in twelve days, and that to-day the finest ocean steamer has not yet exceeded 6,000 tons capacity, and its time of passage is not yet reduced to one-half of what it was forty years ago, the comparison is certainly not to the disadvantage of the Western steamboat men. The imperfection of steamboats and their machinery, therefore, does not explain the relatively backward condition of our internal river commerce.

The second obstacle which I mentioned—the impediments to navigation in the rivers themselves—I need not dwell upon. It is the fact of their existence and the possibility of their removal which brings you here. I do not overlook the fact that the Mississippi river and its tributaries are not in this respect the same rivers that they were. I do not forget that to a certain extent the Government has improved them. Allusion has already been made to some important work that has been accomplished. I believe, however, that I am correct in saying that the first expenditure of public money in any improvement for the Mississippi river proper,—I do not speak of Western harbor improvements, for they are very few,—the first expenditure of public money for that purpose was made after the war. Even this expenditure has been made only here and there, and until a very recent period not, so far as I am informed, on any general and systematic plan.

Why is this so? Is it because our public men, especially of late years, have opposed such improvements? I think it would be hard to find a public man that has undertaken openly to do so, or that has ventured to avow any such purpose even if he had it. We have already seen that thirty-six years ago Mr. Calhoun laid the foundation for such public works as these by a declaration which removed them at once from the sphere of political controversies. We know that distinguished statesmen of all political parties have borne willing tribute to the importance of this work, not to this valley alone, but to the nation. I need not remind you of those earnest and eloquent words with which the late President, in his letter accepting the nomination for that high office, signified his sense of the national importance of the Mississippi river, and declared that Congress ought to prevent it from being any longer a terror to those who dwell upon its banks. I need not remind you that the present incumbent of the same office, in his letter accepting his nomination for Vice-President, declared in emphatic terms that the Government ought to aid works of internal improvement national in their character. Why is it, then,—the question still recurs,—why is it that a Convention like this has still to be held? I think, gentlemen, that we must look to the third of these obstacles which I venture to suggest, for the true explanation,—namely, the failure of those most interested in this great work to wisely direct and effectively concentrate their own efforts. And I respectfully submit to you whether it is not in that direction that the energies of this assemblage can be most wisely put forth.

The most recent history of this movement I think tends to confirm this view, and at the same time to give assurance that this question will not be asked, that this explanation will not continue to be true, much longer.

In 1879, as you are aware, there was introduced in Congress by Mr. Randall M. Gibson, of Louisiana, a bill for the appointment of a Mississippi

River Commission. That bill, changed in no material respect from its form as introduced by him except that the number of persons to compose the Commission was increased in the Senate from five to seven, became a law on June 29th, 1879, under the title of "An Act to provide for the appointment of a Mississippi River Commission, for the improvement of said river from the Head of the Passes, near the mouth, to its headwaters." The President appointed as members of this Commission, in pursuance of the act, General Q. A. Gilmore, General C. B. Comstock, Major Charles R. Suter, Henry Mitchell, B. M. Harrod, James B. Eads, and Benjamin Harrison; three of them being army engineers, one a civil engineer, two connected with the coast and geodetic survey, and one a civilian, and all of them gentlemen of high repute. That Commission promptly set about its work. It made one report in February, 1880, and a second and more elaborate one in February, 1881. It is not my province to speak of what these reports contained, nor of the work and recommendations of that Commission, in detail. I am happy to say that during your deliberations a letter from the President of the Commission will be laid before you, and you will further have the pleasure of hearing from one of its members in person. What I now call your attention to,—and I think the statement is both true and important,—is that the passage of that bill signalized the first effective concentration of effort, or rather, that it gave evidence of concentrated effort towards the first distinct, scientific and systematic plan for the improvement of the great river which has yet been made; and the improvement of that river necessarily includes in due time the improvement of all its navigable tributaries.

In the same year, 1879, was realized the triumph of that engineering work, of which as Americans we are proud, and for which, as business men, I know that you are grateful. I speak of the successful completion of the Jetties and the consequent opening of the port of New Orleans to steamers of the largest size. [Loud applause.] It was something more than a coincidence, that the same year was made memorable by these two great events,—the actual removal of those obstructions at the mouth of the river, with which by other methods the Government had so long contended in vain, and the provision by Act of Congress for the comprehensive, practical and scientific consideration, by men who were not only experts, but experts of the highest character, of what ought to be done towards removing by systematic and permanent methods the impediments to navigation which still remain.

In connection with the Jetties may I ask your indulgence while I call your attention to two statements made at different times concerning the condition of the river below New Orleans, one of them made before the jetties were proposed, and the other after their success had been demonstrated. I desire the more to do so, because of statements which have been occasionally made even within the last year, doubtless under some strange misapprehension of the facts, and which make the contrast I wish to draw the more timely and impressive.

I read from the proceedings of that Congressional Conference held at St. Louis in 1873, the following extract from an address to the members of Congress there assembled, made by Judge Kennard, of New Orleans:

"If you could go with us to the mouth of the Mississippi, we would show you such evidence as would remove the last doubt from the last Thomas among you. Only ten days ago, in making a critical survey of that locality, I found, when we arrived at the mouth of the Southwest Pass, there were lying [that is, either aground or afraid to get aground] thirty odd of the largest class of ships, representative of almost every country in Europe, among which were five or six fine steamers."

Now, let me read you a few lines from a valuable pamphlet recently published by Mr. Alexander D. Anderson, of Washington City, entitled "The Mississippi River and its Tributaries," in which, among other things, he discusses the effect of the Jetties immediately after their completion:

"Another illustration of the effect of these improvements is the record of the exports of a single day during the past year. viz.: "December 20, 1879, a New Orleans paper (the *Picayune*, of December 21, 1879) describes it as follows: 'Yesterday a fleet of fifteen vessels cleared at the custom-house with full cargoes. This fleet embraced eight steamships, two ships, four barques and one schooner; seven of them were for Liverpool, three for Havre, and one each for New York, Bremen, Malaga, Ruatan, and Pensacola. The cargoes of this fleet form the largest exports that ever passed through our custom-house in one day.'"

The newspaper goes on to give the details of these cargoes, from which it appears that they included 46,300 bales of cotton, 40,000 bushels of wheat, 45,579 bushels of corn, and a variety of other merchandise; of which the cotton alone was worth $2,550,000, and the total about $3,000,000. [Loud applause.]

And in the same connection Mr. Anderson quotes the following from a communication to him from the Secretary of the St. Louis Chamber of Commerce, under date of December 29, 1879:

"The Jetties at the mouth of the river have lessened the rates of freight by that route and by the East. The shipments of bulk grain this year from St. Louis by river to New Orleans, have been six million bushels of grain, and would have been three million more had there been a good stage of water."

Within a few days past there has been published in this city an official statement or report by a committee appointed by the St. Louis Merchants' Exchange, for the express purpose of ascertaining and reporting the facts concerning the passage of ships through these Jetties. In that report a list is given by name of ten steamers, each of which had a draught of twenty-four feet and upwards, every one of which steamers has passed up that channel—and it was up the South Pass, formerly impracticable for commerce, but which the Jetties have substituted for the Southwest Pass —without let or hindrance, in the two years since the Jetties were opened.

These facts are no doubt familiar to you all; yet I hope you will have pardoned me for detaining you by their statement, because they all tend to illustrate the subject which I have desired to bring before you—the source and meaning of that public sentiment which you have assembled once more to express to-day, the results which it has so far accomplished, and the conditions upon which it may hope for complete success; and because they throw light upon the significance and value of this latest effort, whose important fruit was the creation of the Mississippi River Commission.

The history and debates of the conventions which have preceded you, teach the same lesson. The President of the Merchants' Exchange, in calling you together to-day, has already alluded to what has been said in those debates by other gentlemen, standing, as you stand to-day, in the attitude of deliberation on this great subject, as to the best means of giving effect to that public sentiment. Again and again the question has been asked, not only what were the difficulties and hindrances which have impeded its rightful operation, but whether the greatest hindrance of all has not been the error on our own part of scattering, if not dividing, forces? Would it not have been better—were it not better now—to concentrate our energies upon the demand for the systematic improvement, first of all, of the great river itself, as the most natural and effective step towards securing all the rest? Again and again, as the proceedings and debates of those conventions bear witness, this danger, this hindrance has been pointed out. Has not the time come when, through our united efforts, it shall cease to exist?

Gentlemen, this great river itself seems, in its source and origin, and in the movement of its great waters to the Gulf, to furnish a striking symbol, an instructive lesson, which the members of this body may profitably consider.

You are gathered here from all quarters of this great valley. From every direction; some of you from great distances; you have come in larger or smaller delegations, representing the sentiment, the experience, the interest and demands of many different communities,—prosperous cities, thriving towns and villages, vast areas of agricultural lands, marvelous for fertility and steadily increasing in production, whose industry and prosperity constitute the life of many great and populous States. So this great river, whose turbid waters, gathered into one mighty current, flow by this city with majestic and ever-increasing volume in their progress to the Gulf,—does it not in like manner represent the confluence of many lesser streams, impelled by the mysterious energies of Nature to unite in seeking a common outlet? Its remotest sources are found in innumerable rills and sparkling brooks, over any one of which a boy might leap, but from whose union are formed, a thousand miles to the north of us, those far-off headwaters which we call the Upper Mississippi; and again, three thousand miles to the northwest, those headwaters which we call the Upper Missouri; and again, almost a thousand miles nearer the Atlantic, the headwaters of the Ohio; and to these streams come continually new accessions from every portion of the immense and various region which they drain, until all unite to form the vast and resistless flood of the Lower Mississippi. And yet we know that this vast flood, resistless as it is, has a peculiar movement and history of its own. Those who know it best tell us that when the volume of its waters is the greatest, when it can no longer be confined within its banks, and spreads for miles on either side, wandering here and there, as it were, in its impatience to reach its destination, its current becomes less powerful, its progress less rapid, its work less beneficent. Its sluggish waters, too widely dispersed, lose their grasp upon the enormous burden of soil and sediment which the swift current has brought down from hundreds of miles above, and by the deposit of which new obstructions now begin to be formed,—new barriers to its own progress, new impediments to its navigation.

But they tell us also that whenever its waters are prevented from thus wasting their strength by diffusion,—whenever they are confined within a narrower channel, either by the ingenuity of man or by the steadfast resistance of their natural banks,—then, even though the volume of the flood be less, its energies are concentrated, the swiftness and momentum of the current rapidly increase, and, gathering itself together for the mighty task, it scours and sweeps from its rapidly deepening channel every hidden obstacle and impediment, and moves on triumphantly to the Gulf. It was by thus enlisting and concentrating the vast physical forces of Nature herself that that great triumph of the Jetties was achieved. Does not the same law control the moral forces of public opinion under this Government of ours? Shall we not find in this the secret of our complete success? [Loud applause.]

I have detained you too long, gentlemen. My office has been a grateful one,—to offer you a hearty welcome from the Merchants' Exchange of St. Louis and the citizens of this city. If I have trespassed upon your indulgence, it was because it seemed to me not inappropriate, upon the very threshold of your action, that we should reflect upon and call attention to the long history and constant growth of that public sentiment which your assembly to-day expresses, and expresses more heartily, more earnestly, more effectively than ever before. That such a body of men, representative in the highest sense, assembled from every quarter of this great valley, should meet without making felt their just desires, without impressing, soberly, earnestly, but imperatively, upon the government of this nation the expediency and the wisdom of yielding that which they rightfully demand,—this, gentlemen, we may well feel confident is one of the things that cannot take place. [Loud and prolonged applause.]

Mr. McEnnis then said: "By request I will introduce Gov. Thomas T. Crittenden, of Missouri, to act as temporary Chairman of the Convention. Gentlemen of the Convention, I have the honor as well as the pleasure of introducing to you Gov. Thomas T. Crittenden, of Missouri." [Loud applause.]

Gov. Crittenden, on assuming the chairmanship, said:

GENTLEMEN OF THE CONVENTION: It is gratifying, indeed, to see such a body of representative men assembled from so large a part of our country for a common purpose. Not how to build up higher walls; not how to construct, under mathematical calculations, stronger forts; not how to enforce a cunning law against the oppressed tillers of the soil; not how to secure a partisan victory for political ends; but how to cheapen bread for the world; how to strengthen our own producers; how to utilize the greatest body of navigable water in the world, with the largest tonnage, at the lowest charge; how to afford to our own people the cheapest and the most easy facility for reaching the great marts of trade of the world. In the language of the New York *Times*, within the area drained by the Mississippi and its navigable tributaries is produced ninety per cent. of the corn, seventy-three per cent. of the wheat, eighty-three per cent. of the oats, sixty-four per cent. of the tobacco, seventy-seven per cent. of the cotton, and sixty-three per cent. of the live hogs of the whole country; and these are the products which make up a large part of our exports, and the exchange of which for foreign commodities constitutes the bulk of our commerce with foreign countries. These figures are great living truths, and they contain and evolve that great problem how to transport these commodities to market at the lowest possible charge, and that problem is, or should be, the only one that has been active in assembling this Convention. Our land is filled with railways passing from east to west, from north to south, with surprising speed, and they are a great desideratum in the elevation of our country which should be duly appreciated, backed by immense capital, managed by men of the largest brain and the keenest activity, which would stand as masters of the situation, if not for this great river and its navigable tributaries which flow through so large a part of our common country, and which with an unfailing hand settle and unsettle the transit question by the laws of Nature and not the whims of man. And this great internal sea of ours causes the managers of those corporations to contend like giants for that tonnage upborne upon the bosom of its waters. It is Nature's highway. unowned by man, and a thousand fleets sweep over it without marking or wearing it out. In the language of our own Eads, he who never opens a mouth in vain, "The garden which it beautifies and enriches contains 768,000,000 acres of the finest lands on the face of the globe. Enough to make more than 158 States as large as Massachusetts. Acres of the choicest soil in profusion sufficient to duplicate England, Great Britain, France, Spain, Austria, Prussia, European Turkey and the Italian Peninsula combined. If peopled as Belgium and the Netherlands are, with not one-half the danger of famine, it would contain 400,000,000 of souls, nearly one-third the population of the entire earth. Human comprehension cannot grasp the grandeur of such an empire. Human wisdom cannot estimate the wonderful value of such an inheritance."

Gentlemen, the question occurs, how to make this inheritance greater, richer and more worthy of being the homes of this marching, trampling, toiling, progressive race of ours. I feel assured that the wisdom of this Convention will solve this important question in the most satisfactory way. When it is determined here to improve the Mississippi river—the great trunk line—then let us proceed to agree upon some feasible plan to improve the tributaries. Let not the smaller question govern the larger one. I touch upon these two subjects with much delicacy, as it will be left to this body to evolve some plan that will work the greatest amount of good at whatever cost to the inhabitants of this valley,—no, to the whole population of our land. Millions have been generously and at times wisely given to construct railroads in our country, and millions upon millions, if necessary, should be as generously given to improve the Mississippi river. It may be asked, improve it how much? I answer: All it requires is that every drop of idle water that now flows to the sea may be harnessed by the hand of engineering skill and made to bear its proportion of the commerce of the world. Paying into the treasury of the Government our proportion of the taxes without grumbling and almost without limit, we shall have no hesitancy in calling upon our representatives in Congress to return those taxes to us for the improvement of our great rivers, without grumbling and if necessary almost without limit. We are a part of the nation—a large part, too—and we desire to be recognized by that Government in such a liberal way as will not only build up our own part of the country, but will also contribute largely to the strength, endurance and stability of the whole country. We are not sectional in our demands, nor selfish in our appeals. We expect to be heard in Congress—we will be heard—because our cause is just. In this great forensic contest Illinois will stand by Louisiana [loud applause], and Minnesota will stand by Kentucky, and but one flag will float over all, and that will be the flag of a paternal government. [Loud applause.] Gentlemen, I have seen, whilst a member of Congress from this State, the evils of "omnibus appropriation bills" for the improvement of our rivers and harbors. Much good is always embodied in those bills, and also an infinite amount of demagoguery and waste of money. It should be stopped before the evil gets too large. It has already made itself very strong in Congress, and if not checked, and that soon, it will dictate its own terms of appropriation. There are too many unnavigable and unwatered streams in those bills inserted by interested politicians for local purposes. Abolish the evil and assert the independence of the great stream and its truly navigable tributaries. Then a victory worthy of the American Congress will have been accomplished, and the money of the people will be judiciously expended. [Applause.] Enough money is wasted on these small streams to perform a large part, if not the whole, of the desired work in the Mississippi river. Such foolishness should be stopped at once. May this Convention strike the key-note in not only suppressing such an evil, but also in marking out a line of policy by which our Senators and Representatives in Congress are to be governed in their future appropriation bills. I thank this Convention for the honor conferred in making me its temporary Chairman, and these distinguished delegates for having honored Missouri with their presence. May wisdom and unity of action govern all your deliberations. [Loud applause.]

At the conclusion of Gov. Crittenden's address, Hon. Nathan Cole, of St. Louis, said:

"Mr. President, I would like to move, at this moment, that Mr. Frank Gaiennie act as temporary Secretary of the Convention."

The motion being duly seconded was put and carried.

Mr. John Hogan, of St. Louis. " I move you, sir, that a committee of one from each State and Territory represented here, be appointed a Committee on Credentials ; and probably it will be better, in order that the committee may be properly selected, and that an opportunity may be given to the States to select their men upon that committee, to adjourn, and I therefore move that the Convention adjourn until to-morrow morning."

Several delegates. " No, no."

Mr. Hogan. "All right ; any way so that the committee can be appointed."

Mr. Roberts, of Pekin, Illinois. " I move that the roll of States be called in alphabetical order, and that each delegation be requested to name one delegate to act upon the several committees : first on the Committee on Credentials, then on the Committee on Resolutions, as this Convention may elect."

A delegate from Arkansas. " I offer an amendment to that. That the chairman of the several delegations act as chairman of those committees."

Mr. Roberts. "As far as Illinois is concerned, I will say that her delegation has been already organized ; that we have a chairman ; and when our State is called, our chairman will announce the several representatives of those committees, and I therefore insist upon my motion."

The Chairman. " Does the gentleman from St. Louis withdraw his motion?"

Mr. Hogan. " My motion, the first part of it, or the part that I wish adopted, is simply that the Committee on Credentials be appointed. The design of the last part was to give an opportunity for consultation with the several delegations.

If the delegations have already appointed a member to serve on that committee, then it can be carried out now. That is all the design I had in view."

Several delegates. "Question! question!"

The Chairman. " Gentlemen, you have heard the motion of the gentleman from Illinois, that the list of States be called; I believe that is the purport of the motion."

A delegate. " List of States and Territories."

The Chairman. " Of the States and Territories; and what was the balance of the motion?"

Mr. Roberts. "And that upon being called, the delegations of the respective States and Territories name a member of the committee from their respective States and Territories."

The Chairman. " That the chairmen of the delegations of the States and Territories, name the respective members to be represented on the committee."

A delegate from Kentucky. " Will the Chairman please state for the information of the Convention how many committees are to be provided for in that resolution?"

The Chairman. " One committee; only one."

The delegate from Kentucky. "A Committee on Credentials?"

The Chairman. "A Committee on Credentials."

The delegate from Kentucky. " Very well, I didn't understand it, and I wished to know."

Mr. George H. Shields, of Missouri. " I desire to offer as a substitute to the resolution now pending, that the delegates from the States and Territories name members of a Committee on Credentials, a Committee on Order of Business, a Committee on Permanent Organization, and a Committee on Resolutions; and as I know that some of the State delegations have not organized yet, in order to give them an opportunity to name members for those committees, I therefore move that the Convention take a recess for fifteen minutes, in order that the delegations may be organized by the respective States and

Territories, and at the termination of the recess be prepared to announce the names of the delegates on these committees to the Convention."

A delegate. "I rise to a point of order. My point of order is, until the Convention is fully organized and a Committee on Credentials has reported, we don't know who constitute the Convention."

The Chairman. "The Chair will sustain the point of order of the gentleman. You have heard the motion of the gentleman from Illinois. The Chair will now put the motion."

The motion was put and carried.

The Chairman. "The Secretary will now call the list of the States and Territories."

A delegate. "I understand that a motion has been made that a recess be taken, in order that delegates may be selected for these committees.

The Chairman. "No, sir; the Chair does not so understand. The gentleman is out of order. The Secretary will proceed with the calling of the roll."

The Secretary then called the roll of delegates. The first State called was Arkansas.

A delegate from Illinois. "I would respectfully ask the Chair as to when this meeting of the Illinois delegation was called. There are several delegates from the State of Illinois, bordering on the Mississippi, who arrived to-day, and do not know of the action that was taken by the delegates who arrived yesterday; and therefore, if it is not too late, I would suggest, for the purpose of perfecting the organization of this Convention with entire harmony, that every State and Territory represented in this great Convention,—probably the greatest and most important that has ever been held in this country, certainly in the Mississippi Valley,—that these States and Territories have the privilege of selecting their members for the Committee on Credentials, Permanent Organization, Order of Business, and Resolutions, so that the representatives from this great valley can act together and can present the names of men from their States that stand high in commercial, political and other relations; and therefore, if not too late, I would suggest that the States act together and select their members for these committees, and afterwards present the names to this Convention, for the purpose of conducting the business of the Convention in an orderly manner." [Several delegates. "No, no."]

Mr. Roberts, of Illinois. "I would inform the gentleman that the Illinois delegation convened at ten o'clock at the Planters' House, in pursuance to a call, and organized by appointing Mr. Holliday chairman of the delegation, and that they then and there agreed on the several representatives for these respective committees. I regret that the gentleman was not present, but that was not our fault."

A delegate. "I suggest that a recess be taken for ten minutes, to allow these difficulties to be settled between the different States."

The delegate from Illinois. "I am requested by several delegates, some of whom were here yesterday, and a large number of whom arrived to-day, to say that they were not cognizant of any meeting of the Illinois delegation having been held at the Planters' House or elsewhere. As far as I may be permitted, I am perfectly willing, as a unit, as a member, as one of this Illinois delegation to this Convention, to submit, for myself, to the action as taken, but we were not apprised of the fact."

Several delegates. "Call the roll."

Mr. E. O. Stanard, of Missouri. "I have no doubt the desire is general to facilitate the business of the Convention as speedily as possible. The Illinois delegation has had a meeting and elected their officers and designated the gentlemen who shall serve upon the committees. Other States may have done the same, but there are several States here, I am told, and one I know—the State of Missouri—whose delegates have never been called together as a body, and that is a delegation in which I am sure there is no organization. Now it seems to me before we proceed to business it would be the part of wisdom that we should take a recess of at least fifteen minutes."

A delegate. " Thirty minutes."

Mr. Stanard. "No, sir; I am making this speech. [Laughter and cries of "Go on."] What I desired to say was this, that I think we should take a recess of at least fifteen minutes, and that each delegation—each State delegation in their seats—should organize. There are more of them together now than will be likely to be got together in any hour of the next twenty-four. [Laughter.] And it seems to me that the first business that we should do, should be for each State to have an organization and designate the gentlemen that they would have to serve on the various committees."

A delegate. " What are the various committees?"

Mr. Stanard. " The various committees have not been designated; but I presume they are such committees as are usual in deliberative bodies of this kind; a committee on permanent organization, on order of business, on resolutions and credentials; at least those four committees. Now it seems to me that we will be in confusion if some step of this kind is not taken, and I hope the gentleman—I understand that the gentleman made a motion that the States be called for the purpose of designating members for the Committee on Credentials."

A delegate. " That was all, sir."

Mr. Stanard. " That was all that that embraced; is that so?"

A delegate. " Yes."

Mr. Stanard. " Now let that matter be held in abeyance, and let us take a recess and organize, as far as the State delegates are concerned."

Mr. Roberts, of Illinois. " If the gentleman will permit me, I will withdraw my motion, temporarily, and agree to his."

A delegate. " It has been carried."

Mr. Roberts. "Well, then, I don't object; if these other delegations are not organized, I don't object to having them."

Mr. Stanard. "I move that we take a recess of fifteen minutes, for the purpose of organization."

The Chairman. "It is moved that this Convention take a recess of fifteen minutes, in order that the delegations may effect an organization and present their names to the Convention."

The motion was put and carried, and a recess of fifteen minutes was taken.

At the termination of the recess the Convention was called to order by the Chairman, who said:

"Gentlemen of the Convention, it will facilitate business very much if each gentleman as he rises will announce his name and the State from which he comes. That request is made by the Press and the Secretary of the Convention, and the Chairman will be very much gratified if it is done."

Mr. D. H. Hart, of Illinois. "I have a resolution I wish to offer to have referred to the Committee on Resolutions, and as I shall not be here to-morrow, I would like to offer it now, and I will pass it to the clerk in order that it may be referred."

A delegate. "We are not organized, yet."

The Chairman. "The first thing in order now, gentlemen of the Convention, is the calling of the States and Territories, in order that the names of the Committee on Credentials may be obtained. The Secretary will proceed to call the roll."

Mr. Rowland, of St. Louis. "Before that action is taken I would request Mayor Ewing be invited to make a short address of welcome to the Convention.

A delegate. "I move that Mayor Ewing have leave to print his speech."

The Chairman. "I will state to the gentlemen of the Convention that Mayor Ewing declines to make an address, and that he would prefer to have the Convention progress with its business rather than to detain it by an address on his part." [Loud applause.]

The clerk then called the roll of States, first calling Alabama.

Mr. T. B. Taylor. "I am placed in rather a delicate position; I am the only delegate from Alabama."

The Chairman. "Have you your credentials."

Mr. Taylor. "Yes, sir; from the Mayor of Montgomery."

The Chairman. "If the gentleman will give his name we will make him a delegate."

Mr. Taylor. "My name is Dr. Thomas B. Taylor."

Mr. Hogan, of St. Louis. "I move that the gentleman from Alabama, by common consent, be appointed upon all the committees." [Applause.]

The question was put, and the motion was carried.

The Secretary then proceeded with the call of the roll of States, and the delegations announced the following as the Committee on Credentials and chairmen of the delegations:

COMMITTEE ON CREDENTIALS.

Alabama—Thomas B. Taylor.
Arkansas—John E. Bennett, Helena.
Iowa—Col. P. G. Ballingall.
Kentucky—B. C. Levi.
Indiana—C. A. Zollinger.
Louisiana—E. K. Converse.
Tennessee—Edward S. Jones.
Kansas—B. M. Brake.
Minnesota—E. W. Durant, Stillwater.
New Mexico—P. J. Kennedy.
Nebraska—Victor Vilquain.
Dakota—J. T. Pettigrew.
Wisconsin—J. R. Berryman.
West Virginia—Frank J. Hearne, Wheeling.

Michigan—Philo Parsons.
Missouri—James Craig.
New York—B. S. Osborne.
Pennsylvania—Capt. J. T. Stockdale, Pittsburg.
Texas—Thomas F. McEnnis.
Mississippi—Col. Green Clay.
Ohio—Joseph Hargrove.
Illinois—Hon. C. A. Walker, Carlinville.

The chairmen of the delegations as reported are:

CHAIRMEN OF DELEGATIONS.

Alabama—Thomas B. Taylor.
Arkansas—Capt. W. H. Fulton.
Iowa—J. W. Thomas.
Kentucky—Eugene Underwood.
Indiana—G. V. Menzies, Mt. Vernon.
Louisiana—Duncan F. Kenner.
Tennessee—J. B. Heiskill.
Kansas—F. P. Baker.
Minnesota—C. C. Sturtevant.
Missouri—E. O. Stanard.
New Mexico—P. J. Kennedy.
Nebraska—H. G. Clark.
Dakota—J. T. Pettigrew.
Wisconsin—Wm. T. Price.
West Virginia—Col. Alex. Campbell, Bethany.
Michigan—Philo Parsons.
New York—B. S. Osborne.
Pennsylvania—R. C. Gray, Pittsburg.
Texas—T. T. Gammage.

When the State of Michigan was called, a delegate said: "Michigan has but two delegates present. More are expected this afternoon. We were not conscious that we had any immediate interest in the affair; but we have the deepest interest in point of sympathy with it, and we sympathize with what the States watered by the Mississippi demand, and we shall second their efforts." [Loud applause.]

When New Mexico was called, Mr. P. J. Kennedy said: "New Mexico has but one delegate, P. J. Kennedy."

Mr. Rowland, of St. Louis. "I move that Mr. Kennedy, of New Mexico, be considered the chairman of the delegation from New Mexico, and also a member of each one of these committees."

The Chairman. "It will be so ordered unless objection is made."

A delegate. "I was just going to make that motion, to apply to all who are single delegates."

The Chairman. "It will be so ordered unless objection is made."

Mr. Craig, of Missouri. "I have investigated, as far as I could, the names of the gentlemen who have been appointed to this Convention from the State of Missouri, and as you will see, I have quite a number of columns of names here; and the gentlemen present, so far as I have been able to ascertain, are all delegates, duly appointed, either by municipal bodies or otherwise, having the right to sit here as members of this Convention; but I will not be able to get my list perfected until to-morrow morning, and even then I will not without the aid of two clerks; and I ask the Convention to give me until to-morrow morning for that purpose." [Laughter.]

Mr. Chase, of Nebraska. "I suggest that when members rise they give their names. We want to know who these men are from the different States. I think it would be well where a delegate represents a State alone, as Mr. Pettigrew, for instance, a member of Congress from Dakota, and who has done us the honor of sitting with us, and as I know him to be straight in every way, that he should be allowed to act upon all the committees; and therefore, I move that he be authorized to act on all the committees as a representative from the Territory of Dakota."

The Chairman. "You have heard the motion, that the Hon. Mr. Pettigrew, of Dakota, be permitted to act upon all the committees, as a representative from that Territory. It will be so ordered unless objection is made."

A delegate. "I now suggest that the members of the Committee on Credentials retire to a separate room."

Mr. Durant, of Minnesota. "I would suggest that the committeemen step back and they will find a room provided for them, and that they perform the committee work as soon as possible and report to this Convention."

A delegate. "I move that the Committee on Credentials have leave to retire for deliberation."

A delegate. "I move that the chairman of each delegation from each State pass in the list of the names of the delegates from his State. I presume, sir, that each chairman on the Committee on Credentials from each State knows who represents his State, and he can pass in the list of names, together with the credentials, if they are required, to save further delay."

A delegate from Indiana. "I wish to call the attention of this Convention to the fact, that by some omission, no placard has been put up for the State of Indiana. I presume other delegates would like to know where that State is located in this Convention, and therefore I suggest the propriety of having some recognition of the State of Indiana and its locality in this Convention."

Mr. Osborne, of New York. "I stand in the same relation with my friend, Mr. Parsons, of Michigan, representing the National Board of Steam Navigation, which has had members for the last ten years in every State bordering on this great water-way, or on the sea-coast. I was appointed a delegate to come from the sea-coast to the city of St. Louis, and join in the deliberations of this body. I am put down in the newspapers as from New York. I represent, in the sentiment of that body, not only New York, but Maine, New Hampshire, Massachusetts, Vermont, Rhode Island,—and I will stop there, unless I switch off to Maryland. [Laughter.] We have no shingle up, but we want our voice heard in this Convention. [Loud laughter and applause.] We recognize as much as any of the representatives from other States that anything that is for the good of the West ought to be good for the East. [Applause.] And for that reason, in the name of the organization that has sent me ten hundred and sixty-five miles—so the railroad time-table says—to come here and represent them, we ask for a shingle, and we want to be represented on the Committee on Credentials. [Laughter.] Excuse me for making all this noise, but I can't ride for thirty-five consecutive hours and some minutes on the cars, and then be an hour late, and not be heard after all. [Laughter.] There were five delegates appointed—good men, some of them you know very well; one of them is in Europe. He couldn't get here to-day, but he will some day. Two more have been appointed. My name is Osborne. I am chairman of the delegation, and I am on the Committee on Credentials, and I have two more delegates to put on any committee that you want."

Mr. Anderson, of Pennsylvania. "As it is really necessary that we should have a mariner to navigate these waters, I move that the sailor-man from New York be added to all these committees,—Mr. Osborne, from New York."

Mr. Osborne. "I will answer for New York." [Laughter.]

Mr. Bain, of St. Louis. "Mr. Chairman—"

The Chairman. "The gentleman from Iowa,—no, from Michigan." [Loud laughter.]

A delegate. "Mr. Bain is from Missouri."

The Chairman. "The gentleman from Missouri, Mr. George Bain."

Mr. Bain. "I merely want to answer the gentleman from Indiana,—that State which is famous for its hoop-poles and Democratic candidates for the Presidency—that we had a placard for that State, and I don't know what has become of it. Perhaps some of the delegates have put it in their pockets. There certainly was a placard put up for that State, so that it could be located in the organization of this body, and I think that Indiana ought to have such a sign, as much as any other State, although it don't exactly border on the Mississippi or any other river. It is certainly too important to be left out of the deliberations of this Convention, and the committee will see to it that it is properly located in this Convention."

A delegate. "Where is the Wabash?"

Mr. Murphy, of Iowa. "I desire to say in behalf of Iowa, that we have had a great many inflictions, but the worst *bane* that ever was put on us was the recognition of that gentleman, Mr. Bain, of St. Louis, as a representative of Iowa." [Loud laughter.]

Mr. Cole, of St. Louis. "Mr. Chairman, I presume the desire of all the members of this Convention is that we should now have the business expedited as much as possible, and if it is in order, I would like to move at this moment that the delegates for each of the committees, on order of business, resolutions, and permanent organization, should be called upon now to report the names of members for those committees. I make that motion."

The Chairman. "Gentlemen of the Convention, the States and Territories will be called now, for the names of the Committee on Permanent Organization of this Convention. Please announce them when the States are called."

Mr. Denman, of Illinois. "I will ask for information, how do we know who are members of the Convention? No committee on credentials has as yet reported, and, although I have not the slightest doubt in my mind that every gentleman here is a delegate, and duly entitled to a seat in the Convention, it seems to me a little premature for such action as this to be taken previous to the report of the Committee on Credentials; let us have that, and know who are here and entitled to seats, before we proceed to permanent organization."

A delegate. "I will ask the gentleman how he got his badge?"

Mr. Denman. "I got my badge from the committee, sir, and remarked afterwards that any man with a little cheek could go and get a badge."

Mr. Wood, of Illinois. "It is plain before we can proceed with any business in this Convention, that it will be necessary for this committee to report. I shall therefore move that the Convention adjourn until half-past three o'clock for the purpose of hearing the report of the Committee on Credentials."

The Chairman. "Gentlemen, I will state to the Convention that we have to vacate this building this afternoon at half-past four o'clock." [Several voices. "No, no."]

The Chairman. "We have to do that. We have to surrender the building at half-past four o'clock."

Mr. Cole, of St. Louis. "I move to amend that we meet at half-past two o'clock, to hear the report of the Committee on Credentials."

Mr. Underwood, of Kentucky. "I wish your attention, Mr. Chairman, for one moment. It seems to me there is a question prior to the question of the appointment of the Committee on Credentials. I see here the names of some States, but it appears that all the States are not named as to who shall compose, or whose delegates shall compose, this Convention. And now, sir, I would like to know, and to hear from the Chairman, what States are to be represented in this Convention." [Voices. "All."]

Mr. Underwood. "All the States of the United States?"

Several delegates. "Yes."

Mr. Underwood. "All the States of the United States, sir?"

Several delegates. "Yes."

The Chairman. "The Mississippi Valley, under the call, as I understand it."

Mr. Underwood. "I supposed, Mr. Chairman, this was

a Convention to be composed of the States of the Mississippi Valley."

Several delegates. "That is right."

Mr. Underwood. "And if it is confined to the States of the Mississippi Valley, we should now understand it; if it is to be composed of all the States of the United States, we should so understand it; and I therefore ask that we shall have some announcement as what is to be the constituency of this Convention."

The Chairman. "I will read, for the information of the gentleman, a part of the call, which I think answers the question:

"'In view of the magnitude of the interests involved and the results to be attained, we would cordially and earnestly invite the various boards of trade of the Valley so largely interested in these results, as well as those from the communities outside the Valley who appreciate the scope of the Convention, to send delegates fully penetrated,'" etc. [Loud applause.]

Mr. Osborne, of New York. "Now, Mr. Chairman, I move that the roll of the Secretary be accepted as the credentials of this body of delegates. It will save time; it will save talk, and it will make harmony." [Loud applause.]

Mr. Bennett, of Arkansas. "I have a little suggestion to make for the speedy prosecution of the business of the Convention. As a member of the Committee on Credentials I would desire to suggest for the consideration of the President of this Convention that the members of the Committee on Credentials meet in a body, and that each member of the Committee on Credentials from each State report the delegates from his own State and hand the list to the Secretary, and let that be the report of the Committee on Credentials. I know it is parliamentary usage for the Committee on Credentials to meet together and then make a separate report; but it will avoid a great deal of confusion and save time, perhaps, to let each delegation report its own members here, and hand the list to the Secretary, and let that be the list of the Convention."

Mr. Osborne, of New York. "I will accept that amendment, sir."

The Chairman. "You hear the motion of the gentleman from Arkansas."

Mr. Craig, of Missouri. "I will ask the Chair if the Secretary has got a roll?"

The Chairman. "Yes, sir; you have heard the motion of the gentleman from Arkansas, that the names of the committee be handed to the Secretary."

A delegate. "I move that the committee be instructed to have a shingle put up representing every State in the Union."

The Chairman. "That will be attended to. You have heard the motion of the gentleman from Arkansas, that a report of the names be reported by the different delegations to the Secretary of the Convention."

The motion was put and carried.

A delegate. "I desire to inquire if the Clerk has a list of the delegates appointed by the municipalities, cities and towns?"

The Chairman. "Yes, sir."

The delegate. "I move that a Committee on Permanent Organization be called."

Another delegate. "I move that the chairman of each delegation report a member of a Committee for Permanent Organization and for Order of Business at the same time."

Another delegate. "All these suggestions are out of order until the Committee on Credentials make their report."

The Chairman. "You have heard the motion of the gentleman from Minnesota, that the chairmen of the different delegations from the different States report two names for the two different committees. It will expedite the business of the Convention if it is done."

The motion was put and carried.

The Secretary then called the roll, and the following Committees were selected:

PERMANENT ORGANIZATION.

Alabama—Thomas B. Taylor.
Arkansas—Hon. Logan H. Roots.
Iowa—Hon. William L. Joy.
Illinois—Gen. Rinaker.
Indiana—J. A. Lemcke.
Kansas—W. H. Caldwell.
Kentucky—J. H. Fowler.
Louisiana—Ex-Gov. McEnery.
Missouri—O. Guitar.
Minnesota—C. C. Sturtevant.
Michigan—Alonzo Sessions, Ionia.
Mississippi—Col. S. H. Parisot.
New Mexico—P. J. Kennedy.
Nebraska—C. C. Housel.
Ohio—John J. Raipe.
Pennsylvania—Charles Meyran, Pittsburg.
Tennessee—R. J. Morgan.
Texas—George A. Wright.
Wisconsin—O. H. Ingram.
West Virginia—John A. Gibney.

COMMITTEE ON RESOLUTIONS.

Alabama—Thomas B. Taylor.
Arkansas—Wm. M. Fishback.
Dakota—P. Donan.
Iowa—Gen. Wm. H. Vandiver.
Indiana—Gen. A. D. Streight.
Illinois—W. T. Dowdall, Peoria.
Kansas—J. P. Root.
Kentucky—H. Verhoff, Jr.
Louisiana—Duncan F. Kenner.
Mississippi—Judge H. F. Simrall.
Missouri—Henry Hitchcock.

Michigan—Alonzo Sessions.
Minnesota—R. Blakesley.
New Mexico—P. J. Kennedy.
Nebraska—J. Sterling Morton.
Ohio—S. F. Covington.
Pennsylvania—Hon. Geo. H. Anderson.
Texas—J. J. Gammage.
Tennessee—H. T. Elliot.
Wisconsin—J. C. Gregory.
West Virginia—F. J. Hearne.

COMMITTEE ON ORDER OF BUSINESS.

Arkansas—H. M. Grant.
Dakota—R. F. Pettigrew.
Iowa—Ed. Russell.
Indiana—J. M. Reynolds.
Illinois—W. D. Dowdall.
Kansas—A. Dorker.
Kentucky—Frank Truck.
Louisiana—A. J. Gomila.
Missouri—Gov. C. H. Hardin.
Minnesota—O. C. Merryman.
Mississippi—C. E. Webb.
Michigan—Philo Parsons.
New Mexico—P. J. Kennedy.
New York—A. H. Dugan.
Nebraska—Henry G. Clark.
Ohio—J. K. Morrison.
Pennsylvania—Joseph J. Sidney.
Texas—W. H. Fleppen.
Tennessee—Smith Hart.
Wisconsin—D. A. McDonald.
West Virginia—John A. Givens.

While the roll was being called, Mr. Covington, of Ohio, said:

"I move that in order to expedite business, the chairman

of each delegation send up the names of all persons appointed on the respective committees."

The Chairman. "That is being done."

A delegate. "I move that we now adjourn until eleven o'clock to-morrow."

Mr. Bennett, of Arkansas. "I desire to offer the following resolution: That the roll of States be called, and that all delegates having resolutions prepared may submit them and have them referred to the Committee on Resolutions for consideration without debate."

The resolution was adopted.

A delegate. "I move that all delegates from the territory contiguous to the Missouri river remain here immediately after adjournment."

Mr. Hogan. "I move, as an amendment to the resolution just offered, that the resolutions be read to the Convention, and then referred without debate."

Mr. Bennett. "I accept the amendment."

A delegate. "It will probably be a very long matter to receive all these resolutions and read them, and I therefore move that the Convention adjourn till three o'clock, in order that the Committee on Permanent Organization may be enabled to report."

The Chairman. "Before the motion to adjourn is put, I desire to read a request which I hold in my hand, that the members of the press who are delegates to this Convention, are invited by the press of this city to meet at three P. M., at the press headquarters, in the Laclede Hotel, Parlor B., for the purpose of a carriage ride to Forest Park and other places in the suburbs."

A delegate. "Please announce where the Committee on Resolutions will meet, and other committees, so that when we adjourn we may know where to go as members of committees."

The Chairman. "The Secretary will read the resolution

that has been offered and amended, before the motion to adjourn is put."

The Secretary then read as follows:

"*Resolved*, That the roll of States be called, and that all delegates having resolutions prepared may submit them after being read, and have them referred to the Committee on Resolutions without debate."

A delegate from Tennessee. "I move to lay the amendment on the table."

A delegate from Illinois. "I rise to a point of order. I made a motion to adjourn, and I understand that it is before the Convention, and that only is in order."

Mr. Stanard. "I hope the gentleman will withdraw his motion to adjourn; it is only about half-past one o'clock.

A delegate. "I call the gentleman from Missouri to order."

The Chairman. "It is moved that this Convention adjourn until three o'clock."

The motion was put and lost.

The Chairman. "The question now is on the motion of the gentleman from Tennessee, to lay the resolution on the table."

The motion was put and lost.

The Chairman. "The question now is on the adoption of the resolution."

The question was put, and the resolution was adopted.

Mr. Elliot. "That resolution has not been voted on yet."

The Chairman. "I will state for the information of the gentleman, that the motion to lay the resolution on the table was lost, and that the resolution has been adopted."

Mr. Stanard. "I understand there is a point of order pending against me."

A delegate from Texas. "I make the point of order that

no resolution can be entertained by the Convention until after the permanent organization, and that we are now in embryo."

The Chairman. "The point of order is well taken. I sustain the gentleman's point of order."

Mr. Stanard. "There are many letters here from distinguished men throughout the entire United States, some of which I am sure this Convention would like to hear. I observe in looking over a long list of distinguished men here from the various States, that there is a gentleman who was a member of the first Mississippi River Improvement Convention, I believe, that ever was held in the Mississippi Valley, and who secured, or was largely instrumental, at least, in securing the first appropriation that was ever made for the improvement of the Mississippi river, and as we have an hour or two to spare, I hope that some of these letters will be read, and that some of these gentlemen who are here will be invited to address the Convention; and in my reference a moment ago, I desire now to state that I referred to Gen. George W. Jones, of Iowa. [Loud applause.] I move that he be requested to address the Convention."

The Chairman. "You have heard the motion; if there is no objection Gen. Jones will come forward and address the Convention."

There being no objection, Gen. Jones came forward, amid loud applause, and spoke as follows:

Mr. President and gentlemen of this glorious, magnificent Convention, I am embarrassed beyond expression at this distinguished honor which is conferred upon me by this Convention in being requested to address you on this occasion. I can conceive of no reason why I should be selected to address you upon this occasion unless it be that I am, perhaps, the oldest member of it. I suppose I am the oldest member of the Convention from the State of Missouri. I came to St. Louis, as the papers have announced, in 1814. My father was a member of the first Convention which framed the Constitution of Missouri, and under that Constitution was elected one of the judges of the Supreme Court of the State of Missouri in 1820. As the gentleman upon my right—from the State of Missouri, I believe (Governor Stanard)—has said, I had the honor of being the introducer of a resolution in Congress, in 1836-7, under which, I believe, the first appropriation of money was ever made to remove the obstruction to the navigation of the Mississippi river at the Des Moines and Rock River rapids. Under that resolution of mine an appropriation of $75,000 was made. General Charles Gratiot, then Chief Engineer of the United States at Washington City. informed me, after the appropriation was made by Congress, that General Jackson, then President of the United States, intended to veto that bill, and suggested to me that I should procure the assistance, if I could, of old members of Congress—I then being about the youngest member in Congress—to wait upon the President, General Jackson, to induce him not to veto my bill.

As I had been introduced to General Jackson when I reached Washington, on the first Monday in December, 1835, by an old friend of his, as a college-mate of his son,—as a class-mate of his son, A. J. Donaldson,—and as I knew that the old hero looked upon me almost as a son, I undertook to wait upon that hero to ask him not to veto that bill. I did so. He said, " My son, I am under the view which I took.—and under my Maysville veto, I am compelled to veto that bill, because of its being in opposition to the views entertained in my veto-message."

I said to him: " Mr. President, I, as a delegate from the Territory of Michigan—I was then the last delegate from the Territory of Michigan— introduced the resolution in Congress asking Congress to make this appropriation for the benefit of my constituents who are the offspring of the General Government, and under the protection of the General Government. I introduced that resolution, sir, so that we could get our bread." We had nothing in the world from Michigan Territory to ship down the river then excepting lead; and we had no means, I told him, of obtaining the flour and the pork and the provisions upon which we were to live, for we raised nothing ourselves in Michigan Territory then west of the Lake, nothing at all, and for that reason I said to him, I have introduced this resolution. He says: " Are you the author of that resolution?" I said: " Yes, sir; and I ask it as a delegate of the Territory of Michigan; and I hope, Mr. President, that you will not veto my bill." He said: " My son, as you are the author of it, I will not veto it." [Loud applause.]

I need not go into the particulars to tell you all of the arguments that I made use of at that time, but it is sufficient to say that as the delegate of Michigan Territory, which then embraced the present States of Michigan, Wisconsin, Iowa, Minnesota, and Nebraska, and all of that country extending to the Pacific ocean,—as that territory was represented by myself, I had some influence with the old hero, and had the honor of seeing my bill approved by his hand.

Now, gentlemen of the Convention, and Mr. President, I hope that you will not expect me to extend my remarks. I suppose I could, as old men are very garrulous, keep you here for a long time, but I would not do so, in consideration of the fact that several motions have already been made, and that you must already be prepared for your dinner, and I therefore ask you to excuse me from saying anything further. [Loud applause.]

The Chairman. "Gentlemen, permit me to state here now, before the members are scattered, that this Convention is respectfully invited to attend a promenade concert in the Chamber of Commerce, this evening at eight o'clock, and to take your wives and sweethearts along with you."

A delegate. "Or somebody else's wife?" [Laughter.]

A delegate from Arkansas. "I move, in order to give the Committee on Permanent Organization time to perfect their organization and to report to the Convention, that we adjourn to meet at half-past two or three—say three o'clock—this evening, in order that the Committee on Permanent Organization may report, because if we do not organize until to-morrow we will not get through this week."

Mr. Bain. "I would suggest that as there is no place to meet here in this room, or connected with this, that the Committee on Permanent Organization meet in the gentlemen's parlor at the Southern Hotel. I make that motion."

A delegate. "I move that we adjourn till to-morrow morning at nine o'clock."

Mr. Hardin, of Missouri. "I suggest that the Committee on Order of Business meet immediately after adjournment."

A delegate from Minnesota. "I wish to say to the Convention that there is present with us to-day the only representative of that first original river convention which was held in the city of Memphis (and which has been described to us by the orator who welcomed us here)—Gen. Rozier, of Missouri; and I would suggest, sir, and move, that Gen. Rozier be requested to address this Convention now. We would like to know the men who are here among us who were the pioneers in this work—the men who were in that convention presided over by John C. Calhoun."

The Chairman. "Gentlemen, I will state for the information of the Convention, that the Secretary is now ready to report where the various committees will meet."

Mr. Rowland, of St. Louis. "Before the report of the

committee is read, I would like to extend an invitation for a committee to meet at the Planters' House."

Several voices. "Report, report."

The Secretary made the following announcement:

"The Committee on Resolutions will meet in Parlor 17 of the Lindell Hotel."

Mr. Bain. "Immediately?"

The Secretary. "Immediately, of course. The Committee on Permanent Organization will meet in the gentlemen's parlor of the Southern Hotel. The Committee on Order of Business will meet at the office of the Executive Committee in the rotunda of the Southern Hotel."

Mr. Rowland. "I move, instead of the office of the Executive Committee, that they meet at the Planters' House, as an invitation has been extended by the proprietors of that hotel."

Mr. Bain. "They will not do anything of the kind."

Mr. Rowland. "I will explain."

The Chairman. "The Committee can make that change if it is necessary."

Mr. Underwood, of Kentucky. "The Committee on Credentials—the place is not indicated."

The Chairman. "I will state to the gentleman that the Committee on Credentials will meet in the Southern Hotel gentlemen's parlor immediately."

A delegate from Iowa. "The Committee on Credentials has already passed a resolution, which the Chairman will pass to the Secretary now. I make a motion that these committees meet at four o'clock, and report to-morrow at ten. The idea that the Committee on Resolutions can report this afternoon is impossible. There will be lots of talking, and it will be impossible to report this evening, and I move that this Committee report to-morrow morning at ten o'clock."

Mr. Fishback, of Arkansas. "I have a motion to adjourn, which is always in order, and ought to have been put."

The Chairman. "The gentleman from Arkansas moves that this Convention adjourn until this afternoon at four o'clock."

The motion was put and lost.

Mr. Craig, of Missouri. "I move that the Convention adjourn to meet at ten o'clock to-morrow morning."

The motion was put and carried, and the Convention thereupon adjourned.

SECTION 2—SECOND DAY.

OCTOBER 27, 1881.

The Convention re-assembled at 10:30 A. M., and was called to order by Governor Crittenden, temporary President.

The President. "The Convention will be opened with prayer by Rev. Dr. Eliot, of this city."

PRAYER BY REV. W. G. ELIOT.

"Almighty and most merciful God, Thou who art the Ruler of the universe, King of kings and Lord of lords, we pray that Thy blessing may rest upon us here.

"We thank Thee that we are permitted this day to meet together as brothers in the interest of peace, of good order, and of national union. We thank Thee for the great American brotherhood to which we belong. We thank Thee that we have come together to consider those things which are for our common good; that here we remember that we represent sister States of the great republic; that here we are members of one body. And we thank Thee that we have at last learned, though it has been through sadness and tears, that being members of one body, when one member suffers, all members suffer with it, and when one rejoices all rejoice with it. Therefore we pray that Thou wilt give us wisdom in our councils and strength in our purposes. We pray that Thou wilt teach us that we are not working for separate benefit, but for the common good. We pray that Thou wilt teach us to remember that Thou governest all, and that no councils which are begun or continued without Thy blessing can succeed.

"We thank Thee that Thou hast prospered our great and beloved country so far, leading us through ways that we had not known, through sorrow, through tears, through battle, through blood, to this glorious union of hearts and purposes.

" O most merciful God, may Thy blessing still rest upon us, Thou who hast taught us that we are but one family. Through one great common grief which almost bereft us at the time of thought and reason, Thou hast taught us we are but one family. Grant that we may carry this feeling forward with greater and greater earnestness and more tender affection. And may Thy blessing rest upon our country, upon its rulers and its legislators. Grant that they may have wisdom and truth to guide them, and that they may not care for party interests in comparison with the great interests of the whole land.

" And now, trusting ourselves to Thee, feeling our own weakness and our own ignorance, thanking Thee once more that we are here together for a united purpose in the interest of peace and good order and national union, we would glorify Thy name forever through Jesus Christ our Lord. Amen."

Mr. Hardin, of Missouri. "You have a committee appointed on Order of Business, and they are ready to make a report."

The President. "Let the report be presented."

Mr. Hogan, of Missouri. "Before that report is read permit me, if you please, to make this suggestion. The United States Government have appointed a Commission for the improvement of these water-ways that we are looking after. That Commission, by request, has appointed a delegation from its body to represent it in this Convention and make known its plans. I suggest that the Convention invite that delegation to take seats upon the platform, and unite with us in the investigations that we are about to inaugurate."

The President. "Gentlemen, you have heard the motion of the gentleman from Missouri, Mr. Hogan, that the United States Commission, appointed to investigate the subject of the Mississippi river and its tributaries, be invited to take seats upon this platform."

The question was put and the motion carried unanimously.

The Secretary then read the report of the Committee on Order of Business, as follows:

To the President and Delegates of the Mississippi River Improvement Convention:

GENTLEMEN:—The Committee on Order of Business respectfully recommend the following programme for the action of the Convention:

First—Prayer.

Second—Permanent organization.

Third—Reception of communications to the Convention.

Fourth—Reception of resolutions to be referred to the Committee on Resolutions without debate.

Fifth—The parliamentary rules of the House of Representatives of the United States to govern the Convention.

Sixth—Speeches limited to ten minutes unless extended by the Convention.

Seventh—That each State in the Mississippi Valley be entitled, upon all reports and resolutions which may be presented to the Convention by the Committee on Resolutions, and all amendments which may be offered to the same, to cast the same number of votes as they respectively do in the election of President of the United States, to wit:

Alabama	10	Mississippi	8
Arkansas	6	Missouri	15
Illinois	21	Nebraska	3
Indiana	15	Ohio	22
Iowa	11	Tennessee	12
Kansas	5	Texas	8
Kentucky	12	West Virginia	5
Louisiana	8	Wisconsin	10
Minnesota	5	Pennsylvania	29

The States of New York and Michigan each four votes, and the Territories of New Mexico and Dakota one vote each.

J. M. REYNOLDS,   C. H. HARDIN,
 Secretary.   *Chairman.*

The report was adopted unanimously.

The President. "Is the Committee on Permanent Organization ready to report?"

Mr. Logan H. Roots, of Arkansas:

"MR. PRESIDENT AND GENTLEMEN OF THE CONVENTION: On behalf of the Committee on Permanent Organization I would state they considered very earnestly the importance of permanency *after* this Convention should cease, but they decided that it was not their province, but that that should be left to the Convention, to decide through what machinery they will prosecute the important work after the adjournment of the Convention. There were many names presented before them for consideration, as the officers of this Convention,—more indeed, I believe, than were presented to either National Convention of the Republican or Democratic parties for nomination to the Presidency of the United States. [Laughter.] But they have selected and unanimously report the following list:

"For President of this Convention, the Hon. Mark H. Dunnell, of Minnesota.

"They have recommended a Vice-President from each of the States and Territories who responded to the roll-call upon yesterday, their names being as follows:

Arkansas—John D. Adams.
Iowa—George W. Jones.
Kentucky—Eugene Underwood.
Indiana—M. M. Hurley.
Louisiana—George C. Waddell.
Tennessee—H. T. Elliot.
Kansas—D. G. Stockwell.
Minnesota—O. C. Merriman.
Nebraska—C. S. Chase.
Dakota—J. T. Pettigrew.
Wisconsin—William Wilson.
New York—B. S. Osborne.
Pennsylvania—R. C. Gray.
Texas—W. H. Fleppen.
Ohio—S. F. Covington.
Illinois—H. Fullerton.
Missouri—James S. Rollins.
Michigan—Philo Parsons.
Mississippi—H. F. Simrall.
Alabama—Thomas B. Taylor.
New Mexico—Governor Sheldon.
West Virginia—Alexander Campbell.

"They further recommend for Secretary of this Convent on, George L. Wright.

"For Assistant Secretaries, Frank Gaiennie and Nicholas Bell.

"All of which is submitted as the unanimous report of this committee. The formal document will be submitted when written by our Secretary, Mr. Caldwell, of Kansas."

A delegate moved the adoption of the report, and it was adopted unanimously.

Mr. Roots. "I move that a committee of three be appointed to wait upon Gen. Dunnell and escort him to the chair."

The motion was carried.

The President. "I appoint John F. Phillips, of Missouri, Mr. Campbell, of West Virginia, and Mr. Roots, of Arkansas."

The committee conducted the President elect to the platform.

The President *pro-tem.* "I have the honor to introduce to you, Hon. Mark H. Dunnell, of Minnesota, permanent President of this Convention. Please permit me to state that from long association with him in Congress, I here fully endorse the action of the Convention, and say that you could not have made a wiser choice." [Applause.]

The President then said:

"GENTLEMEN OF THE CONVENTION: In accepting the position you have assigned me in this Convention, allow me to return to you my sincerest thanks and assure you that it shall be my endeavor to preside over your deliberations impartially and to the best of my ability. We have met here from twenty States of the Union, besides the Territories represented,—delegates from the Gulf to the sources of the Mississippi,—to deliberate, to vote, to resolve upon questions of exceeding interest, not only to that section of country which we here represent, but also to the entire Union. We are here to consider how we may the better develop the mighty resources which a good Providence has placed within our reach in this mighty valley of the Mississippi. '[Applause.] The questions which will come before us are intensely practical. They lie out before us at once. We are the great producing section of the republic, and the question which interests us as delegates, the question which interests those we represent, is, How shall these vast products find the markets of the world with the least possible loss in transportation. [Applause.] We find here in our great Valley, the mighty Mississippi, which stretches from the Gulf all along to its source, fed by great tributaries, whose representation is made here in your presence at this time.

"How shall these waters best subserve the great purposes for which they were given to us? Shall these waters be unvexed by the steamboat and the barge? Shall they be vocal with protestations against all other modes of transportation? Shall these waters be subservient to the mighty interests of this mighty valley? Within a few years the Mississippi Valley has aided very materially in solving questions which interested the patriots of America. Out from this valley went supplies that the markets of the world demanded, that gave to us that balance of trade which has brought on all the attendant blessings that have come from it. The balance of trade was given to us by the products of the Mississippi Valley. [Loud applause.] Out from this valley went the source of our present national credit; and from this region of the republic went the solution of questions which were beyond the reach of statesmanship.

"Gentlemen of the Convention, there are others here to present the arguments which come from an array of statistics; there are others here to be heard to-day. Resolutions are to be offered, to be followed by debate, and the great work of this Convention is with you.

"In closing, let me again thank you for the honor, and let me make this suggestion: That the higher success will be reached by this Convention if we shall preserve a large degree of order ; and it will be my endeavor as your presiding officer— aided, as I no doubt shall be by you—so to preserve the ordet of this Convention, that when it shall have closed we may not be led to say that its results were less successful than they ought to have been, because its proceedings were not conducted in order. [Applause.] Then, gentlemen, I shall ask for a high measure of order in the midst of these exceedingly interesting deliberations." [Loud applause.]

The President. "It will now be in order to present communications to the Convention, according to the order of business which you have adopted for this forenoon."

Mr. Taylor, of Alabama. "I have in my pocket a plan for the improvement of the Mississippi river and its tributaries. The main plan is this: I believe the bed of the river is a chain of slack-water lakes, separated by shoals. My plan is to cut a canal through those shoals to the center of the river, or thereabouts, so as to connect the slack-water lakes, so that the best navigation can be secured to the Gulf. I believe, sir, it is perfectly practicable. I believe when I can get the engineers of the United States to understand me fully that they will agree to it. With your permission I will lay my plan before this Convention."

The President. "Refer it to the committee. The gentleman will forward any communication he sees fit to make. If I am correctly informed these communications are to be received without debate. I am informed by the Secretary he has a communication in his possession which, under the order of business will now be in order."

The following communication from the President of the Mississippi River Commission was then read:

Office of Mississippi River Commission,
Steamer "General Barnard."
Vicksburg, Oct. 17, 1881.

To the President of the Mississippi River Improvement Convention, St. Louis, Mo.:

Dear Sir: It has been my intention to be present at the meetings of your Convention, in order to afford any information that might be desired with regard to the plans, prospects and expectations of the Mississippi River Commission.

I find, however, that imperative official engagements will require my presence elsewhere. I have, therefore, thought proper to submit the following statement in writing, which may be presented to the Convention, should it be deemed desirable to do so.

Under the organic act of June 28, 1879, it was made the duty of this Commission:

First—To direct and complete such surveys of the Mississippi river, between the Head of the Passes, near the mouth, and its headwaters, as were then in progress; and to make such additional surveys and examinations of the river and its tributaries as the Commission might deem necessary.

Second—To consider and mature such plan or plans as will correct, permanently locate and deepen the channel and protect the banks of the Mississippi river; improve and give safety and ease to navigation; prevent destructive floods, and promote and facilitate commerce and the postal service; and, with such plans, to prepare and submit estimates of the cost of executing the work.

Third—To report specifically upon the practicability, feasibility and probable cost of three certain methods or plans of improvement, designated in the act as the "jetty system," the "levee system," and the "outlet system."

Fourth—The Commission was also authorized, prior to the completion of all necessary surveys and examinations, to submit plans and estimates of cost of such immediate or initial works, constituting a part of the general system of works recommended, as might be advantageously begun at once.

In the first report of the Commission, submitted in February of last year, the so-called systems of improvement mentioned in the law were discussed, viz.: the "outlet system," the "levee system," and the "jetty system."

The outlet system, being one of diffusion and waste, and not of concentration, did not commend itself to our judgment. It has been claimed that outlets, either natural or artificial, which shall draw off the flood-waters of the river and convey them away by independent routes to the sea, will tend to prevent the recurrence of destructive floods by supplying additional avenues for their escape. The general proposition that if a river cannot carry its own waters within its own banks, outlet channels will supply a remedy against overflow, certainly sounds reasonable at first hearing. It is true, however, in certain cases only. It is not generally true of sedimentary streams, flowing through alluvial lands, and it is not true of the Mississippi river. The character and useful magnitude of such a stream are determined by its behavior in times of flood; and there is no more certain way to dwarf its dimensions and destroy its navigation than by depleting it of its flood-waters. Once check its velocity by outlets, or by any other means, thus impairing its power to carry its load of solid matter to the sea, and the inevitable result is that a deposit of sediment takes place, and the bed of the stream is raised. The consequences are that the sectional area and flood-carrying capacity are both diminished and flood-surface raised. Surely the last condition of that stream is worse than the first, for it is smaller than before and less able to retain its flood-waters within its own banks. If new outlets are made to meet this contingency, the flood-current is still further checked, and the bed is raised higher by increased deposits.

It is submitted, therefore, that the permanent effect of outlets is to injure the navigation and increase the frequency and magnitude of floods.

With regard to a system of improvement by means of levees, it may be said, that while levees are, upon a large portion of the river, necessary to prevent destruction to life and property by overflow, and while they enhance the safety and ease of navigation, and facilitate trade and commerce by affording convenient landing-places above the reach of flood, and while they aid and promote the postal service by the protection they afford to the roads and railroads in their rear, upon which that service is conducted, the construction and maintenance of a levee system cannot be regarded as a necessary auxiliary to any judicious plan designed for channel improvement only. There is little doubt that levees do exert some direct action in enlarging the bed of the river during those periods of flood, when, by preventing the overflow of adjacent lands, they actually cause the water to rise to a higher level within the river-bed than it would attain if not thus restrained; for the simple reason that, other things being equal, the deeper the water in the bed of a stream the greater will be the velocity and the greater its scouring power. Levees are regarded, therefore, as a desirable, though not an essential, adjunct in the method of improvement recommended by the Commission. They are necessary to prevent destructive floods; they are desirable and useful for other purposes already stated; they are desirable, although not necessary, for purposes of channel improvement. The Commission, in its first report, recommended that all gaps in existing levees, between Cairo and New Orleans, be closed.

It may be said, in this connection, that some members of this Commission attach more, and others perhaps less, importance to levees as a factor in the problem of channel improvement than that above indicated.

The plan of improvement recommended by the Commission is based upon the simple, and, I believe, unquestioned fact that the bad navigation of the river is caused by the caving and erosion of its banks, and the excessive widths, and the bars and shoals resulting directly therefrom.

Two well-known conditions characterize the entire length of the river below Cairo: First, that bad shoals and bars and dangerous navigation are always accompanied by a low-water width exceeding 3,000 feet; and, second, that wherever the width does not exceed 3,000 feet there is a good channel the year round. In other words, bad navigation is produced by a wide river, and good navigation by a narrow one. The same principle applies to the portion of the river between the mouths of the Missouri and the

Ohio rivers. The evident remedies for the existing evils are: First, to stop further enlargement by protecting the caving banks; and, second, to narrow the stream to a suitable and approximately uniform width at all places where the widths are excessive and the navigation bad. Wherever necessary, therefore, the caving banks will be graded to a proper slope and protected by suitable revetments against further erosion.

Where the widths are too great the channel will be narrowed by forces developed in the stream itself, through the agency of high permeable dikes placed either longitudinally or transversely to the channel, as circumstances shall require. By these light open works, constructed largely of poles, wire and brush, the area to be raised will be converted into a series of silting basins, within which the water, constantly flowing through the barriers with diminished velocity, will deposit its heavier materials. In this way the bed of the stream will be gradually raised during the high-water season, forming new banks and developing new shore-lines for the amended channel.

These methods of improvement have been successfully applied at various points on the Missouri and Mississippi rivers, and are in no sense experimental, except in the details of construction.

For beginning the work projected by this Commission, and for which the sum of $1,000,000 was appropriated at the last session of Congress, an efficient equipment has been ordered, and it is expected that active operations will be started within the coming month, upon the Plum Point reach, above Memphis, and the Lake Providence reach, above Vicksburg. These two reaches constitute an aggregate length of about seventy miles of the worst navigation below Cairo. The works are expected to secure a low-water depth of ten feet, with possibilities considerably beyond that limit.

Although this Commission have given especial attention and study to the requirements of navigation on the main river below Cairo, they have carefully inspected the plans of improvement now in process of execution by the Engineer Bureau of the War Department upon that portion of this stream between Cairo and St. Paul, and are of the opinion that their completion will establish a low-water navigation of not less than eight feet between Cairo and St. Louis, and not less than six feet between St. Louis and St. Paul, with capabilities in both cases of greater depths, through an extension and enlargement of the works.

It is hardly necessary to add that the work thus undertaken is one of unparalleled magnitude; that great difficulties are to be encountered; that it is only by patience and perseverence, and upon the stepping-stones of mistakes corrected, that success can be hoped for, and that the final result will depend as much on the support and co-operation of the people as on the efforts of the Commission, or other agents of the Government.

Three members of the Commission. Judge R. S. Taylor, of Fort Wayne. Ind.; Mr. B. M. Harrod, of New Orleans, La., and Major Chas. R. Suter, Corps of Engineers, will be in St. Louis during the Convention, and they have been constituted a committee to represent the views of the Commission, should your Convention desire a conference, or further information, beyond that set forth in this communication.

Very respectfully, your obedient servant,

Q. A. GILLMORE,
Lieut.-Col. of Engineers and Bvt. Maj.-Gen., President of Commission.

The President. "I hold in my hand a communication from James B. Eads. It will now be read."

The following was then read:

St. Louis, October 18, 1881.

To the Executive Committee of the Mississippi River Improvement Convention:

Gentlemen: I am in receipt of your kind invitation to address the Convention at its coming meeting upon the improvement of the Mississippi river.

I greatly regret being compelled to forego the pleasure of accepting this invitation. On the 23d inst. I sail from New Orleans for Mexico; and were I to postpone sailing upon that date I would be forced to abandon the trip during this year, as I could not again secure a vessel in time to enable me to carry out the purposes of my visit and return at the date when my presence in this country is imperatively demanded.

I now go to Mexico for the purpose of crossing the Isthmus of Tehuantepec, and inspecting in person the line of the proposed ship railway.

I need hardly assure you of my deep interest in all matters pertaining to the improvement of that great river which has been the study of my life, and if any views I could present would add, however little, to the great good which the Convention will doubtless accomplish, I should be most happy.

Although I will be unable to attend the meeting of the Convention, I will still be engaged in a work which is closely connected with the improvement of the Mississippi river and the successful consummation which cannot fail to be of untold value to the commerce of the Mississippi Valley.

The removal of all obstructions from the mouth of the river opened to our commerce the markets of the East, the ship railway will open to it the markets of the West, and will in effect be the opening of the Mississippi river into the Pacific ocean.

Hence, while I cannot be with you, I will still feel that I

am working with you for the accomplishment of an end which will result in the greatest benefit to our commerce and the increased wealth and happiness of our people.

I am, very respectfully yours,

JAS. B. EADS.

The President. "I have a letter from Hon. Randall L. Gibson, member of the House of Representatives from Louisiana, and Senator-elect, written from Paris, which will now be read."

The letter was read as follows:

HOTEL D'OXFORD ET CAMBRIDGE,
13 RUE D'ALGIER, PARIS.

HENRY LOUREY, *Chairman.*

SIR: I thank you for your courteous invitation to attend the Mississippi River Improvement Convention, to be held in St. Louis on the 26th inst. I sincerely regret my inability to attend.

To all those who have sought to secure recognition of the Mississippi river and its tributaries from the National Government, and adequate appropriations for their improvement, it is not necessary to say how indispensable is the cordial union of the efforts of all the Representatives in Congress from the Mississippi Valley and all the friends of river improvement.

Without harmony and union and great energy nothing can be accomplished. This is not a new question, and before proceeding further, or taking a new departure, it is important that the members of your Convention should know what has been done and what is proposed in Congress.

The final measure for a scientific and comprehensive treatment of the Mississippi river was proposed in the Forty-fourth Congress, June, 1876, and the speech made by Capt. J. B. Eads before the Committee on Commerce in support of it marked the commencement of the struggle. You will find it annexed to some remarks of mine on the subject in the *Congressional Record* of February 5, 1879.

After several years of constant struggle, the bill offered May 10, 1879, became a law, having been approved June 28, 1879. I enclose you a copy of the act entitled "An Act to provide for the appointment of a Mississippi River Commission for the improvement of said river from the Head of the Passes, near the mouth, *to its headwaters.*" Section 4 confers the powers upon the Commission. You will find them ample for the purpose. I think that an effort should be directed towards securing from the executive branch of the Government intelligent supervision of the labors of the Commission and recommendations in favor of adequate appropriations. The President may make and unmake the Commission. Everything depends on the intelligence and energy with which the Commission performs its duty and the President may see the law faithfully executed. Much of course will depend upon the Secretary of War, who is especially charged with the supervision of the work. You may ask why it may be deemed necessary to establish a special Commission for the Mississippi river? I answer that the nature of the work itself required a systematic plan, embracing every part of the river and all its phenomena. All the parts of this great river are closely connected; like the members of a living organism, they are mutually interdependent. The work that might confer great advantages at one point might inflict intolerable injury to another. The effort to remove the shallow waters, or sand-bar that causes them, at Providence, will merely transfer them to a point lower down, flooding the country below in seasons of high water and presenting the same obstacles when the river is low, unless the plan be so comprehensive as to include the lower as well as the higher sections of the river. Every improvement of the tributaries, every channel deepened, every furrow made and farm drained concentrates all the more rapidly the rain-fall of the vast region extending from the Alleghenies to the Rocky Mountains, and precipitates it into the great basin from Cairo to the Gulf.

The report of the Commission shows that this vast basin, overspreading its banks owing to these causes, is gradually but surely filling up, having increased in width about seventy per cent. since the first survey, and growing more shallow year by year, until, as the lamented Garfield said in his letter of acceptance, it has become a "terror to the people living upon its banks, and the navigation more hazardous and expensive and its trade and commerce more and more insecure."

Into this great basin, or inland sea, empty forty-three mighty rivers, while the distance from Cairo to the Gulf is only about 500 miles in a direct line. By the river it is about 1,100 miles, presenting a coast line of over 2,200 miles.

While the tributaries should be improved, it must be apparent that the main trunk-line should not be neglected; that that they are so intimately connected as to be interdependent.

In the second place, a Commission was necessary to secure the support of any plan for the improvement of the Mississippi river. The fact is, the Mississippi is in nobody's district. No Representative felt it to be his duty to secure appropriations for it. Any appropriation to be expended in any one place on the Mississippi river could be lost, for it involved the attempt at piecemeal work, which, from the nature of the case, as I have shown, could amount to nothing. And in point of fact, it was only after the Commission was established and presented its plan that we were able to induce Congress to vote a reasonable appropriation. Before that we could get nothing. We were divided in our views; each member had his own plans; there was a diversity of opinion. Nothing could be done, and nothing was done. The Commission suited us all, and we got more for the Mississippi river and its tributaries the last session of the last Congress than in any half-dozen sessions before. In fact, it was the first time that Congress had ever recognized the claims of the Mississippi Valley,—every part of it.

The Commission having the power under the existing law and ample appropriations, will do their work wisely and well. If they do, Congress will vote every dollar you can fairly ask. If they do not, it will be broken up, and we will fall back upon the old plan, by which the members of Congress would secure a small appropriation each for that part of the river, or more likely for its tributary in his own district, or rival towns and cities; or steamboat interests will send their "parliamentary solicitor" or lobbyist to procure an appropriation for some little local improvement. Our efforts should be to uphold the Mississippi River Commission; if necessary, to extend its powers and to increase its members; we should see that the members are adequately paid, and that the best men in the country are kept upon it.

I hope your Convention will have a successful session. We need an earnest and enlightened public sentiment to sustain the effort of your Representatives in Congress.

Yours, faithfully,

R. L. GIBSON.

The President. "I have a letter from Hon. James B. Beck, one of the Senators from the State of Kentucky, which will now be read."

The following letter was read:

UNITED STATES SENATE CHAMBER,
WASHINGTON, October 15, 1881.

GEORGE L. WRIGHT, ESQ.

DEAR SIR: My failure to answer your kind letter inviting me to address the River Convention October 26th, was because I wanted to be there, and could not see my way clear to accept, because of this session. It is now clear that I cannot be with you. I regret it. I regard the improvement of the Mississippi river, from St. Paul to the mouth, and of the great tributaries of your great river, as one of the most important questions now before the country. Competing highways alone make cheap transportation possible, and free water-ways make railroad combinations very difficult. I hope to be able to be heard on that question here next winter, as I can't be with you now.

Yours, truly, J. B. BECK.

The President. " A letter will now be read from Hon. A. D. Gorman, one of the Senators from the State of Maryland."

The Secretary then read the following:

WASHINGTON, D. C., October 7, 1881.

MY DEAR SIR: I have the honor to acknowledge the receipt of your invitation to attend the Convention to be held in your State on the 26th of October, to deliberate on the question of improving the condition of the Mississippi river and its navigable tributaries.

I regret very much to say that my engagements are such as to make it impossible for me to accept the same.

The question of cheap transportation is one that concerns every section of our common country. That the improvement of the great interior water-ways will go far towards the solution of the problem, no one who has considered the subject, will for a moment question; what other steps are necessary are not so well defined.

I regret that I cannot hear the views of your representative men, but trust, however, to receive from you a copy of your proceedings and debates.

Thanking you and your committee for your kind invitation, I am yours, truly,

A. D. GORMAN,
United States Senator, Maryland.

The President. "A letter will now be read from Hon. Abram S. Hewitt, of New York."

The Secretary read the following:

NEW YORK, September 21, 1881.

HENRY LOUREY, ESQ., *Chairman, St. Louis, Mo.*

DEAR SIR: I have the honor to acknowledge the receipt of your invitation to attend the Mississippi River Improvement Convention, to be held on the 26th of October, 1881. I regret that the condition of my health will not permit me to be present. I appreciate fully the value and necessity of making the Mississippi river and its navigable tributaries thoroughly efficient highways for commerce. I have always been in favor of their improvement upon a well-devised system, which will insure successful and permanent results. I am equally opposed to all propositions designed for the promotion of private interests or to furnish jobs for contractors, and I trust that the results of your deliberations will be to put in intelligible form some plan of improvement which will secure the favorable opinion of competent engineers. You may count, therefore, upon my cordial co-operation in Congress and out of it, in any movement which shall tend to make our natural highways a check upon the railways of the country, which, until they are properly controlled by Government supervision, are liable to be used merely for private ends, and not for the public welfare.

I have the honor to be, very respectfully,

Your obedient servant,

ABRAM S. HEWITT.

The President. "A letter will now be read from Hon. B. F. Jonas, a Senator from the State of Louisiana."

The letter was read as follows:

UNITED STATES SENATE CHAMBER,
WASHINGTON, October 17, 1881.

GEO. L. WRIGHT, ESQ., *Corresponding Secretary, St. Louis.*

DEAR SIR: I am in receipt of your postal of the 13th, and also received your invitation in September.

I have delayed answering because of the uncertainty as to the duration of the session of the Senate.

If it should adjourn on Saturday next (as seems probable), or in time for the Convention, I shall be present, as I feel the deepest interest in the subject of its deliberations.

Very truly yours, B. F. JONAS.

The President. "A letter will be read from Hon. Thomas L. James, Postmaster-General of the United States."

The Secretary read the following:

POST-OFFICE DEPARTMENT,
WASHINGTON, D. C., September 22d, 1881.

DEAR SIR: I have the honor to acknowledge the receipt of your invitation to be present and participate in the deliberations of the Mississippi River Improvement Convention on the 26th of October next, and to say, in reply, that I regret my official duties will prevent me from being with you on that occasion. Very respectfully,

THOMAS L. JAMES,
Postmaster-General.

The President. "A letter has been received from Hon. George B. Loring, Commissioner of Agriculture, which will be read."

The following was read by the Secretary:

DEPARTMENT OF AGRICULTURE,
WASHINGTON, October 15, 1881.

DEAR SIR: It would give me great pleasure to take part in the deliberations of the River Convention to be held in your city on the 26th inst, as I consider its object a very important one, and I regret that my engagements for that day make it impossible for me to attend.

Very respectfully,
GEORGE B. LORING,
Commissioner of Agriculture.

The President. "A letter will be read from Hon. Joseph R. Hawley, Senator from the State of Connecticut."

The Secretary next read the following:

UNITED STATES SENATE,
WASHINGTON, October 15, 1881.

DEAR SIR: I thank you for the invitation to the River Convention, October 26th, and should find it both agreeable and instructive to be there, but that is impossible, and I must confine myself to the newspaper reports.

Yours, truly, Jos. R. HAWLEY,
United States Senator, Connecticut.

The President. "A letter will be read from Hon. R. G. Horr, member of Congress from the State of Michigan."

Mr. Horr wrote as follows:

EAST SAGINAW, October 16, 1881.
GEO. L. WRIGHT, *Secretary.*

DEAR SIR: Your kind invitation reached me in due time, and I now write to say that it will be impossible for me to be with you on the 26th inst. I need not say that the object of your meeting meets my hearty approval, and I can assure you that the improvement of your river will ever receive my active support. Yours, most truly,
R. G. HORR.

The President. "A letter has been received from Hon. Thomas Updegraff, a member of Congress from the Third District of Iowa."

The Secretary then read the following letter:

MCGREGOR, IOWA, October 18, 1881.
GEORGE L. WRIGHT, ESQ., *St. Louis.*

DEAR SIR: Great as I esteem the importance of improving and maintaining the navigation of the Mississippi and its tributaries, circumstances prevent my attending the River Convention soon to be held at your city. Wishing the Convention abundant success, and thanking you for your kindness,

I am, very truly yours,
THOMAS UPDEGRAFF.

The President. "There are no other communications on the table to be presented to the Convention."

Mr. Hogan, of Missouri. "Mr. President, at the request of several gentlemen, members of this Convention, and in accordance with the suggestion of General Gillmore, President of the Mississippi River Commission, I respectfully suggest that at this time it would be proper for this Convention to hear from the delegated members of that Commission who are now present, and, as General Gillmore says, will be prepared to present to this Convention their thoughts on this subject. I think the members of this Convention would be glad to hear from at least one of the members of that Commission now; I therefore make that motion, sir, that they be requested now to address the Convention."

The motion was seconded.

Mr. Roberts, of Illinois. "I wish to suggest to the gentleman that there will probably be some resolutions to offer, that, under the rules, will have to go the Committee on Resolutions, and as that would be the next order of business, I would suggest that the persons having these resolutions to offer, put them in first so that the Committee can be considering them. I have a resolution myself that I wish to offer and have read and referred to the Committee on Resolutions. If the gentleman will withdraw his motion for the time—"

The President. "The gentleman from Missouri moves that the Convention now listen to some remarks from some member of the River Commission. That motion has been seconded. As many as favor the adoption of this motion will say 'aye.'"

A delegate. "Wouldn't it take a two-third vote of the Convention to suspend the regular order of business?"

The President. "It probably would."

A delegate from Illinois. "I make that point of order, that it requires a two-third vote to suspend the regular order of business."

Mr. Stanard, of Missouri. "I hope that my friend (Mr. Hogan) will withdraw his motion for the time being; not that I would show any disrespect to the Commission at all, because I am anxious to hear from them, but it seems to me there is force in the suggestion of the gentleman from Illinois that it will be eminently proper at this time that gentlemen of the Convention have an opportunity to hand in their resolutions, as the Committee on Resolutions have not reported, and would like to know of any resolutions or papers gentlemen of the Convention may have to present, and have the opportunity of considering them, so that an early report may be had from the Committee on Resolutions. I hope the gentleman who made the motion asking some member of the Commission to speak, will withdraw that motion temporarily, and that the order of business may be proceeded with until the resolutions have been presented."

Mr. Hogan, of Missouri. "I had not any idea of precluding resolutions. I didn't know there were gentlemen here who might want to present resolutions to be referred. I had forgotten about that. My sole object was to get the thought of the Commission into the minds of the committee and of the Convention before proceeding with business. I have no objection to deferring it until after the resolutions proposed are referred to the Committee on Resolutions, and then hope the other will be done."

The President. "The Chair understands the gentleman to withdraw his motion, and next in order will be the reception of resolutions to be referred to the Committee on Resolutions without debate."

Mr. Roberts, of Illinois. "I have a resolution I wish to offer, and ask that it may be read and referred to the Committee on Resolutions."

The resolution was read as follows:

Resolved, That it is the sense of this Convention that the future policy of the government of the United States for the improvement of the Mississippi river and its tributaries, should embrace the enlargement and deepening of the Illinois and Michigan canal, and the improvement of the Illinois river, so as to afford deep-water navigation from Lake Michigan to the Mississippi river.

The President. "These resolutions, under the order, will go to the Committee on Resolutions."

Mr. Roberts, of Arkansas. "I suggest that the States be called alphabetically."

The President. "A gentleman has suggested that the States be called in order and resolutions come from delegations. The Secretary will read the list as printed."

The Secretary then read the list of States as printed.

Mr. Jones, of Tennessee, offered the following:

Resolved, That in constituting the commissions to administer the appropriations to the Mississippi and its tributaries, some recognition is due to the practical experience of river men, who have spent their lives in navigation of the streams to be improved; who have made the movements of the waters the study of years; who know their channels as the faces of familiar friends, and have watched their changes and pryed into the causes of them; whose business makes them most interested in practical improvements, and most competent to advise upon the means to be adopted to make the watercourses fit avenues of commerce.

Resolved, That the attention of Congress and the River Commission is respectfully called to the fact that there are now in existence certain railroad bridges which operate to obstruct navigation, with draws of inadequate width, or not properly placed as to the navigable channels, or placed diagonally across the currents, and that said bodies be requested to make proper inquiry, and institute the proceedings necessary to the removal or the correction of the evil.

Referred to the Committee on Resolutions.

When the Secretary called "Kentucky," Mr. Underwood of that State said:

"We have at present no resolutions prepared, but members of our delegation desire to have time yet to prepare some, and I would like to ask if it would be in order to present resolutions from any of the respective delegations at any future period of the deliberations of this Convention?"

The President. "Resolutions coming from delegations or members might be referred directly to the Committee on Resolutions. There will, perhaps, be no occasion for their presentation at any other than this time, if we follow strictly the order of business."

Mr. Covington, of Ohio. "I would like to renew the proposition of the gentleman from Kentucky (Mr. Underwood), and if you will allow me to explain a single moment, since the calling for resolutions, it has occurred to me that nothing has been presented, or probably will be presented, referring to the light-house system as established on Western rivers. It is, to my mind, one of the greatest aids to commerce, and it is a system that should be maintained, whatever the cost may be. Every navigator of the Western rivers will admit there has been nothing done for Western rivers from which so much benefit has been derived, for the expense incurred, as from the light-house system. I would be pleased if the Convention will allow me to draw up a resolution on that subject, and present it. I think there would be no objection to it."

The President. "I hear no objection."

Mr. Gould, of Missouri. "In answer to the gentleman from Ohio upon this subject of the Light-house Board, I have prepared a resolution that I had designed to offer to the Convention at the time Missouri should be called. You have passed the 'M's' and I didn't hear it; I was engaged, perhaps. I would offer a resolution and ask that the same be read."

The President. "Missouri will be called in order."

Mr. William T. Price, of Missouri, offered the following resolution:

Resolved, That the several delegations in attendance on this Convention are hereby declared committees, whose duty it shall be to press upon the attention of the Congress of the

United States the propriety and the necessity of liberal appropriations being made and prompt and vigorous efforts being put forth to improve the navigation of the Mississippi river and its navigable tributaries, by the publication of statistical and other information, memorials of State Legislatures and such other methods as to them may seem best calculated to secure the result.

Referred to Committee on Resolutions.

Mr. C. E. Mears, of Wisconsin, offered the following:

WHEREAS, The United States Government has already commenced the improvement of many of the navigable tributaries of the Mississippi river, by appropriation of money by Congress and the judicious expenditure of same by the United States Engineer Corps, which expenditure is greatly benefiting the entire Mississippi Valley; therefore,

Resolved, That we recommend continued appropriations by Congress for the improvement of the navigable tributaries of the Mississippi river until they are in perfect condition, as the importance of their commerce demands.

Referred to Committee on Resolutions.

Mr. Taylor, of Kansas City, offered the following:

Resolved, That the Secretary be instructed to address a letter to each Congressman whose constituency are interested in the deliberations of this Convention, requesting him to briefly define his position as to a liberal appropriation for the improvement of the Mississippi river and its navigable tributaries, and that they be published in the St. Louis daily papers.

Referred to Committee on Resolutions.

Mr. Philo Parsons, of Michigan, offered the following:

Resolved, That it is the deliberate conviction of Michigan, which, from her vast territory, contributed States bordered by the Mississippi, that wise and liberal appropriations, ample in amount, should be appropriated for the improvement of the great Father of Waters and the splendid tributaries.

Same reference.

Mr. McPike, of Illinois, offered the following, which were also referred to the Committee on Resolutions:

WHEREAS, The general and thorough improvement of the Mississippi river and its navigable tributaries are properly recognized of national importance, and,

WHEREAS, To give practical force to the efforts now being made to accomplish such end, this Convention hereby pledges its combined and earnest energies to urge upon Congress and our representative men the propriety and necessity of early, concentrated and persistent action to secure its achievement; therefore, be it

Resolved, By this Convention assembled, that we urge upon Congress the adoption of a regular system of national improvement of said thoroughfares, to deepen that channel and render them a great highway, over which the freighted wealth of this unequaled valley—its cereal and mineral products in their varied forms—may find not only an easy and cheap, but also a safe transit to the markets of the world.

Resolved, That recognizing its overshadowing importance to all other or integral parts of public improvement proposed or possible, ask we from Congress definite and specific appropriations disconnected from any other system or policy of public expenditures.

Mr. John I. McBride, of Illinois, offered the following:

WHEREAS, The washing in of the alluvial lands along the Mississippi river tends to widen the same and create bars, and thereby causing shallow water and impeding navigation; therefore, be it

Resolved, That it is the sense of this Convention, that after the work of keeping the snags removed and maintaining the signal light-house service, the next work of first importance which should receive attention, is that of preventing the washing in of the banks, and, secondly, the narrowing of the channel in the most necessary places, as has been recommended by the River Commission.

Referred to Committee on Resolutions.

Mr. Thistlewood, of Illinois, offered the following resolution:

Resolved, That this Convention, imposing implicit faith in the wisdom and the ability of the present Mississippi Commission, as organized by act of Congress, does hereby indorse their plans for the improvement of said river, and would most earnestly petition our representatives in Congress to use all honorable means to secure such a liberal appropriation as will enable said Commission to vigorously prosecute their important work, in a manner commensurate with the magnitude of so important a public highway.

Referred to Committee on Resolutions.

Mr. Fishback, of Arkansas, presented the following resolutions, which were referred to the same committee:

WHEREAS, The preamble to the Constitution of the United States declares that one of the objects of our Union is to promote the general welfare by a combination of effort of all the States and through the General Government.

WHEREAS, The enormous development of our internal resources and the rapidly expanding increase of our foreign commerce render cheap and easy transportation from the interior to the seaboard one of the chief elements of our general welfare; and

WHEREAS, Of the two leading methods of transportation one is artificial, constructed at enormous cost, and operated at heavy expense, while the other is furnished by nature free of cost; the former owned by private individuals and subject to private control and private avarice or caprice; the latter free to the competition of all and subject to the exclusive control of the United States Government; and

WHEREAS, The Congress, while it has given to these artificial highways, which are the property of private individuals, nearly one hundred millions of money, and nearly two hundred millions also of acres of our national lands, has left the great natural and national highways of the Mississippi Valley with appropriations totally inadequate to the purpose of rendering their navigation certain; and

WHEREAS, It is inconsistent with the general welfare that the large interior basin lying between the Rocky Mountains and the Alleghenies, comprising upward of one-half, and by far the most fertile part of our national domain, with 16,000 miles of navigable streams, and nearly 20,000,000 of people, and yielding more than half of the agricultural products of the country, should be forced to abandon its natural and cheaper highways because of their uncertainty, and to carry its best and rapidly increasing productions to the seaboard across mountain ranges, over artificial highways, and at such heavy expense as to sometimes amount to a total interdiction, and at all times to a serious detriment both to the consumer and the producer; therefore,

Resolved, first. That in the opinion of this Convention the general welfare of our country can in few other ways be so largely promoted as by a systematic and comprehensive plan of opening the navigable streams of the United States, and keeping them open at all seasons, thus rendering impracticable those capricious or avaricious combinations among common carriers which in the past have proven so disastrous to legitimate commerce.

Second. That, as the initial part of such a plan, it is of especial and commanding importance both to the foreign and domestic commerce of our country, that the Mississippi river, from St. Louis to its mouth, be made to afford unfailing navigation at all seasons, and as early as practicable, and that at the same time the navigation of its upper waters and tributaries be opened and improved more or less rapidly, as the traffic of their adjacent territories respectively may demand.

Third. That these natural highways being subject to the exclusive control, and by our Constitution confided to the peculiar care of the General Government, it is the duty of the Congress of the United States to make whatever appropriations may be necessary to carry out objects of such vital importance to the general welfare.

Fourth. That a committee consisting of one from each State represented in this Convention, and five from the city of St, Louis, be appointed by the Chair, whose duty it shall be to collate and tabulate statistical information in regard to : First, the probable cost of rendering permanently navigable the Mississippi river from St. Louis to its mouth. Second, the probable cost of rendering permanently navigable its tributaries respectively from their mouths to their heads of navigation. Third, the amounts, both in value and quantity, of produce which are now carried across the country out of their natural courses by railways and which would seek the seaboard by rivers if navigation were rendered certain at all seasons. Fourth, the amounts, both in value and quantity, of productions now transported along the respective routes of our rivers, both by the rivers themselves and by the parallel railways along their respective valleys. Fifth, the relative cost of river and rail transportation. Sixth, the comparative amounts which have been appropriated by the Congress to the natural and peculiarly national highways of the Mississippi Valley for their improvement, and to private corporations for constructing artificial transportation lines from the interior to the seaboard, and such other information as may seem to them advisable, and report the same to this Convention to-morrow at 12 M., to the end that it be laid before the people and the Congress of the United States.

Mr. Hartwig, of Missouri, offered the following:

WHEREAS, The rapid progress made in this country during the past forty years is in a great measure due to the skill of American inventors and American engineers; and,

WHEREAS, There is a growing feeling among the people of the great Mississippi Valley, and especially among our old and experienced river navigators, that some mechanical device could be adopted that would cheaply and rapidly deepen the water in the channels of our Western and Southern rivers, and thereby give relief at once to the river commerce of the West and South; and,

WHEREAS, The unprecedented increase of produce shipments by the Mississippi river during the last twelve months makes it the imperative duty of the General Government to test any plan or device that in the opinion of practical river navigators promises good results; therefore, be it

Resolved, first, That the Congress of the United States is hereby urgently requested to appoint a commission consisting of twelve old and experienced Western and Southern river navigators, whose duty it shall be to investigate any and all mechanical devices for improving navigation that may be brought to their attention for cutting or dredging through and deepening channels across sand-bars, and after a careful and exhaustive examination into all the details, report to Congress the device or character of machinery which in their judgment is best adapted for that purpose and which promises the best results.

Resolved, That Congress is hereby requested to make sufficient appropriations to test any mechanical device reported on favorably by said commission and put same to work on the Mississippi or Missouri river during the summer of 1882.

Referred to Committee on Resolutions.

Mr. Stanard, of Missouri. "I hold in my hand a preamble and a set of resolutions prepared by the delegation of the Merchants' Exchange of the city of St. Louis, representing as they do their views upon this important subject,—the subject under consideration. I ask that the resolutions be read."

The resolutions were read as follows:

To the representatives of the commercial communities of the Mississippi Valley in convention assembled at St. Louis, Mo.

Believing that the Mississippi river and its navigable tributaries, the great inland water-ways prepared by the Creator for the use of the people, are a most important and valuable part of the national domain, free to all, beyond the reach of monopoly and affording to the whole people that competition in transportation which benefits producers and consumers alike; and further, that cheap transportation is the great necessity of an agricultural people, the indispensable condition of the easy conveyance to distressed markets of their staple products, bulky in proportion to value; that the familiar economical truth that the cheapest transportation of such products is by water, is especially applicable to these great water-ways of the West; provided, the same be kept free from snags, sand-bars, treacherous banks and other obstacles to navigation, do therefore resolve and declare

First. That it is the manifest and imperative duty of the government of the United States to cause to be made such improvements of the great rivers of that valley, to wit, the Mississippi, the Missouri and the Ohio, neither of which is within or subject to the jurisdiction of any one State, as will permanently secure the safety and ease of the navigation thereof from source to mouth; thereby cheapening freights, reducing insurance and other burdens and expenses, promoting the vast inland commerce of the nation and creating new avenues of foreign trade, and thus not only inviting increased production and population, but assuring greater prosperity to the whole people.

Second. That the appropriations for such improvements should be separately made for each river, and be adequate to the continued prosecution of work once begun until the same is finished, so as to avoid the wasteful destruction of work partially completed, by reason of the delay or stoppage thereof for want of sufficient appropriations; and be it further resolved,

Third. That this Convention recognizes with extreme satisfaction and emphatic approval, in the passage of the acts of Congress of June 28, 1879, "for the appointment of a Mississippi River Commission," and in the comprehensive and scientific surveys and important recommendations made by the distinguished engineers appointed on that commission, as set forth in their reports of February 17, 1880, and January 8, 1881, the first well-considered and effective step towards the complete and permanent opening of the Mississippi Valley to the markets of the world; but would also strongly express its regret at the refusal of the last Congress, after creating the Commission, and notwithstanding the deliberate and emphatic approval of their plans by the House Committee on the improvement of the Mississippi river, to appropriate the amount estimated and recommended by the said Commission for doing the work by them carefully laid out and prepared; and be it further resolved,

Fourth. That in the deliberate and earnest judgment of this Convention, delegates to represent the interests in that behalf of more than one-half the States and Territories of the Union, inhabited by more than one-half of its entire population, from whom is collected seventy-two per cent. of the entire internal revenue of the nation, whose internal commerce is already one-half that of the whole United States, more than twelve times greater than the total foreign commerce of this nation, and larger than the total foreign commerce of the world; but upon whose industry is each year levied, by the obstacles to the safe and easy navigation of the Mississippi river and its navigable tributaries, a needless direct tax by way of increased freights and insurance, demurrage, wreck and repairs, of not less than ten millions of dollars ($10,000,000), it is the important duty of Congress and the right of the people for whom this Convention is authorized to speak, that the legislation thus wisely begun be made effectual and permanent by enlarging the powers of the River Commission to include the active prosecution of the works already recommended by them, and by the regular and separate appropriation from year to year of such sums as said Commission, acting under the reasonable supervision of Congress, shall report as necessary to that end, so that this great and indispensable work, material in every sense, shall no longer be delayed.

Fifth. And be it further resolved, that the comprehensive and scientific scheme of river improvement thus inaugurated should as rapidly as possible include the complete and permanent improvement and maintenance of all the navigable tributaries of the great national water-way aboved named.

The resolutions were referred to the same committee.

Mr. Bernheimer, of Missouri. "Recognizing the fact in one section that the improvement of the Mississippi river means the improvement of its channel and the facilitating of commerce, I ask the Convention to recognize the fact for the South, that it deserves the improvement and protection of the banks bordering on it, for the protection of the surrounding country. For that purpose I beg to offer a special resolution for levees, as follows:

Be it resolved, By this Convention that we deem it not only eminently fitting, but urgently the duty of the General Government to afford relief and render protection to those sections to the great Mississippi Valley which are annually subjected to inundation by the floods of this great river,—the national highway to the sea.

We deem this work of national importance, and urge upon Congress to make special provision for the building and maintenance of a perfect system of levees throughout the sections requiring the same, thus reclaiming many millions of acres of valuable lands, public as well as private, which will otherwise be left an idle waste, to the detriment of the whole country.

Referred to the same committee.

Mr. C. H. Mansur, of Missouri. "We have heard a good deal, both by resolution and in speeches, of the importance of unity of action, and I want to see if members will abide by what they propose, and pledge themselves not to support any man for office who is not in sympathy with Mississippi river improvement, and will ask their friends to refrain from supporting all such candidates. [Cheers.] I offer the following resolutions:

WHEREAS, The United States is in a condition of profound peace, at home and abroad; and

WHEREAS, The year A. D. 1882 is an off-year in politics; and

WHEREAS, The improvement of the Mississippi river and its tributary streams is a subject of vital importance to the present, as well as future welfare of the tens of millions of people inhabiting and to inhabit its great valley, transcending far questions of mere party politics, which it should be above and beyond; and to the end that our members in Congress, as well as the people of the whole country, may know that this Convention is in earnest; therefore, be it

Resolved, That the members of this Convention hereby pledge their honor, each to the other, that in A. D. 1882, within our respective districts and within our party allegiance and lines, we will neither support for a nomination, or if nominated, will neither work for, nor support for any election any person who will not pledge himself, if elected, to abide by, work and vote for, on the floor of Congress, such measures and appropriations as may be adopted and recommended by this Convention.

Resolved, That this Convention recommend to the voters of the Republican and Democratic parties of the several Congressional Districts lying within the area of the Mississippi Valley, to pursue the same line of policy outlined in the above resolution.

Referred to same committee.

Mr. Given Campbell, of Missouri, offered the following:

Resolved, That this Convention suggest to the Governors of each of the States of this valley the propriety and importance of the appointment and maintenance by each State of at least one agent who shall actively promote the objects of this Convention.

Referred to same committee.

Mr. Gould, of Missouri. "Are resolutions still in order from Missouri?" [Laughter.]

The President. "Resolutions are still in order from Missouri."

Mr. Gould. "I hold in my hand two resolutions. [Laughter.] As I see the Secretary has some difficulty in deciphering resolutions that are sent up, and is somewhat embarrassed, by permission of the President, I will read the resolutions. I would remark, in the first place,"—

Cries of "Read!" "read!"

Mr. Gould. "I will read, then; don't be alarmed; Missouri is still in order. Resolutions of this character"—

Renewed cries of "Read!"

Mr. Gould then read the following:

WHEREAS, The Government has within the last few years extended the benefits of the light-house system to Western and Southern rivers to a limited extent, thus adding greatly to the facilities of navigation, so far as it has extended, and showing the necessity of increased service; therefore,

Resolved, That this Convention, looking to the immediate improvement of the navigation of the Mississippi river and its navigable tributaries, recommends to Congress the pressing necessity of adding another district to the present number, the same to extend from Cairo to New Orleans and embrace the Southern tributaries, thus enabling the present force to devote much needed service to the upper streams above Cairo, which cannot now be accommodated, with the amount of service granted by Congress.

Mr. Gould. "As the Convention is entertaining propositions a little wider than was apprehended when these resolutions were drawn,—they have not been drawn with very much care; simply suggestions, as it were,—and as I see the Convention is receiving various propositions outside"—

Cries of "Read!" "read!"

Mr. Gould. "With your permission I will read this."

The President. "Observe order, gentlemen. The gentleman is in order. Proceed with the reading."

Mr. Gould (reading)—

WHEREAS, Congress has enacted a general bridge law, whereby railroad and other companies are authorized to bridge navigable streams without properly protecting the passageways through bridges built with draws, thus often causing loss of life to raftsmen while attempting to pass through the draw, and a great loss of time to steamboats and barges, and not unfrequently the loss of the same when attempting to pass them in windy weather and dark nights, thus increasing the risk and causing additional cost in insurance to the transportation of the products of the country; therefore be it

Resolved, That inasmuch as it is entirely practicable to protect such draws, and at small cost, by building cribs or sheer-booms, or driving spiling above the opening and alongside the draw-pier, thus rendering the passage of all kind of water-craft comparatively safe, by dropping through with lines, when necessary, we therefore respectfully ask that Congress will, at its next session, enact a law compelling all owners of bridges across navigable streams, that are built as draw-bridges, to furnish the necessary protection, within a reasonable time.

The resolutions were referred to the Committee on Resolutions.

Mr. George H. Shields, of Missouri. "If Missouri is still in order I desire to offer some resolutions, and as I don't write very well, I will read them:

"*Resolved,* That the immediate and comprehensive improvement of the Mississippi river and its navigable tributaries to the fullest extent of their improvable capacity, in order to secure safe, permanent and reliable channels of sufficient depth and breadth to afford, at all seasons of the year, ample facilities for the water transportation of the immense productions of the great Mississippi Valley, is demanded of the Government of the United States by every consideration of commercial, agricultural and society advancement, and by justice and an enlightened policy of promoting the prosperity and defence of the whole nation.

"*Second.* That we favor any meritorious project for increased water transportation facilities, by which the general interests of the whole country may be conserved, and we commend all such schemes to the careful consideration and intelligent support of Congress, if truly worthy; but we deem the immediate and permanent improvement of the Mississippi river and its navigable tributaries, according to some comprehensive plan, embracing the whole subject, of paramount importance, and we demand of Congress that the matter be considered on its own merits, and free from all complications or connection with other internal improvements.

"*Third.* That we believe the appointment, under the act of Congress, of the "Mississippi River Commission," a step in the right direction, and we earnestly demand that the reasonable requests of that body, which we believe to be composed of wise, scientific and practical men, for public moneys to carry out the needed improvements, under a general and comprehensive plan, should be cheerfully granted."

Referred to Committee on Resolutions.

Mr. Livingstone, of Illinois, offered the following resolution, which was referred to the Committee on Resolutions:

Resolved, That there be appointed by this Convention a permanent executive committee to further the objects of this Convention, to consist of at least one from each Congressional District which is represented here, which will have power to collect and publish information on the subject, and to appoint committees to attend the sessions of Congress from time to time, to urge upon that body ample appropriations for the improvement of the Mississippi river and its tributaries, and to take such measures as they may deem necessary to secure the objects embraced in the call of this Convention.

Mr. McEnery, of Louisiana. "These resolutions are offered by the entire delegation."

Resolved, That we heartily approve the expressed determination of the Federal Government to improve navigation by adequately constructed levees, preventing destructive floods and giving ease and safety to trade, commerce and the postal service on the great national highway, the Mississippi river.

Also, that we approve the steps already taken in the appointment of a mixed commission of engineers from the scientific corps of the Government and from civil life, to plan and execute this great work, and in appropriating sums of money, both for the necessary surveys and examinations and for commencing work under the plan proposed by them; and, in view of the greatness of the object sought, the necessity of uniformity of system and administration to the success of such work, and in the interests and rights of 30,000,000 of citizens, we demand that the efforts of the Government shall be both persistent and liberal.

That the course indicated by the legislation of the last Congress should be maintained on the Mississippi river, and extended over the tributaries, and that appropriations shall be adequate to the magnitude of the work and the necessity of pushing it forward as rapidly as the increased commercial necessities demand.

Finally, in exemplification of the wise appropriation and judicious expenditures of the public money, under a system and in an enterprise similar to that which we are now advocating, we point to the triumphant success and the great commercial results of the Jetties of the South Pass. This great work has already established new and more extended lines of commerce, giving freer access to the ports of the world and saving many times their cost as profit to the producer in reduced rates of transportation.

The full development of their benefits will only be attained when similar improvements are extended to the entire length of the Mississippi river and its great tributary streams and full protection be given to the dwellers on the banks.

The resolutions were referred to the Committee on Resolutions.

Mr. Loyal, of Louisiana. "Mr. Chairman, I had prepared an article to be read before this Convention, and submitted it to the delegation of which I am a member; they advocated my not pushing the question; I therefore have not done it, but inasmuch as I have devoted considerable attention to the subject, I filed it with the Secretary; I wish it, if so ordered, to be referred to the Committee on Resolutions."

The Chairman. "There will be no objection."

Mr. D. C. Basey, of Missouri, offered the following:

Resolved, That the Chairman of this Convention appoint a committee of three from each Congressional District to petition their Congressmen to use their influence and vote for as liberal appropriation as may be asked by the River Commission, which was appointed by last Congress, to improve the Mississippi river and its tributaries.

Referred to Committee on Resolutions.

Mr. J. C. Livingstone, of Louisiana, offered the following:

Resolved, That the protection and improvement of the river transportation of the Mississippi Valley means a confined channel of sufficient depth from navigable headwaters to the sea.

Referred to Committee on Resolutions.

The following was presented by James F. Robinson, of Arkansas:

Resolved, That the purposes of this Convention can be best attained by simply indorsing the law creating the Mississippi River Commission, approving the plans of the Commissioners, and using all legitimate means to procure from Congress the necessary appropriations to carry out their plans.

Referred to the Committee on Resolutions.

The following was offered by Mr. Walker, of Minnesota:

Resolved, That for the purpose of expediting the great work of improving the 16,000 miles of water-way comprising the Mississippi and its navigable tributaries, we do most earnestly insist and recommend that Congress make immediate provision for the rapid progress of the work by adding to the Mississippi River Commission at least eight more members, five of whom shall be from the regular corps of engineers of the War Department of the United States, so that it may be susceptible of division into three working parties of five each, three of whom shall be United States engineers.

Referred to Committee on Resolutions.

Mr. P. J. Kennedy, of New Mexico. "Coming as I have come some fifteen hundred miles to represent the Territory of New Mexico, I desire to say that previous to going to New Mexico I spent twenty-seven years of my life on the Mississippi river building levees, confining the water to its channel, and keeping the country, as well as I could, protected from overflow. I have a report, which I have made out in the form of resolutions. As resolutions are now in order, I present them to this Convention, and ask the Secretary to read them.

The Secretary then read the resolutions as follows :

Resolved, That the importance of the subject of reclaiming and protecting from overflow, by the annual floods of the Mississippi river, of the great region within its delta, cannot be overestimated. The Mississippi river is the natural drain of a vast area of our territory between the Rocky and Allegheny mountains, and from our northerly boundary to the Gulf of Mexico, and embracing over 1,200,000 square miles. It embraces portions of the States of Missouri, Illinois, Arkansas, Tennessee, Mississippi and Louisiana, and contains about 38,700 square miles, or, in acres, in the aggregate, 24,768,000 ; of this amount there are 4,000 miles of seamarsh, and irreclaimable, leaving 22,208,000 acres of fertile land, wholly idle and useless, on account of its annually being inundated by the waters of the Mississippi.

The soil is rich alluvial deposit and inexhaustible. Plantations so situated as to be free from the invasion of the floods, without fertilizers, produce crops of sugar, cotton, rice and corn, as when first redeemed from the [forest. The land subject to overflow, if protected by levees and reclaimed, is capable of sustaining not less than 20,000,000 people. Its productions would be the richest in the world, averaging two bales of cotton to the acre ; 2,000 pounds of sugar, besides molasses, etc., to the acre, and forty bushels of corn ; and other cereals, as well as vegetables and fruits, grow in profusion. In fact, the wealth of the overflowed lands of the Mississippi Valley are exhaustless and inexhaustible, and yet this favored region is decaying, becoming a waste and a wilderness, because of the annual floods of the river which divides its centre.

The work to reclaim this vast region should be the solemn and immediate duty of the General Government, and to restore them to the hands of the husbandman.

First. Because the work is one national in its character. The Government, to be just, should control its floods, so that the natural servitude owed by the Delta regions, should not operate injuriously to citizens, because of their being located in that region.

Second. The work is national in its character, because it affects the safety and fortunes of five States, and indirectly affects the people of the entire Mississippi Valley. It cannot be called a sectional improvement, as it is designed at once to confer benefit upon the people who live in the lands subject to overflow, render safe their lives and property, and to improve a region which will, in a few short years, repay a hundred-fold the appropriation the Government should give.

Third. It is national, because the more perfect levee system of one State is useless unless there are equal and uniform levee systems in other States.

In the language of Prof. C. G. Forshey, a distinguished engineer, who made a study, for more than thirty years, of the Mississippi, its currents and levees: "No State alone can build its levees, because of the independence of its topography. A system to be efficient in one, must comprehend them all. The interior is a basin, or series of basins; the water, whenever let in, submerges the basins alike. These States, then, must share a common fortune, and hence it must appeal to a power that comprehends many States in its operations. Congress alone has that power."

Congress can provide for the general welfare. Scarcely a river harbor or bay upon our coast but annually receives its thousands that the highways of commerce may be safe and open. In building the levees of the Mississippi, Congress will promote and render safe the vast commerce of the greatest river of the world, by removing its bars, deepening its channel, and by expediting the transportation of freight, mails and passengers.

If the levee system became general, and the waters of the river were confined to its channel, bars would be washed out and the channel deepened. According to the opinion of Captain Eads: "It (the river) scours out increased room for itself wherever its current is accelerated, and its deposits are everywhere found where its current is retarded." He cited, to prove his assertion, that "when the 'Bonne Carre' crevasse occurred in 1874, that when the current is checked by the depletion of the river by a crevasse, deposits of sediment will occur below the crevasse, because the slackening of the current, caused by the channel below being then too large for the diminished needs of the river, would cause the water to deposit a part of its sediment, and thus raise the bottom of the river below the crevasse until, by the contraction, the natural current was restored." He also says that " we know that shoals are produced below crevasses, etc., and that they will disappear when crevasses are closed."

There can be no doubt that crevasses are forming bars constantly and obstructing the commerce of the river, and the outlets, if not closed, will deepen and widen and the bars will grow and become more serious by their obstructions. It is well known that the transportation and delivery of mails, freight and passengers are hindered and delayed by the floods for want of landings. Many ideas have been advanced as to the best methods of relief from overflows, to wit: One, reservoirs; two, straightening the channel; three, outlets; and four, levees.

The reservoir system is to hold back by a system of artificial lakes during floods, the volume of water held back to be retained for improving low-water navigation; but the Board of Engineers appointed by the Government to examine and report a permanent place for the reclamation of the alluvial basin of the Mississippi river, says: "In theory this system is very attractive, but in practice it promises no relief for the lowlands of the Mississippi, simply because there are no available sites for reservoirs sufficiently large to produce the desired effect."

Secondly. Straightening the channel is the idea of diminishing the natural resistance opposed to the flow of the water by cutting off the bends of the river, and thus lowering the surface. There are good reasons why cut-offs, judiciously located, should be made; among others is, that caving banks are caused by a curved channel, and if the channel is uniform, or nearly so, in width, the caving caused by the curving will be trifling.

Thirdly. Is that of making or creating outlets to drain the surplus water from the river and discharging it through new channels. Though there are many objections to them, *i.e.*, that they may deluge the adjacent country; that great deposits will be left in the lakes in which the deposits are withdrawn, thereby destroying the navigation of the lakes, and may even change the channel of the river, and also cause a diminution of the velocity of the current, and thus perhaps increase the height of the floods.

Fourthly. Is that of a system of protecting by artificial

banks erected in the natural banks of the river. We all know that great good has resulted from the levees already built. There is no doubt that the plan is the best to be adopted in the Valley, to the exclusion of all others. The history of other countries shows that the levee system is the only one; for instance, those in the Rhine, below Arnheim, protect the most fertile part of Holland. They are exposed at high water to as strong a current as the floods of the Mississippi, and the occurrence of crevasses, as they take place during high water on the Mississippi, are not known there.

The levees as now existing, compared with the interests they protect, are insignificant to those of the rivers like the Po, Rhine, and Vistula, and yet they have done great good and benefit to the lands protected. There is no doubt that the location of permanent levees, made to conform to a plan for straightening and correcting the channels, even using the cut-offs, will save thousands of square miles from inundation and overflow, and add most vastly to the glory and wealth of the country.

All the engineers appointed by the Government agree and advise, however they may differ upon plans or other points, that it is of the highest importance to repair the present levees and build additional ones, so that the commerce of the great region of the Valley, and the lands embraced therein, be protected. Every section of our country demands that this work be immediately done; then there will be reopened plantations, farms will be worked, and farming utensils of all kinds will be needed, factories will start, and the people inhabiting these reclaimed lands will want the thousand articles produced by Northern skill and industry. Therefore I would ask this Honorable Convention that they request their members of Congress that a bill be introduced that $50,000,000 be appropriated for making and repairing outlets and levees in the Mississippi Valley; the work to be done under the direction of the Secretary of War and the Engineers of the United States, also that the work be completed within five years. And I am thoroughly convinced, that if such a bill be passed, and the work done as it should be, that it will repay the country a hundred-fold for the expense.

Referred to Committee on Resolutions.

The President. "A communication has been sent to the President of this Convention from the Hon. James S. Rollins, of Missouri."

The communication was submitted as follows:

COLUMBIA, MO., October 24, 1881.

To the President of the Mississippi River Improvement Convention:

DEAR SIR: Having been appointed by Gov. Crittenden a delegate at large to the convention over which you preside, I may not be able to attend on account of the delicacy of my health, and beg therefore to present through you to the convention this communication.

Forty-five years ago I was a delegate from Boone county to a convention held in the city of St. Louis on the 20th day of April, 1836, for the promotion of internal improvements within the State of Missouri. This was the first Convention ever held in the State for this object, and so far as I have knowledge, the first Convention of the kind ever held west of the Mississippi river.

The following were the delegates from the county of Boone: R. W. Morris, Wm. Hunter, John W. Keiser, Dr. James W. Moss, D. M. Hickman, John B. Gordon, James S. Rollins, and Granville Branham; and of these I am the only survivor.

The following gentlemen were the delegates from the county and city of St. Louis: Edward Tracy, John O'Fallon, Archibald Gamble, M. Lewis Clark, Henry Walton, Henry Von Phul, Wm. Ayres, S. B. Grant, Samuel Merry, James C. Laveille, Thornton Grimsley, Lewellyn Brown, George K. McGunnegle, and Pierre Chouteau, Jr.; and of these M. Lewis Clark, now of Louisville, Ky., is the only one living; and of all the members composing that body, so far as I can ascertain, there are not more than four or five of the number living. At that time the Hon. John F. Darby was mayor of the city, and aided largely in dispensing its generous hospitality. He lives to a green old age, an historic wonder, abounding with pleasant recollections, observations and anecdotes of the city from the time it was a small French village to the present day.

Great changes have occurred since the holding of this convention in the city of St. Louis, containing at that time a population not exceeding 10,000, and the State itself a population of about 250,000. Missouri was at that time a frontier State.

The country between the western border of the State and the Rocky Mountains, and which now comprises the Indian Territory, the great States of Kansas, Nebraska and Colorado, was regarded as a sandy and sterile desert. The States of Iowa, Minnesota, and the great territories lying west of them, and stretching beyond the Rocky Mountains, extending to the mouth of the Columbia river, embracing Oregon and Washington Territory, were almost wholly uninhabited, save by hostile Indians, vast herds of buffalo and other wild game that roamed over the plains and through the mountains. It was only now and then that the puff of the steamboat was heard upon our rivers, and the shrill whistle of the locomotive had never yet startled the denizens of the forest in this almost boundless valley. Since that time the empire of Texas has been added as a State of the American Union; New Mexico, Arizona, and California with its 700 miles of coast upon the Pacific ocean, not to speak of the still further off territory of Alaska, have since been added to the domain of the United States.

In the proceedings of the convention above referred to I had the honor to introduce a resolution asking the appointment of a committee to memorialize Congress for a donation of public lands to be appropriated under the authority of the Legislature of Missouri to those objects of internal improvement contemplated by the convention. This resolution was unanimously adopted. The Hon. Hamilton R. Gamble, Edward Bates and myself were appointed upon this committee; and, so far as I know or now remember, this was the first memorial ever presented to Congress asking a grant of land to aid in promoting objects of internal improvement in the Mississippi Valley; and allow me to say with becoming modesty that I have stuck to this text with unflinching fidelity from that day to this!

It would be an interesting and illimitable theme to point out what has been accomplished in this direction in the way of population, development and progress in the western half of our country during these forty-five years. To do so would far exceed the appropriate limits of a letter like this. Let the imagination of intelligent minds fill in the gap and be amazed at the wonderful growth and grandeur of our country. So much for reminiscence.

Allow me to say, according to my poor view, and judging of the future by the past, with the increased intelligence and enterprise of the people, the impulse to public improvements which science has wrought in the application of steam and electricity in every department of human labor and industry; in the art of navigation, in the building of railroads and telegraph lines, in leveling and tunneling the mountains, in improving and utilizing every species of machinery, and removing obstacles seemingly insurmountable, opening up the way for the effective and rapid development of all the hidden sources of our vast internal wealth, that the American people are just entering upon another stage of change, improvement, amelioration and expansion which in the closing years of the nineteenth century will insure for them a transcendent power that will eclipse all their achievements hitherto in advancing civilization, intellectual and moral growth, material wealth and political power. So much for prophecy.

The intelligent Convention over which you preside, composed of a representation from eighteen States and Territories bordering upon and directly interested in the improvement of the navigable waters of the Mississippi Valley, has a great work before it in devising a scheme which will be acceptable to the people of every part of our country, and whereby the national Congress may be induced to make such appropriations from the national treasury, under a systemized plan of improvement of the great rivers, which in the end will afford to all the people who inhabit it the easiest and cheapest outlet through these natural channels of commerce for the products of their toil and labor to the markets of our own country and of all other countries where there are such exchanges of production necessary to meet the wants and add to the comforts of peoples living in distant parts of the habitable globe. Your enlightened body will not be without guidance upon this important subject. Superadded to the great intelligence of its large representation you will have the experience, the wisdom and the recommendations of other similar bodies who have gone before you, the reports of learned scientific men showing the necessity and feasibility of these improvements, with statistics of the population, the present wealth and the production of that vast and fertile area of our country, showing the interests to be subserved and benefited by these appropriations and improvements, as well as the still greater wealth to be added to the aggregate wealth of the nation. It is not necessary for me, in this short communication, to present these statistics here. You will have before you the able and admirable address of the Commission appointed by the Governors of States upon the commerce and improvement of the rivers of this valley, including also the address of the Hon. Eugene Underwood, President of the Commission, presenting in a very able manner the considerations and arguments in favor of the National Government taking hold and devising a plan whereby the improvement of the navigation of these great rivers may be accomplished and perfected.

The arguments presented in the able papers to which I have referred have not been, nor can they be answered.

To accomplish this great work the aid of the General Government is absolutely essential, and without which it cannot be done. For the attainment of this object we cannot rely upon the separate and sometimes conflicting action of independent States. To achieve so great a work we need the united effort of the whole people of our great country.

These are two great and vital schemes, which must in the future command the attention and unite the energies and intelligence of the National Legislature. These are for the General Government to make the necessary appropriations to improve and make safe and easy the commerce of those rivers, national in character, and in which a large majority of the people are interested. The other is to make similar and needed appropriations from the National Treasury in aid of the varied system of free public education existing under the laws of different States and established for the enlightenment of the entire youth of the country without regard to sex, color or condition.

Without intelligence, and that enterprise which intelligence brings, neither the commerce nor the physical condition of the country can ever be properly improved; and without the maintenance of a free system of public schools established in all the States, and with the aid of the National Government, we cannot have that general intelligence so essential to the enjoyment of rational freedom and the upholding of the free Government under which we live.

By the omnipotent aid of this system of free public schools we must wipe from our escutcheon the dark stigma of having one million five hundred thousand free men (according to our last census) entitled to the ballot,—the sacred right of suffrage,—who can neither read nor write.

We are ever to remember that our possibilities and capabilities as a country do not lie merely in our rivers, though affording more miles of navigation than any other nation; nor in our independent and magnificent central position; nor in our soil, though richer than that washed by the Nile itself; nor in our mountains of iron, or our fields of coal, or mines of lead, and the precious metals, or quarries of marble, or in any other natural advantage. however great and wonderful. But they do consist far more in the people we are to have,—in our children and youth, those who, in fact, are soon to make up and constitute the nation itself (for let it be forever remembered that the people are the State, and nothing else),—those who are to possess and use all its vast and untold resources and means of enjoyment, who are to develop its civilization, and to create for it the name and glory which it is to have among the nations of the earth.

But we must not lose sight of our theme—the improvement of the navigation of the Mississippi river and its tributaries. It is a vast enterprise. The danger is that we may ask too much by attempting too much at the same time. It occurs to me, that if the Convention would recommend to the Congress of the United States the improvement of the navigation of the Mississippi river from its source to its mouth, with appropriations sufficient to enter vigorously upon the work, as an entering wedge for the improvement of its larger tributaries in the future, it would be far better than to attempt any log-rolling scheme, by which bills are often loaded down and defeated. The strength of the friends of the measure would not then be frittered away, for there is no man who will ever in the future wend his way into the hall of either house of Congress from this valley who will deny that the Mississippi river is a national stream and entitled to this recognition by making necessary appropriations for its improvement. Any one who would vote against a proposition like that may at once be set down as incorrigible and opposed to all schemes and appropriations by the General Government for the improvement of the navigation of any river, whether it be local or national in its character. With the main river properly improved under the direction of able and enlightened engineers, and with its banks made secure from the Jetties to St. Paul, its navigation made easy, safe and economical, the commerce of this great valley would seek its outlet mainly through this channel, and it would force at once the improvement of the navigation of all its tributaries worthy to receive such aid, and which would be promptly afforded either by the government of the States through which these rivers flow, or both by the State and the General Government. In other words, the improvement of the Mississippi river proper would lead quickly to the improvement of all its tributaries, whose people living along its line would seek an outlet for the products of their labor, and the furnishing of their supplies through the common channel. My suggestion would, therefore, be, in order to obviate any objection, to concentrate all your forces upon the question of obtaining a sufficient appropriation for the improvement of the entire length of the Mississippi river proper, and as far as the main stream may be made navigable. It can never be out of place, nor can the quotation be too often repeated, the description given of this river by our former great Senator, Mr. Benton, many years ago, in which he says: "Wonderful river! connected with seas by the head and by the mouth, stretching its arms towards the Atlantic and the Pacific, lying in a valley which is a valley from the Gulf of Mexico to Hudson Bay; drawing its first waters not from rugged mountains, but from the plateau of the lakes in the center of the continent, and in communication with the sources of the St. Lawrence and the streams which take their course north to Hudson's Bay; draining the largest extent of the richest land; collecting the products of every clime, even the frigid, to bear the whole to market in the South, and there to meet the products of the entire world. Such is the Mississippi, and who can calculate the aggregate of its advantages and the magnitude of its future results?"

But I need not go further. The time is at hand when the claims of the Mississippi Valley can no longer be ignored. The sceptre has already departed from Judah! The potent voice of the Senators and Representatives from eighteen States lying within and bordering upon this great valley can no longer be stifled or silenced. Whatever may be the result of the action of this Convention, it is a mere question of time as to when the voice of the people of this valley will be heard and obeyed. Every intelligent mind must see and feel that the political power of the Government is rapidly concentrating here; that here is to be the seat of empire, from whence will emanate your laws, your great national politics, and whereby the destiny of the continent will be directed and controlled. A lack of concert of action, temporary causes, the division of trade and commerce by artificial means, may hinder and prevent for the time being the ultimate control, as I have predicted it; but this mountain- and lake- and gulf-locked valley, unsurpassed in the extent of its resources and undeveloped wealth, capable within itself of sustaining a population ten times greater than the population of the United States,—this great valley of the Mississippi, which drains a thirty-sixth part of the land surface of the globe itself, and which, rising near the lakes of the north, so near as to make their shores tributary to its valley, and flowing through more than twenty degrees of latitude, affords a variety of production for commercial interchange, compared with which the productions of the Amazon, the shores of the Mediterranean, or the valley of the Danube, or the Black and Baltic seas, must, under the highest development, remain utterly insignificant. The Mediterranean system and the valley of the Amazon, of the Baltic and Black seas, are limited in their products by the climatic uniformity of a single zone. But here is a valley developing north and southward, almost from the frigid to the torrid zone, in extent of area 2,231,000 square miles, all of it a part of our great country, and under the jurisdiction of the Congress of the United States,—a land upon whose distant mountain-tops the snow never melts, and in whose green valley beautiful flowers never cease to bloom. This vast valley, with its inconceivable riches from the soil, and beneath its soil; from its cereals, its cotton, tobacco, hemp, fruits; from its ores, timber, its water-power, its game, its populous towns and cities, its growing manufactories, with everything, in fact, needed for human sustenance, comfort, happiness and civilization, with possibilities even beyond conception or comprehension; lying, too, in the centre of the continent, with no Alpine barriers to oppose its outlet,—what to-day is its chief want, its commanding necessity? It is that the very channels which the Almighty has furnished shall be improved and made available by man's skill and labor. Why, it would seem to be in the very order of Providence that the National Government should do its part! And it must be done in order to enable the people to enjoy the very beneficence of our Creator; and that it will be, there cannot be a rational doubt.

The people, gentlemen, of this great valley, nay, I say of the entire country, and of all who are well-wishers of the success of free government on the American continent, look with hope, and anxiety and with confidence to the deliberations of your body, so to direct the legislation of the country as to insure the success of these great enterprises at the earliest practicable time.

I am, with very high regard, your obedient servant,
JAMES S. ROLLINS.

The President. "This communication will become a part of the proceedings of the Convention if there is no objection. The Chair hears none."

The Secretary read the following communication:

ST. LOUIS, October 24.

GEO. L. WRIGHT, *Corresponding Secretary River Improvement Convention:*

DEAR SIR—The Committee on Exhibition of the St. Louis School and Museum of Fine Arts desires to extend to the delegates attending the Convention a cordial invitation to visit the galleries of the Museum.

It is the desire of the officers and members of the Board of Control that the Museum should be known as it really is, as an institution established for the advancement of the West and South, and not for local use alone.

I send herewith a package of tickets, which may be made use of by those who wish.

Very respectfully,
HALSEY C. IVES, *Director,*
W. G. ELIOT, *For the Committee on Exhibition.*
Chancellor.

The following communication was also read:

MERCANTILE LIBRARY,
ST. LOUIS, Oct. 26, 1881.

The St. Louis Mercantile Library Association extends a cordial invitation to the delegates attending the Mississippi River Improvement Convention to visit its rooms during their sojourn in the city.

The reading-room is supplied with the principal newspapers from all parts of the country, and is open from nine o'clock A. M. to ten o'clock P. M.

Very respectfully,
JOHN N. DYER,
Librarian.

Mr. Roots, of Arkansas. "I move that the thanks of this body be returned to the bodies extending these cordial invitations, and that as many members as can conveniently, accept the same."

The motion was seconded and carried.

A delegate. "A gentleman from Kentucky, high in the position he occupies, has requested me to present these resolutions to the Convention, and have them referred. I now make the motion if there is no objection."

The resolutions were read as follows:

Resolved, That the attention of Congress and the River Commission is hereby directed to the advantages to be derived from slack-water navigation from the Ohio river to the Atlantic seaboard, by connecting by canal the waters of the Kentucky river and the Cumberland river (via Cumberland Gap) with the waters of the Tennessee river, and of the Savannah river; and

Resolved, Furthermore, that the Congress of the United States be and is hereby requested to make adequate appropriation for surveying and determining the cost of construction of the aforesaid important cheap transportation water-way from the mouth of the Kentucky river to Savannah, Georgia.

A delegate. "I wish to make the point of order that it is not germain under the call of this Convention."

The President. "The resolutions can be referred. I overrule the point of order."

Mr. Osborne, of New York. "I offer the following:

"*Resolved*, That we, as a Convention, protest against the pernicious practice of indiscriminate Congressional appropriations to brooks, mill-streams, puddles, ponds, clam-bays, oyster-harbors, and all classes of imaginary, useless and unimportant bodies of unnavigable water." [Cheers and laughter.]

The resolution was referred.

A delegate from Nebraska offered the following:

Resolved, That in the opinion of this Convention the Missouri river, with its 3,000 miles of navigation and flowing past and through four States and three Territories, should be placed by the Government in charge of a commission of engineers, organized as is the Mississippi River Commission.

Mr. Roots, of Arkansas, offered the following:

Resolved, That the permanent Secretary of this Convention, acting in connection with the Committee which issued the call for this Convention, be and hereby is authorized to print and distribute ten thousand copies of the proceedings of this Convention, and to also print and distribute such other statistics and information as may in his judgment be considered sufficiently worthy and important.

Mr. Roots. "It seems to me this should be adopted without reference; I suggest its immediate consideration; I don't propose to discuss it."

Mr. Kenner, Chairman of the Committee on Resolutions. "I would state on behalf of the Committee on Resolutions, that they have a resolution of a similar character under consideration, and they would ask this be referred to that Committee."

Mr. Roots. "I have no objection to its reference."

The President. "It will be referred."

Mr. Birch, of Missouri. "I was not present when my

State was called. I desire to offer a resolution. With the permission of the Chair I will read it:

"*Resolved*, That the improvement of the Mississippi river and its navigable tributaries is the highest practical political duty of the people who inhabit the Mississippi Valley; and that, until it shall be fully resolved upon on a scale commensurate with the great agricultural and commercial interests involved, the citizens of this valley should subordinate all other business politics and act as a unit in the enforcement of this imperative necessity; and be it further

"*Resolved*, That as a means for its inauguration and completion, we recommend the levy of an export duty upon the agricultural products of the country of one per cent. as a special improvement fund, with which, within twenty years, we will be enabled successfully to solve this great problem."

Referred to Committee on Resolutions.

Mr. Childs, of Missouri, offered the following, which was also referred to the Committee on Resolutions:

Resolved, That it is the sense of this Convention that any system of improvement of the Mississippi river and its tributaries that may be adopted by this Convention, or by Congress, shall commence at the mouth of the river and follow the same to the sources of the streams improved.

Mr. Kenner, of Louisiana. "As Chairman of the Committee on Resolutions I ask that we be allowed to withdraw to a room in another part of the building, in order to take into consideration the various matters which have been submitted to us this morning."

Leave was granted.

Mr. Hogan, of Missouri. "Resolutions having been offered and referred, I now renew the motion which I made a while ago, that a member of the River Commission now be heard from, in explanation of their plans, if they wish."

Mr. Stanard, of Missouri. "I second the motion."

The motion was put and carried.

The President. "The Convention has voted to hear a statement from the Mississippi River Commission, and any gentleman from that Commission will now be in order."

Judge R. S. Taylor, of Fort Wayne, Ind., a member of the Mississippi River Commission, then came forward, and having been introduced by the President, spoke as follows:

MR. PRESIDENT AND GENTLEMEN OF THE CONVENTION: It is with a real sense of embarrassment that I appear in your presence in response to your kind invitation. I feel an intense solicitude with regard to the deliberations of this Convention, but being here as your invited guest merely, I do not feel at liberty to say the thoughts that are in my mind quite as freely as I otherwise might. I can, however, without impropriety, congratulate you upon the success which has thus far attended your meeting, and particularly upon the number and variety, and the general excellency of the resolutions that we have heard read. It is an old saying, you know, that "the road to hell is paved with good resolutions." [Laughter.] We have had enough of them to-day to macadamize the whole route. [Laughter.] But when it is done we will travel the road the other way.

The members of the Mississippi River Commission look with interest upon the outcome of this Convention. Two years ago they entered upon the discharge of the duties imposed upon them by law. They have been during those two years engaged in work preparatory only. They have been engaged in an extensive system of surveys, in careful examination and observation, in the comparison of all the data that could be gathered from previous surveys and observations, in consideration of all that was known about the river by engineers, by river men, and by all. Upon some of the great questions involved they have reached definite and final conclusions. They have adopted a plan of improvement, which has been laid before Congress, and approved by that body. An appropriation of one million dollars has been made for the purpose of commencing the improvements thus recommended. The Commission have made extensive preparations for the execution of the work thus committed to them. They have in hand a fleet of nearly two hundred boats, great and small, finished, or in course of construction, together with a vast collection of machinery, material, and equipment. They stand to-day upon the threshold of their work. Whether that work shall be carried forward to completion and usefulness, or abandoned at its inception, with the loss of all the costly preparation which has been made for it, will depend upon the measures that may be taken by Congress. Congress, however, is a body which, like many others, moves as it is moved upon. And in this Convention is easily recognized a force to move upon Congress as no other influence can. There are some things, therefore, which I would like to say, if I felt at liberty to do so, as to that which I would like to see done, and that which I hope may not be done by this Convention. [Several voices: "Go on! go on!"]

There is one thing which I need not hesitate to say, and that is this: The mere assembling of this Convention is its greatest success; and its influence will be sensibly felt in the formation of public opinion, in the legislation of Congress, and in the progress of the improvements contemplated, if it shall make no mistake hereafter. Your work was half done when you met in this hall. The presence, in this city, of this vast body of representative men, coming together from sixteen States of the Union, is itself the mountain in the landscape, dwarfing all else by the breadth of its base, and the sublimity of its height. You could return to your homes without having said a word of formal utterance, and yet feel that your coming had not failed of its purpose. How greatly, therefore, is it to be hoped that that which has been so grandly and wisely done already, may not be marred by one unwise word.

It is most important of all things, that in the proceedings of this Convention there shall be final unanimity and harmony. Its voice, to be effective, must be like the verdict of a jury, unanimous. You heard from the distinguished gentleman who delivered the eloquent address of welcome yesterday, a beautiful illustration drawn from the great river itself. Let me borrow it, and carry it a little further. The Father of Waters, having traversed the continent, and created in its course an inland sea twelve hundred miles long, made one fatal mistake at last,—it divided at its mouth into four or five shallow channels, and so shut the gate between itself and the great sea. Let me hope that this Convention will form no delta at its mouth, and that the voice of it shall come forth from one throat, and speak with one tongue.

There are some other things, gentlemen, to which I might, perhaps, with propriety allude for a moment. My personal connection with this work is of recent duration. Coming to it, I find that the Mississippi river, great among rivers as the Bible among books, is, like the Bible, the subject of great difference of opinion among those who have studied it much. I have brought to my study of the question one qualification which is deemed to be absolutely necessary in a juror, and that is, a profound ignorance of the subject. [Laughter.] And so as an ignorant and impartial juror, I have endeavored to consider dispassionately all sides of what I have found to be a great controversy. I have heard many very contradictory views expressed. I have heard a score of different plans proposed for the improvement of the river. I have been told, for example, that the thing to do is to straighten the crooks, and run the water from St. Louis to the Gulf by the shortest line possible. I have been told, on the other side, that every cut-off is a calamity, that it increases the velocity above and below, and so aggravates the caving of banks, enlargement of bends, and formation of bars, as to result finally in restoring the river's original length. I have been told on one side that the only relief for the lower river consists in letting off the water of its great floods by side cuts into the swamps and bayous, through which it can find its way to the sea by other channels. I have been told on the other side that the result of this would be like taking blood from the arm of a strong man;

that the enfeebled current would be no longer able to carry its load of sediment, and would drop it in shoals and bars. I have been told on the one side that the great want of the river is levees; that by the erection of a complete system of levees along the entire river, the water will be confined in one fixed channel, the current increased in depth and velocity, and so enabled to scour its own bed deeper and deeper. On the other side I have been told that the sure consequence of levees is to cause increased deposit of sediment on the bottom of the river; that by that means the whole river—bed, water and banks—will be bodily lifted up, higher and higher, until the Mississippi will run down to the sea on the top of a great embankment, from which it will be in perpetual danger of slipping off into the cotton fields and sugar plantations adjacent.

Now, in the midst of such a maze of contradictory theories what is an ignoramus like me to do? The thing that seems to me wisest is this: I go back to the safe analogies of theology and religion; I look to see who have studied these questions most, and with best opportunities to understand them. I find upon the river and its tributaries engineers sent out by the Government for the express purpose of studying their phenomena, and devising methods for their improvement. Among them are men who have given the better part of their lives to the study of these great questions, and who have conducted extensive and costly experiments in practical works of improvement. I find upon the Commission military engineers of world-wide celebrity, who come to it from other fields of labor, rich in learning and experience, and unembarrassed by previous prejudices in relation to this particular work. I also find upon the Commission two civil engineers of the greatest ability, who have made the Mississippi river one of the chief studies of their lives: Mr. B. M. Harrod, of New Orleans, and your own illustrious fellow-citizen, Mr. James B. Eads [Cheers.],—a man to whom the city of St. Louis owes a debt of gratitude which she can never repay; who has brought to your doors the commerce of the land by the beautiful bridge that stands upon your wharf, and the commerce of the sea through the Jetties at the Gulf. To these I may add the Chief of Engineers at Washington, whose official duties have required him to investigate all the questions involved as carefully as though he had been personally in charge of the work.

Now, I find, on examination, that all these men,—on the Commission and off of it,—while disagreeing on some matters of detail, as do good and wise divines upon infant baptism, perseverance in grace, and the like, are, as to the great plan of salvation, in entire harmony. [Laughter and applause.] I say to myself, therefore: "These are the orthodox leaders, and to their coat-tails I will pin my faith." When I find such men as Gillmore, Comstock, Mitchell, Suter, Benyuard, Ernst, Harrod and Eads,—men who have brought to the investigation of these great problems every prerequisite of genius and education, and who have pursued it by separate and independent paths, concurring at last upon all the fundamental principles involved, I am bound to believe that the conclusions which they have reached are entitled to our confidence, as the best that are attainable in the present state of human knowledge.

If you will allow me, gentlemen, I will go a little further on the subject of the plans of the Commission. I am not an engineer, and therefore I can speak of those plans, and of their merits, with a degree of propriety which would illy become, perhaps, any other member of the Commission. My place upon it is peculiar. It is like that of one member of a committee appointed by the Governor of a State not ten thousand miles from here, to revise the laws. The Constitution required that the laws should be made so that they could be understood by a man of ordinary intelligence. [Laughter.] The Governor appointed a committee of three to revise them; two of them were lawyers and the other was a man who didn't know anything about law, and not much about anything; and in explanation of the appointment the Governor said if the two lawyers could make the laws so the other man could understand them, the object would be attained. That is my place upon this Commission,—to see whether the engineers can lay their plans so that I can understand them. [Laughter.]

I will not detain you, gentlemen, by going into details, but will confine myself to a few very general observations. All the plans of the Commission rest upon this primary proposition: that the improvement of the river consists essentially in so regulating the width of its channel that it shall bear a proper ratio to the volume of water discharged, and in confining the water to such regulated channel, so that it shall, by its own force and velocity, keep its bed scoured out clean. Upon this, as the final desideratum in every such case, all engineers in the world agree, so far as I know.

The problem presented in the application of this principle of improvement to the Mississippi river is a little different from any that ever before taxed the ingenuity of men. There is not on the face of the earth any other river having a channel so long and wide, carrying a volume of water so great, through banks composed of such soft and friable material. To regulate the banks of the Mississippi river by means of any solid wall, or stone revetment, or any structures of plank or timber, which could by their strength and solidity resist the force of the current, is impossible. That which cannot be done by force or strength, must be done, if at all, by stratagem. The forces of the river, so mighty to tear down, must be taught to build up. The water must be made not only to dig its own channel, but to construct its own banks. The material for this work is the sand and soil borne down by the current. To compel the water to drop this sediment just when and where it is needed to build new banks, and nowhere else, is the task which challenges the strategy of the engineer.

While the Mississippi river has the strength of Samson, and tosses islands and bars from side to side, as though they were light as chaff, it has at the same time the weakness of Samson,—it is easily seduced. You remember how Delilah came it over him. [Laughter.] The amount of solid matter which the river holds in solution is enormous, and it carries it from mountain to sea without exertion or fatigue. But one inexorable law follows it like a decree of fate,—it must run with its load, or let it fall. If it slacken its speed but for a moment, the specks of earth which it carries trickle to the ground thick as flakes of snow. And it is by the knowledge of this weakness, and by skilfully taking advantage of it, that the engineer is able to make the tremendous forces of the river obedient to his will. The devices proposed for this purpose are very simple and very cheap. They consist of slight structures of piles, of wire, and of brush, combined and applied in various forms,—structures so slight that you would hardly believe it possible that they could produce the great results expected from them.

It was not my intention, gentlemen, to enter into any detailed account of these devices; but I am tempted by your forbearance, and your manifest interest in the subject, to go a little farther in that direction. And I will, if you please, take one example of common occurrence on the river, and one method of improvement applied to such a case, and explain the process to you so minutely, that any one of you could do it himself,—if he had the money.

I will suppose the case of a portion of the river five or ten miles long, and two miles wide, with a bed so broad and level, that in extreme low water it will not show a depth anywhere exceeding four feet. The problem is to convert this broad shallow stream into a narrow deep one. The engineer determines first upon a width of, say, three thousand feet for the new channel, which he then locates upon such lines of direction and curvature as seem to conform best to the courses of the current above and below, and the laws that control the movements of flowing water. I will suppose the entire space across the river-bed to be represented by the width of this hall, and the proposed new channel to be represented by the central tier of seats in front of me. The two aisles on the right and left will then represent the shore lines of the improved river, and the side tiers of seats the spaces to be built up with earth to form the new banks. In the example supposed, these spaces will be each about three-quarters of a mile wide.

These must be filled with earth over their whole surface to a depth of thirty or forty feet,—a pretty extensive undertaking, as you will readily perceive. The next step in the work is to drive a row of piles along each side of the proposed new channel, which I have represented by these two aisles. Among these piles are interwoven long, slender, willow poles, in and out, from pile to pile, like gigantic basket work, and extending fifteen or twenty feet above low water mark. The proposed new channel is thus inclosed on each side by a strong, coarse screen, through which water will flow quite freely, but with much diminished velocity. At right angles with these screens, and at intervals of three or four hundred feet, transverse screens of exactly the same character are constructed to the bank on each side of the river.

Thus the space which it is desired to cover with earth is all fenced in with these permeable screens, and subdivided into compartments by partitions of the same kind, so that it resembles, in a vague way, a vast beer-garden, a thousand acres in size, and cut up with rustic trellises and arbors.

Then, as the dirty water of the Mississippi comes meandering along, it slips through those screens, into this garden, as innocently as any country greenhorn was ever taken in in St. Louis. [Laughter.] But the moment it passes the screen, it finds its velocity slackened,—the law of its being is upon it, and it must let go part of its load. So down go the little particles of sand and loam to the bottom. And by the time the water wanders round through all the compartments of the beer-garden, and gets out at the lower end, it finds itself, like a good many men who venture into strange places,— minus a good share of its portable property. [Laughter.]

Now, I have no doubt, this strikes you as a very whimsical and trifling scheme for the accomplishment of so great a work. And I am sure you would be amazed, as I have been, to see the results produced by it. I understand that you are going to take an excursion down the river to-morrow. I am sorry it is so high, because if it were not, you could see on that occasion the very thing which I have been describing to you. At Horsetail Bar, where Capt. O. H. Ernst, of the United States Engineers, has been at work about two years, you could see a space several miles long, embracing more than a thousand acres of land, which has been filled from fifteen to twenty feet deep with solid earth, all coaxed from the Mississippi river by tickling its flanks with willow brush. At the same time, the river, being confined by these contraction works to a three thousand feet channel has scoured several additional feet of depth in its own bed. You will understand, of course, that the description I have given you is but an illustration of one mode of dealing with one form of river-bed in which improvement is required.

As the general question presents itself to me, it is reduced to these very small and narrow limits: the plans now proposed for the improvement of the Mississippi river are the best that the knowledge, experience and skill of the present age can suggest; if they cannot be made successful, no man knows now where to turn for success; and if the river can be controlled by some such simple and inexpensive means as those now proposed, then its improvement is possible; if not, not.

There are some other topics, gentlemen, connected with the duties of the Commission, to which I would allude if time permitted. The Commission is required by law to consider specifically the subjects of reservoirs, of outlets, and of levees. These have all received the attention of the Commission. Their views upon them, so far as matured, have been expressed in their reports to Congress. One of those subjects—that of levees—has been, and must continue to be, a topic of special study and investigation. The Commission have collected and presented in their reports many important facts bearing upon it, and others will follow. It is a subject too vast in importance to be lightly considered, or hastily disposed of. It remains in the hands of the Commission, to be dealt with as experience, future emergencies, and the appropriations made by Congress shall indicate.

Gentlemen, if you will allow me, I will add one other thought. It is not alone in its relations to commerce, trade and wealth that I see the importance of this river improvement. When the finger of the Almighty outlined this great valley, it pointed to the seat of empire [cheers], and that which was predestined by Nature has been, and is being, fulfilled by man. It has been decided, not without contention and bloodshed, and yet, as I believe, with final unanimity, that all the vast area of that valley shall be inhabited by one people, speaking one tongue, owing glad and proud allegiance to one government [applause], and bound together by the nearer ties of one common brotherhood. And to all its people, from the eastern mountain tops to the western, from Lake Itaska to Port Eads. this great central river is a common pride and a common charge; and that it shall be so regulated as that its utmost advantages shall be derived for all, and that the burden which it imposes shall be shared by those who share its benefits, is a problem worthy of the solicitude of the nation.

Passing down the river not long ago, I floated on its broad, smooth channel over the very spot where the batteries of Island No. 10 bellowed forth the awful notes of war. Further below, at the very spot where the Sultana went down, her decks crowded with Union prisoners, their faces turned towards liberty, friends and home, I saw a green island, built up by the river, where the cypress and cottonwood wave over the grave of those ill-fated heroes.

Not long since a party of gentlemen of my acquaintance, two of them distinguished actors in the siege of Vicksburg, one of them in the army of the besiegers and the other in the army of the besieged, went out together to look, with the critical eyes of army engineers, upon the lines of defense and attack in that memorable contest. They came back after several hours' absence, tired and dusty, having been utterly unable to find the place for which they sought. Thus do the elements themselves. the river with its flood, the sky with its rains, and the green grass with its sod, seek to obliterate and cover the scars and memories of war. [Applause.] And shall not we. following the example of inanimate nature, say in our hearts: "The war is over with all its bitter memories and resentments forever." [Applause.]

I say. therefore, that it is a good time for the people of the great Northwest and the great Southwest to join their hands in the great work of improving the noble river which is their common inheritance and their common benefactor. From such a partnership, in an enterprise so truly beneficent and national, we shall have good reason to expect. not only extended commerce, great material prosperity, and increased wealth, but, what is more and better, that unity of hearts, and hopes, and interests, in which are the sure guarantees of the indissoluble unity of the States and the nation. [Prolonged applause.]

Mr. Hogan, of Missouri. "I move that the Convention return a vote of thanks to the gentleman for his eloquent address, and to the Commission he represents."

The motion was carried by a rising vote.

Mr. Murphy, of Iowa. "If we can resolve ourselves out of the day of resolves, I suggest that before the benediction is pronounced we ascertain who are members of this Convention. Hence I think it would be in order to hear from the Committee on Credentials, and their report. I make the motion that we hear from the Committee on Credentials."

The President. "I understand from the Secretary, that on yesterday the Convention decided to accept the roll as it was called yesterday in the Convention, as containing the names of the members of the Convention."

A delegate from Missouri. "The gentleman was out yesterday getting a drink, when the Convention disposed of this question."

Mr. Murphy. "I confess the soft impeachment, and the gentleman from Missouri was with me." [Laughter.]

A delegate. "There are a number of delegates who came in since yesterday whose names should be recorded."

The President. "I am informed that all those to whom the gentleman alludes have been enrolled, and have received their badges."

Mr. Kennedy, of New Mexico. "I move that we adjourn to half-past three."

The motion was put and lost.

Mr. Hogan, of Missouri. "I don't wish to be regarded as obtrusive at all, but I wish to employ all the time we have got as advantageously as possible. The Committee on Resolutions are now out; we can do nothing permanently until they report; but, sir, there are a number of distinguished gentlemen here from various States and places, who have been invited—some of them I know—to address this Convention; and I would like now if they could be invited to occupy the time not otherwise employed."

Mr. Walker, of Minnesota. "I second the motion. We have engineers in attendance who are engaged on the great work going on between St. Louis and St. Paul—eight hundred miles of river—in charge of Capt. McKenzie, who is here, and in connection with the remarks of the River Commission we should like to hear from Capt. McKenzie as to what progress is being made on the work in his charge. I move he be invited to address the Convention."

Mr. President. "The Chair would state that next in order is speeches limited to ten minutes, unless extended by the Convention. In the absence of any motion, Capt. McKenzie will now be heard, if there is no objection."

Capt. McKenzie. "I consider myself a little out of place as a speaker. I consider my part the practical part of carrying out the work. It would be unnecessary for me to speak with regard to the expectations of the work which is going on. I would merely say in a few words, that the work which has been going on for the past three years between the mouth of the Illinois and St. Paul, has now passed the experimental stage. The work that has been done has proved that the plans that have been adopted will, in time, give a good and permanent channel, and that all that is now required is the means with which to carry on this work. [Applause.] We have, at many places, already deepened the channel, and, in fact, removed what were, a few years ago, considered the most troublesome obstructions on the upper river. The general plans we are following are simply to confine the river in one uniform channel, and when this is accomplished we shall have a permanent channel of six feet from St. Paul to St. Louis. I thank you, gentlemen, for having expressed a desire to have me address you, but I would ask that with these few remarks I have made, I be excused, inasmuch as I would greatly prefer, as heretofore, to carry on the practical work, than to appear as a public speaker."

Mr. Stanard, of Missouri. "I move to cut off speechmaking; I believe time will be saved. I move that we adjourn till half-past two o'clock, for a session this afternoon."

The motion was put and carried, and a recess was taken till the time mentioned.

AFTER RECESS, October 27, 1881.

The Convention re-assembled at half-past two, President Dunnell in the chair.

Mr. Hogan, of Missouri. "I suggest that, inasmuch as the Committee on Resolutions are not ready to report, we have some few speeches from gentlemen that I am satisfied will interest the Convention. I would like, if I am in order, to make a motion to that effect."

The President. "The Convention will naturally at this stage proceed to the order, which says 'Speeches limited to ten minutes, unless extended by the Convention;' this is a part of the order, and speeches of ten minutes are now in order."

Mr. Hogan. "I suggest that the Convention call on Mr. Cannon, of Illinois."

The President. "Hon. Joseph G. Cannon, of Illinois, is present, and we shall be glad to have him address the Convention."

Mr. Cannon said:

GENTLEMEN: I am here as a looker-on in Venice, and did not come with the intention of addressing or making suggestions to this Convention. And what I may say now will be exceedingly brief. I could not hope, from a general standpoint, to give so happy a discussion of the matter before the Convention as the gentleman from Indiana, Mr. Taylor, who addressed you before lunch, and certainly I am not competent to give a close and scientific discourse touching the matter of interest before you. I am here to look on and gather the temper of this Convention, first, from personal observation; second, I am here because my interest, and the interest of the people with whom I live, demand that some action shall be had to settle the transportation question. [Applause.] I live over in Illinois, on the extreme eastern border, one hundred and thirty miles south of Chicago. The interests of my people primarily, from a commercial centre, are with Chicago and not with St. Louis, yet after all that is said and done, wherever we can go to trade, our interests are the same in the Mississippi Valley, and that includes the whole of the valley. Somebody said yesterday,—and he didn't get it large enough,—that there were twenty-four hundred millions of bushels of cereals produced in this country per annum. The census report shows, that of the twenty-seven millions, my own State of Illinois produced one-sixth; our sister State of Iowa produced one-eighth, and our sister State of Missouri one-ninth. I need not specify farther; it was nearly all produced in the Mississippi Valley. I am reminded in connection with this,—from my residence in Illinois and the West, in fact having resided here nearly all my life, from boyhood,—that after navigation opens in the spring, for us who are a little farther north and east, that then we get reasonable freight rates brought about by competition, by lakes and canals. When the ice king lays his strong hand upon those northern waters, then we are at the mercy of those who transport by rail. They are human; they propose to make all they can when they have not full and free competition; perhaps anybody would do that. I am not here to abuse them. I suppose it is natural that they should. Now, then, my interest and your interest is to devise a means, if we can, by which this competition shall not be for six months in the year, but perpetual. [Cheers.] The water for a large portion of the year above you on the Mississippi to the Gulf is open, and for twelve months in the year,—and I feel that is about all the months there are in the year,—from Cairo south, the Mississippi never closes, if I am correct as to my facts. Now, then, if we can have a line of transportation that way, we will soon have all the necessary railroads to reach Cairo or to reach other points, Why, here is this great Wabash system that is reaching out throughout the length and breadth of the country. In the last three years, the Wabash system has got a line from my town in Illinois, Danville, to Cairo, so you will see other roads reaching, not only to Cairo, but to St. Louis, and in that way I think the question will be solved.

Now, then, there has been something said in resolutions that have been read to-day, and something otherwise, that to make yourselves practical you ought to demand that appropriations for the Mississippi river, and perhaps its principal tributaries, should be made separate; that is, that you should have strength enough in the American Congress—representatives enough—to make appropriations for these improvements, without reaching out and taking in other rivers or harbors. Now, then, if you had the strength that would be a very desirable thing to do; in fact, if I had my way about it, and it were practical, I would have each appropriation, everywhere and for everything, stand upon its own merits. If you have not strength, then you have to do the next best thing. And let me tell you about the river and harbor bill last winter. I have been a representative for my people up here in Illinois for eight years, and am now upon my fifth term. Last winter the river and harbor bill that was reported was the first and only bill I ever voted for. The manner in which they make up ordinary bills for all appropriations was to have them go into one bill, and they generally made them strong enough that the bill could command two-thirds of the votes of the House, and thereby suspend the rules and pass it. This bill was so good it could not command the necessary two-thirds; and it was a more liberal bill to the Mississippi river and her important tributaries, than was ever before reported. It was by the Commerce Committee; and I believe you have a citizen of your own State, Mr. Clardy, who was on that Committee and worked faithfully for your interests and the interests of your country. We had a representative from Illinois, Mr. Henderson, We want these appropriations, and the people demand them. They demand a settlement of this question, and if they can't get it settled one way they will another. Many advocates throughout the country say, "Lay the positive arm of positive law on railroad corporations and regulate them in that way." That can be done, provided it is practical; public opinion that is intelligent and determined, and born of necessity, always makes the laws and judicial decisions. If any man had said ten years ago that the Granger decision, so called, made by the Supreme Court of the United States, ever would have been made, the whole legal profession everywhere would have said "No, that never will be." Yet an intelligent public opinion in this republic of ours brought about those influences; and it is right and proper they should have done so. Yet, after all, it is possibly, it is probably, not practical to regulate this whole thing by positive law. We had better bring the forces of trade and competition to bear, if we can, and never resort to positive law until other things have failed, touching the regulation of these great questions. Why, your own great engineer of world-wide fame is helping to settle this question; and he is working, and you have worked with him, and the country has worked with you all in harmony with the forces of Nature, and of trade, in settling it. I recollect very well that in 1873 I attended a Convention here; the first one and the last one I ever attended, until this. I recollect a number of gentlemen went from here to Galveston and down to the mouth of the river and back home; a number of members of Congress needed to be informed, and were informed, and this question was pressing upon the country. The first result was the Eads' Jetty bill, and you have the Jetties in successful operation. Now that Convention has accomplished great things, and will accomplish still greater; so I say it is policy to work in harmony with the forces of Nature in improving the great water-way, and be in harmony with the forces of trade underlying the law of demand and supply. And I think you are starting out in that way, and I bid you Godspeed, because this fair Mississippi Valley of ours, that produces this wheat, and this corn, and this hay, and this cotton; that produces almost anything and everything that can be produced almost anywhere else in the world, also produces fair women and brave and intelligent men. Is my ten minutes up?

The President. "Nearly."

Mr. Cannon. "Then I yield the balance of my time to the next good-looking man that shall address you."

Mr. Childs, of Missouri. "We have here a delegate, Gen. Rozier, who was a member of the Convention in 1845, and we should like to hear from him."

The President. "Gen. Rozier is called upon."

Gen. Rozier said:

MR. PRESIDENT AND GENTLEMEN OF THIS CONVENTION: I feel profoundly grateful to you for your kindness on this occasion. I suppose that the interest felt in the improvement of this great valley of the Mississippi may have occasioned, probably, that my name should have been suggested to you. I believe to-day, though somewhat of a young man, that I am the only delegate, with the exception of one man in the city of St. Louis, who was at the great convention that took place in Memphis in 1845, when John C. Calhoun presided. Gentlemen, the questions there were what you have. The great principle in question was whether the General Government could appropriate any money for the improvement of rivers and other improvements. It was well discussed. They had reports not only upon the navigation of the rivers West; but the railroad questions came up, the hospital questions came up, improvements of the great river of the West, and other matters in that line, and the improvements of levees, and the reclamation of vast quantities of swamp lands. Gentlemen, the same principle came there that is now agitated in the valley of the Mississippi. The question with Mr. Calhoun and his Democratic friends at the time was whether the Constitution permitted of any improvement upon the country by Congress. How was that decided? There were there such men as Gov. Jones of Tennessee, John Bell of Tennessee, C. C. Clay of Alabama, men of genius representing Kentucky and Ohio, and Western States; there it was declared that in a national point of view, that the great national rivers, which, by the act of 1789, by Congress adopted—that those highways were only subject to improvement and appropriation by Congress. We heard them speak of the Balize; Mr. Calhoun, in that Convention, declared then, as we declare to-day, that the Balize had to be opened for the commerce of the vast Mississippi with the commerce of the world, and it had to be done at what cost it might be. That was the understanding; and not only that: Mr. Calhoun and the convention took the ground that the great national highways came under the charge of the Government just like any other seaport upon the coast, for the protection of the General Government; and that was the doctrine; and yet to-day this question is advocated, Are we to go beyond the great national rivers? Your map points out exactly the grand Mississippi that flows from the north to the Gulf of Mexico, and the Ohio, and the Missouri; they are the great national highways we can only protect, and not run into every small rivulet of the country for an appropriation. No, I will not delay this Convention, and I cannot delay it; as I suggested here to-day, there are only two members living of that Convention, and that is myself and the Hon. James E. Yeatman, of St. Louis.

Gentlemen, there is one practical thing, and I will not delay you. There was a very respectable and highly intellectual man in Missouri, who has been connected with the Marine Department from the time Commodore Perry ruled upon the Lakes, and I recollect well his remark in 1873, when in the Senate of Missouri, I reported there on the commerce and the tonnage and losses upon Western rivers. He wrote this in answer:

"The great Benefactor has intrusted us with the great plan of improving Western rivers for the benefit of mankind." We not only contemplate to-day the vast resources of the valley of the Mississippi; here we are with sixteen millions of people, with one hundred and twenty-nine members of Congress in the Lower House and thirty Senators, and yet the valley of the Mississippi has been unprotected, and those improvements which are necessary to be made have not been made. In the last twenty years we have lost three million dollars by the destruction of steamers on Western rivers annually, which would amount to sixty millions; besides that, in the estimates for the twenty years, we have had four hundred and sixteen individuals lost by casualties of the river. There are only three modes by which you can improve these vast Western rivers; and how is that, sir? By these gunboats,—that is, the boats for the purpose of extracting snags from the river, which is practical in all its operations. I recollect here but a few years ago that fifty miles from your city one log lay above an island, and nine boats were wrecked on it within six months, and yet the snag-boats came there, and they removed this thing in two hours. That is not all. We want the channel improved and deepened, and we can only do that by following the natural course of the river, and trying to put, likewise, improvements upon this alluvial soil, and hugging the bluff shore of Missouri from here and to the Balize,—that is the shore on this side of the river. Isn't it a remarkable fact after you pass St. Louis and go down to Benton, in Scott county, that on the whole western side of the Mississippi there is not a bluff that stands there; it is alluvial soil. I don't want to go into this matter any further than this, to say that I have always felt a vital interest in the improvements of the West; and this great and magnificent river we have to-day, ought to have the attention of Congress, and appropriations ought to be made for that purpose, and the time has come. I care not whether the present members of Congress are in favor of it or not, you cannot stop the vast commerce and agricultural interests of the country. You might as well say it is feasible to build a dam and stop the waters that wash your city, as prevent the progress of this country, and improvement of the great Mississippi. I will go further than this. The city of St. Louis to-day ought to raise a monument to Capt. Eads' name. You ought to have a monument to Fulton, pointing to the great river of the West, in the application of steam; it has done so much for the West. You ought to have a monument to Capt. Eads, pointing to the Balize, opening commerce, not only to the Gulf of Mexico, but to the world. I have said enough.

Mr. Hogan, of Missouri. "We have with us Hon. H. S. Shallenberger, of Pennsylvania, and I would like to have him say a few words to this Convention. I would like to have him make a few remarks."

A delegate from Illinois. "Some of us want to go home to-night; we want to hear the resolutions; we will, of course, remain here as long as we possibly can to hear speeches, and hope they will be made, but we would like to hear the resolutions and act upon them, or at least have them before the Convention, so that we may go home satisfied of what will be its results; therefore I suggest that we have the resolutions. I will move that the Chairman of the Committee on Resolutions be now requested to make his report.

The motion was seconded, put, and carried.

D. F. Kenner, of New Orleans, Chairman of the Committee on Resolutions, then presented the following report.

MR. PRESIDENT: The Committee on Resolutions, after careful consideration of the objects of the Convention, as set forth in the call under which it has assembled, and of various resolutions which have been submitted to the Committee as expressing the views, not only of individual delegates, but of delegations from widely distant parts of the Mississippi Valley, touching those objects and the best mode of promoting them, have instructed me on behalf of the unanimous Committee to report to the Convention the preamble and resolutions herewith submitted, with the recommendation that the same be adopted by the Convention.

[Signed]   DUNCAN F. KENNER,
Chairman Committee on Resolutions.

The representatives of the commercial interest and agricultural and other productive industries of the Mississippi Valley, in convention assembled, at St. Louis, Missouri, believing that the Mississippi river and its navigable tributaries, the great inland water-ways, prepared by the Creator for the use of the people, are a most important and valuable part of the national domain, free to all, beyond the reach of monopoly, and affording to the whole people that competition in transportation which benefits both producer and consumer alike; and further, that cheap transportation is the great necessity of an agricultural people, the indispensable condition of the easy conveyance to distant markets of their staple products, bulky in proportion to value, and that the familiar economical truth, that the cheapest transportation of such products is by water, is especially applicable to the great water-ways of this country, provided the same be kept free from snags, sand-bars, treacherous banks and other obstacles to navigation, do therefore resolve and declare :

First. That it is the manifest and imperative duty of the Government of the United States to cause to be made such improvement of the Mississippi river, and its navigable tributaries, as shall permanently secure the safe and easy navigation thereof, thereby cheapening freights, reducing insurance and other burdens and expenses; promoting the vast inland commerce of the nation and creating new avenues of foreign trade, and thus not only inviting increased production and population, but assuring greater prosperity to the whole people. Especially is this duty obvious, and our demand justified, in view of the donations already made by Congress in land, amounting to nearly 200,000,000 acres, and in bonds issued or guaranteed, nearly $100,000,000 more, in aid of artificial highways, the property of private individuals, and necessarily furnishing, even at lowest rates, the most costly form of transportation on a large scale, as compared with appropriations not yet amounting to $25,000,000 in all, for the improvement of 15,000 miles of natural water-ways, whose freedom from tax imposed or monopoly is protected by Constitutional guarantees, while the cheap service and unrestricted competition they afford is the most effectual corrective of exorbitant charges by any route to the seaboard. That the appropriations for such improvements should be separately made, with due provisions for assuring the people of their faithful applications to the same, and should be adequate to the continued prosecution of the work once begun until the same is finished, so as to avoid the wasteful destruction of work partially completed by reason of the delay or stoppage thereof for want of sufficient appropriations; and be it further

Resolved, That this Convention recognizes with extreme satisfaction and emphatic approval in the passage of the act of Congress of June 28, 1879, "For the appointment of a Mississippi River Commission," and in the comprehensive and scientific surveys and important recommendations made by the distinguished engineers appointed on that Commission, as set forth in their reports of February 17, 1880, and January 8, 1881, the first well-considered and effectual step toward the complete and permanent opening of the Mississippi Valley to the markets of the world; but would also strongly express its regret at the refusal of the last Congress, after creating said Commission, and, notwithstanding the deliberate and emphatic approval of their plans by the House Committee on Improvement of the Mississippi, to appropriate the amount estimated and recommended by said Commission for doing the work by them carefully laid out and proposed; and be it further

Resolved, That in the deliberate and earnest judgment of this Convention, delegated to represent the interests in that behalf of more than one-half the States and Territories of the Union, inhabited by more than one-half of its entire population, from whom is collected above 70 per cent. of the internal revenue of the nation, whose internal commerce is already one-half that of the whole United States, more than twelve times greater than the total foreign commerce of the nation, and larger than the total foreign commerce of the world— but upon whose industry is this year levied, by the obstacle to the safe and easy navigation of the Mississippi river and its navigable tributaries, a needless direct tax, by way of increased freights and insurance, demurrage, wrecks and repairs of not less than \$10,000,000. It is the imperative duty of Congress and the right of the people, for whom this Convention is authorized to speak, that the legislation thus wisely begun, be made effectual and permanent by enlarging the powers of the River Commission to include the active prosecution of the works already recommended by them, and by the regular and separate appropriations, from year to year, of such sums as said Commission, acting under the reasonable supervision of Congress, shall report as necessary to that end; so that this great and indispensable work, national in every sense, shall no longer be delayed; and be it further

Resolved, That the scientific and comprehensive system of river improvement, by a competent commission, thus inaugurated, should be applied to the complete and permanent improvement and maintenance of all the navigable tributaries of the great river; and be it further

Resolved, That this Convention recognizes, with great satisfaction, the benefits already resulting to the navigation of the Mississippi river and its principal tributaries by the extension of the light-house system thereto; and expresses the earnest hope that the partial lighting of those rivers may be speedily enlarged, by increasing the number of districts and lights to such an extent as the Light-house Board, in consultation with the River Commission, shall find necessary to render such service completely efficient; and be it further

Resolved, That the President of this Convention be and he is hereby authorized and requested to appoint, at his early convenience, a committee of twenty-one, who shall be charged with the duty of preparing, as soon as practicable after the Convention adjourns, a memorial to the Congress of the United States, on behalf of the delegates composing this Convention, and the people whom they represent, in support of, and in accordance with, the foregoing resolutions, embodying such statistics and information as said committee may deem expedient; that they cause to be printed a sufficient number of copies of said resolutions and memorial, together with the proceedings of this Convention, for wide distribution, and that a copy thereof be placed in the hands of each member of the United States Senate and House of Representatives, as soon as practicable; and that said committee be, and they are hereby authorized to take such further action touching the proper presentation of said resolutions and memorial to Congress, and procuring the due consideration thereof as they may deem best.

Mr. Hardin, of Missouri. "I move that the report be adopted."

The motion was seconded.

Mr. Roberts, of Illinois. "Before that is adopted, I wish to say, I offered a resolution before recess, in regard to the deepening of the Illinois and Michigan canal, which the Committee seems not to have reported on. I want to offer this again before the Convention, and offer it as an amendment before this Convention. I ask to read it, and if necessary, Illinois wants to be heard upon it.

"*Resolved*, That it is the sense of this Convention that the future policy of the Government of the United States for the improvement of the Mississippi river and its navigable tributaries should embrace the enlargement and deepening of the Illinois and Michigan canal, and the improvement of the Illinois river, so as to afford deep-water navigation from Lake Michigan to the Mississippi river.

"Now, if I am in order, I want to present a few reasons why I think this should be adopted as the sense of this Convention."

The President. "The gentleman moves, as I understand him, the resolution which he has read, as an amendment to the report of the Committee on Resolutions."

Mr. Roberts. "Yes, as an amendment to the report."

Mr. Doniphan. "I rise to a point of order, that there is a supplementary report yet to be brought to the attention of the Convention."

Mr. Roberts. "There is a motion to adopt the report as it has been read. Whatever may come afterwards I don't know, but I suppose it is in order now to offer this as an amendment to the report that has already been read."

The President. "I think the gentleman is in order."

Mr. Doniphan. "My point was, I would like to have the full report of the committee."

The President. "That is another question; the report was read as a whole, and the motion was made to adopt it, and it was in order; then a gentleman makes an amendment to that report; the gentleman, therefore, is in order."

Another delegate. "I rise to a point of order, that that subject is not within the call of the Convention; to make a recommendation for this canal would be going beyond the navigable streams and tributaries of the Mississippi river. [Applause.] The point is that this seems to bring in a recommendation that would extend beyond what I understand to be the scope of this Convention; that the whole extent is the Mississippi river and its navigable tributaries."

Mr. Kenner, of Louisiana. "If the gentleman will allow me to make an explanation in justice to the Committee, I would be obliged to him. I mislaid an additional resolution which the Committee had authorized me to report to the Convention; I could not put my hand on it. If you will allow me, I will read that resolution."

Mr. Roberts, of Illinois. "I will yield for that purpose."

The President. "As I understand, this resolution was intended to be a part of the resolution."

Mr. Kenner, Chairman of Committee on Resolutions. "Yes, or as a separate report."

The Secretary then read the following supplemental report of the Committee on Resolutions:

MR. PRESIDENT: Your Committee on Resolutions have also instructed the undersigned, its chairman, at the request of the member of the committee from Iowa, to submit to the Convention, without recommendation, the following resolution: DUNCAN F. KENNER.

Resolved, That, in the interest of cheap transportation, and to afford a choice of water routes to the seaboard, we regard connections between the navigable waters of the Upper Mississippi river and the great lakes, as of great importance; and that Congress, in making the appropriations to improve the navigation of the Mississippi river and its tributaries, ought not to overlook or disregard the e tablishment of free water communication between the valley of the great river of the West and tide-water of the East.

Assistant Secretary, Bell. "The chairman of the committee directs me to state that it is offered by the member of the committee from Iowa, and is placed before the Convention by the committee without recommendation."

Mr. Roberts, of Illinois. "If I am in order, I would like to be heard upon this resolution."

The President. "A gentleman has raised a point of order. The Chairman is not familiar with the phraseology of the call, and hence could not now rule upon the point of order that has been raised."

A delegate. "I would like to say this much in explanation of my motion. I think it is clearly not within the scope of the Convention to admit that resolution. I simply do this to expedite the business of the Convention. If that resolution is allowed to come in, there may be hundreds of others just like that. I understand that this Convention was called together for a particular purpose. I am for that resolution, but I am satisfied that the callers of this Convention did not intend the scope to be so great, therefore I insist upon my point of order."

A delegate from Illinois. "The gentleman in making his point of order claimed that the gentleman from Illinois was outside the call of this Convention. The geographer in preparing the map for this Convention left off a city which we of Illinois, and all members from the Northwest, are a little proud of,—a city called Chicago. [Laughter.] It is a small place; it does very little business."

A voice. "Where is it?"

The other delegate. "I can't tell you; it is not on the map. It does very little business; but that city, small as it is, too insignificant to be represented upon that map, has already expended three million dollars in making a canal for the passage of the waters of Lake Michigan through the Illinois river into the waters of the Mississippi. In connection with that, and in carrying out that measure for the improvement of the Illinois river, the State of Illinois has already expended one million dollars in the construction of a lock and dam at one point, and another lock and dam at another point, making one hundred miles of slack-water navigation. And that they have received no aid from the Government, but, in place of that, money has been expended on the lower end of the Illinois river, and not one particle of good has been accomplished by it. Now, then, we wish to have this matter brought before the National Government. In the river convention held at Quincy two years ago a resolution was adopted, and some appropriations have been made by Congress, to establish reservoirs in an unknown region of Minnesota."

A delegate. "I rise to a point of order. Is the gentleman speaking upon the point of order, or discussing the merits of the proposition?"

The delegate from Illinois. "I am speaking to the point of order; I propose to make this point, that the Illinois river is a navigable tributary of the Mississippi river, and it is within the purview of this call."

A delegate. "I rise to a point of order, that the gentleman is not speaking to the point of order, but discussing the merits of a proposition not before the Convention as yet."

Mr. Simrall, of Mississippi. "I rise simply to explain what I understood to be the sentiment of the Committee on Resolutions on that subject, and my own as a member of that committee. We did not undertake to pass judgment upon the merits of the proposition. We rather thought that the scope of the resolution was outside, probably, of the object of this body; but, inasmuch as the subject referred to in the resolution is one of a vast importance to the commerce of this valley, we thought it best to remit the resolution to the judgment and decision of the whole Convention. I make this suggestion as to the order of procedure: Some of us are very far from home, and at considerable personal inconvenience have come to this body. The body of that report met the unanimous vote of every member of the committee from all parts of this valley. Let us at this time dispose of the body of the report—the resolutions assented to and recommended by the committee; when that is done let this debatable proposition, about which contrariety of opinion may arise, come before this body and be disposed of upon its own merits. I have said more now than I intended. I have but a single word more to add, if it is in order; therefore, I would move that this body proceed to consider that part of the report of the committee, in which the committee reported to this Convention certain resolutions for its adoption."

The President. "That motion is now pending, and the gentleman from Illinois has moved to amend that report, and the gentleman upon the left has raised the point of order that the resolution is not in order, and the Chair sustains the point of order." [Loud applause.]

Mr. Roberts, of Illinois. "I was speaking on the point of order. I suppose it would be fair that I should be heard."

The President. "If the gentleman was speaking on the point of order he will be heard, and the ruling withheld."

Mr. Roberts, of Illinois. "I understand this call embraces the improvement of the Mississippi river and its navigable tributaries. I believe it has been known for more than half a century that the Illinois river is a tributary of the Mississippi, and that it has been navigable, and is a much better stream for navigation to-day than any stream of its size in the United States."

A delegate. "I ask whether a point of order is debatable."

The President. "Yes, the point of order is debatable. The gentleman is now speaking by permission of the Chair."

The delegate. "The gentleman can state his point of order, but not discuss other questions."

The President. "The gentleman is right in that; the gentleman (Mr. Roberts) must confine himself to the point of order."

Mr. Roberts. "The question whether the Illinois river is a navigable stream and is a tributary, is a question, and I suppose we have a right to be heard upon that. This call does not designate what streams are tributary to the Mississippi,— what are navigable. If this call had outlined and given us the names of certain streams that this Convention was called to take into consideration, that might have been excluded, but it did not elect to do that; it says all of the navigable tributaries. Now, the question is, whether the Illinois river is a navigable tributary; and that is a question of fact, and gentlemen have a right to have that passed upon; and have I not the right to discuss the question now from that standpoint, as to whether it is a navigable tributary of the Mississippi river? If it is a navigable tributary, then my resolution is germain. Now, I have offered this as one of the representatives of Illinois upon this floor; Illinois is something of a State; Illinois has something of a representation upon the floor of Congress; she has a voice there that will be heard when these resolutions,—to which I can give my hearty support,—come to be considered before the Congress of the United States. Does this Convention want to stifle the voice of the State of Illinois,—the great State of the valley of the Mississippi river? Do you want to say to the representatives that represent the people of Illinois upon the floor of Congress, that you wouldn't even consider a resolution that is of vital importance to Illinois and the valley of the Mississippi river? Now, I am only asking for the sense of the Convention, that in future the Government of the United States shall take into consideration this question. It is well known that the State of Illinois, after spending one million dollars in making the Illinois and Michigan canal, and improving the Illinois river last year, provided for the cession of that great highway to the Government of the United States. Now this question of fact—"

A delegate from Indiana. "I rise to a point of order, that any member stating a point of order, has not a right to discuss the question at issue. I hope the Chair will so rule, otherwise there will be no end."

The President. "The point of order is well taken. The member from Illinois must confine himself to the point of order."

A delegate from Missouri. "If the Illinois river is navigable, it is already included in the resolution, and it is not necessary to go over the ground again."

A delegate from Arkansas. "I would like to ask if the canal you speak of is a tributary, why is it any more necessary to mention it than the river I live upon?"

Mr. Roberts, of Illinois. "I will reply to that, if I am in order."

The President. "Will the gentleman allow the Chair to state, there are a large number of delegates who desire to pass upon the body of the report as first read. The supplemental resolution will give to the gentleman from Illinois an opportunity then to present his resolution. The Chair decided upon the point of order, perhaps, with haste; but it was inclined to do so that this course now indicated by the

Chair might be pursued for the comfort and convenience of all."

Mr. Roberts, of Illinois. "I will yield, with the understanding that I may have the floor for this resolution when the report of the committee is passed upon."

The President. "The gentleman will have the opportunity. He shall be recognized for that purpose."

Mr. Chase, of Nebraska, arose in the rear of the hall and secured recognition by the Chairman, amid constant calls for the "Question! question!"

He said: "Final action upon the resolutions is an important matter—too important to be taken without further debate. Upon one proposition—the one generally received—that the Missouri is tributary to the Mississippi, they sound all right. But, sir, when and how, is this grand and reverend assemblage, who do not entertain this proposition—those who claim that, as a matter of fact, the Mississippi is a tributary of the Missouri. [Laughter.] These audible smiles, gentlemen, are no answers to this proposition. Let us see whether there is not sense in it. The two rivers vary but little in length. The Mississippi, from its source to its mouth, is put down as 3,160 miles long. The Missouri, before it reaches the Mississippi, is 3,100 miles long, while the Mississippi, when joined by the Missouri, has only traveled less than half that distance. Surely, if the Mississippi is the 'Father of Waters,' the Missouri is the mother. [Laughter.] And then the Missouri gives its own caste to the Mississippi after their junction. The Missouri, brought into existence by those beautiful springs and most beautiful cascades of the far-off Rockies, which hang like so many silver ribbons from those craggy peaks, speeds on to the embrace of the Mississippi, and greeting her with a kiss, imprints upon her cheeks, never more to be eradicated, her own dusky hue, the hue of an incomparably rich soil—a hue which a thousand Indian summers has never faded. That complexion the Mississippi carries with her to the Gulf of Mexico, and for several miles from its mouth, ere it is retouched by the deep blue of the ocean wave. I have, myself, many times witnessed this fact. Even the Ohio—noble stream that it is—when it joins the Mississippi mingles with this Missouri tint, only to be engulfed by it. Which river, then, is the tributary? Is it the Missouri, which joins the Mississippi with 3,000 miles of water, or is it the Mississippi, which joins the Missouri with 1,200 miles?"

A member. "You are not speaking to the question. I call the gentleman to order."

Mr. Chase. "State your point of order, sir. I am in order." [Laughter.]

The same member. "Mr. President, I call the gentleman to order. He is not speaking to the point."

The President. "The gentleman from Nebraska is in order."

Mr. Chase. "We, of the Missouri valley, have always treated you and the entire delegation from Missouri with generous consideration. St. Louis has no warmer friends than she can find in the Nebraska delegation. I have spoken on several occasions, years ago, before the Merchants' Exchange, on matters of mutual interest to our people, and your people, and I appeal to my long-time friends, Mr. Hogan, Mr. Stanard and other St. Louis gentlemen, to say whether Omaha and St. Louis have not always been friends. Why, then, does Missouri object to the tenor of my views?"

A member from Missouri. "You are charging this on Missouri, and the point of order was raised by a member from Indiana."

Mr. Chase. "It might probably come from Indiana, but I was surprised that it should come from Missouri. [Applause.] The gentleman from Indiana may yet find out that I am no novice at this convention business. I have been in many gatherings similar to this. While scarcely out of my minority I was a delegate from Buffalo, where I was then reading law, to the famous river and harbor convention at Chicago, in 1847, and always since have taken a deep interest in works of internal improvement, which I believe, when several States are interested, should be aided by the National Government. I have noticed the apparent drift of this Convention from the beginning—the Mississippi drift—but I know St. Louis and Missouri too well to believe they could be otherwise than generous to the Missouri river country. The Nebraska delegation came here to represent that country so far as our State is concerned. We have a large amount of grain and other products to ship, and we demand cheap transportation for them, both for the benefit of the consumer, as well as the producer. We raised in that State this season 100,000,000 bushels of cereals, young as we are, and a very large portion of this finds a market outside the State. While we do not desire to antagonize railroad interests, we will barge our grain to you down the Missouri, if you will carry it that way to market at a lower freight tariff than any other route. Our grain interests, too, are largely supplemented by cattle and hogs, and other bulky marketable products, which, if reduced to the barrel, could as well be barged as railed. What we want, and what we intend to have, at all hazards, is fair play for the new Northwest.

"Improve the Missouri and give her waters a chance, and she will soon shovel out a feasible channel for all your commerce on the Mississippi.

"Mr. President, I notice my time, ten minutes, is almost up; I beg pardon for using even that short time in a Convention like this, of so many hundred men, many of them men of practical experience in river navigation. I believe in the assertion that no one present has ever before, in a commercial convention in this country, looked upon so many gray heads,—shall I say, to speak the truth,—bald heads [laughter], grown bald in studying out a way to readily navigate the great inland seas of the West? But, sir, we could not answer for silence; how should we go home, and the Missouri valley remain practically unprovided for. Had I not been interrupted, I would have had time to tell you more about Nebraska, as well as something about her chief city, Omaha, a city now of 40,000 people, and from whence we shipped last year 10,-000,000 bushels of grain, 160,000 beef cattle, and transacted a commercial city business of $50,000,000. But time forbids. Come and see us, and when you leave our productive acres, you will all be Missouri valley men, I assure you." [Cheering.]

The President. "The Chair is compelled to state that this hall can be had but thirty minutes longer by this Convention to-day, and I trust the gentlemen will not unnecessarily consume the time of the Convention."

A delegate. "The subject-matter of the amendment of the gentleman from Illinois is embraced entirely in the supplemental report."

Cries of "Question!"

The President. "The question before the Convention is upon the adoption of the report of the Committe on Resolutions."

A delegate. "I ask for the reading again of that portion having reference to the enlargement of the powers of the Mississippi River Commission, so far as it refers to the extension of those powers to the navigable tributaries of the Mississippi."

The portion was then read.

The President. "It is moved and seconded that the report of the Committee on Resolutions be adopted. As many as favor this motion will say 'aye.'"

The question was then put, and the report was unanimously adopted.

The President. "The Secretary will now read the supplemental report."

The Secretary then read the supplemental report of the Committee on Resolutions, as printed on page 118.

A delegate from Arkansas. "I offer an amendment to that: that the Arkansas river, from Fort Smith, be opened clear to Wichita, Kansas."

The question was put on the amendment, and it was lost.

Mr. Hardin, of Missouri. "I think the report has not been adopted, because the rules require a call by States."

The President. "If the gentleman is correct, the States should be called. The present Chairman was not a member of the Convention yesterday, and was not aware of that rule."

Mr. Rozier, of Missouri. "I move the suspension of the rule, so that the report of the Committee on Resolutions be adopted."

The question was put on the motion, and it was carried.

The question was then put on the adoption of the report of the Committee on Resolutions, and it was adopted unanimously.

The President. "The question before the Convention is the supplementary report, which has been read, and the gentleman from Illinois (Mr. Roberts) is in order."

Mr. Roberts, of Illinois. "I now offer this resolution of mine."

The President. "You offer it as an amendment or a substitute?"

Mr. Roberts. "I offer this as an amendment to the resolution:

"*Resolved*, That it is the sense of this Convention that the future policy of the Goverment of the United States for the improvement of the Mississippi river and its navigable tributaries, should embrace the enlargement and deepening of the Illinois and Michigan canal, and the improvement of the Illinois river, so as to afford deep-water navigation from Lake Michigan to the Mississippi river."

Mr. Roberts. "Now, in advocacy of this, I have only one word to say."

A delegate. "I rise to the same point of order. I have no objection to his speaking of the Illinois river, but when he speaks of the Illinois and Michigan canal, I rise to a point of order."

Mr. Roberts. "If the gentleman has ever traveled over that country he will see that the Illinois river runs to the city of Chicago and the lakes. It seems to me there is a disposition, in common parlance, to sit down on this resolution, but Illinois wants to be heard—or part of it at least. Now, the little town at the head of navigation on the Illinois river is the city of Peoria, the second city in the State of Illinois. It pays more revenue into the treasury of the United States to-day than the city of St. Louis."

Cries of "Whisky!"

Mr. Roberts. "Yes, I want to see whether Illinois has a right to be heard. I will call the attention of the Convention for one moment to the receipts of grain in the city of Peoria, saying nothing of the receipts at other towns bordering on the Illinois river. The receipts of grain for the year 1880, were 26,041,335 bushels. There was shipped off 20,666,225 bushels. She paid into the Treasury of the United States, in revenue last year, $10,752,319. She manufactured 18,475,565 gallons of whisky. Now, I know this is a cold-water Convention, but I don't believe that this cold-water Convention would object to getting the product of the taxes that is collected from whisky to furnish money to carry out the views of this Convention. Therefore, I shall not detain this Convention. I want this Convention to understand that Illinois is on the map; that the city of Chicago is on the map; that the Illinois river, from the Mississippi to Chicago, demands the attention of this country, as well as other tributaries to the great river, and I move the adoption of this resolution."

The President. "As many as favor the adoption of the amendment will say 'aye.'"

The question was put, and the vote was taken by division.

The President. "It is evident there is a very large majority against the adoption of the amendment."

Mr. Stanard, of Missouri. "Mr. Chairman, and gentlemen of the Convention ; I desire to make an announcement while the Convention is full. [Laughter, and a voice ' Peoria.'] You remember I was instrumental in your getting lunch two hours ago. I desire to make this announcement on behalf of the Local Executive Committee, relative to the plan of entertainment, which will be given in honor of this Convention here in this theatre this evening. There has been some confusion relative to the tickets, and I desire to announce on behalf of the Executive Committee, in charge of this and other matters of detail relative to your entertainment, that those members of the delegation who have not already received their tickets, or if they find it inconvenient for them to get them, that they will be admitted here to-night on their badges. I am requested to make, also, an announcement that concerns the citizens of St. Louis, more than the Convention, that those who have subscribed for the expenses of the Convention and entertainment, —I refer to the merchants of the city of St. Louis,—that their tickets have been sent by messengers to their stores this afternoon, and should they not receive them, that they will be admitted at the door, Mr. George Bain, being Chairman of the Entertainment Committee, and having the list, and knowing who are entitled to admission. I desire to make another statement on behalf of the Local Executive Committee. It is this, that to-morrow at 12 o'clock it is the design of the merchants of the city of St. Louis, that there shall be a 'grand excursion take place on the river, on barges and boats, etc., on which occasion a collation will be served, and we want every delegate to this Convention to remain and attend that excursion, and we will make it as agreeable as it possibly can be."

Mr. Kennedy, of New Mexico. "I move the adoption of the resolution—the supplemental report."

The question was put.

The President. "The 'ayes' appear to have it."

Mr. Rowland, of Missouri. "I wish to say that an invitation is extended to the People's Theatre. The delegates will require nothing but their badges."

A delegate. "I move you, that inasmuch as there is a difference of opinion as to whether the supplemental report was adopted, that that matter be laid on the table."

The question was taken by division.

The President. "The 'noes' have it, and the resolution is still before the Convention."

The question was put on the adoption of the resolution, and it was not adopted, the vote being, ayes 84; noes 131.

Mr. McEnery, of Louisiana. "I give notice that on to-morrow I will move a reconsideration of the vote by which this resolution was defeated."

Mr. Rowland, of Missouri. "I move that the Convention adjourn till ten A. M., to-morrow, October 28, 1881."

The motion was carried, and the Convention adjourned.

SECTION 3—THIRD DAY.

OCTOBER 28, 1881.

The Convention was called to order by the President at ten A. M.

The President said. "By a mistake yesterday, the Vice-Presidents who were elected were not invited to take their places upon the stage; if there are those in the audience now who were elected as Vice-Presidents, they will please come forward and take their places with those that are now on the stage."

A delegate from Iowa. "There was a mistake in our delegation. Hon. Mr. Craig, of Dubuque, was elected Vice-President."

Mr. Chase, of Nebraska. "Does taking seats on the platform preclude us from taking part in the debate?"

The President. "It does not. Gentlemen of the Convention, the following telegram has been received, which I will now read:

"WASHINGTON, D. C., Oct. 27, 1881.

"To MICHAEL McENNIS, *President:*

"I sincerely regret that I cannot visit St. Louis at this time and take part in the proceedings of your Convention. The measure which you assemble to consider is one of great national importance, and is entitled to prompt and favorable consideration by Congress. Official engagements imperatively detain me here, and deprive me of the privilege of enforcing my views by public address.

"JAMES G. BLAINE."

The President. "Just before the adjournment of the Convention yesterday, a motion was made to reconsider the vote of the Convention rejecting the supplemental resolution reported by the Committee on Resolutions; that was entered, and if there be no objection, that motion will now be entertained."

Mr. McEnery, of Louisiana. "Just before the Convention adjourned yesterday, I notified the Convention that on to-day I would move a reconsideration of the vote by which this supplemental resolution was lost; and now, sir, I move a reconsideration of that vote; and in making that motion, I desire to submit to the Convention one or two reasons that induced me to make this motion."

The President. "Will the gentleman allow the resolution first to be read, and then his remarks will be in order."

The resolution was then read as follows:

Resolved, That, in the interest of cheap transportation, and to afford a choice of water routes to the seaboard, we regard connections between the navigable waters of the Upper Mississippi river and the great lakes, as of great importance; and that Congress, in making the appropriations to improve the navigation of the Mississippi river and its tributaries, ought not to overlook or disregard the establishment of free water communication between the valley of the great river of the West and tide-water of the East.

Mr. McEnery. "Now, Mr. President, after the adjournment of the Convention yesterday, I met several delegates, not only among my own delegation, but from other States, who informed me that they had misapprehended the resolution which had been read to the Convention, and rejected by the Convention; they had confounded it with the resolution introduced by the gentleman from Illinois (Mr. Roberts), that singled the Illinois river out of the tributaries to the Mississippi river that should receive the favorable consideration of Congress; and, as a matter of course, acting under that conviction, they voted against this resolution. Now, gentlemen of the Convention, this resolution announces the abstract proposition that it is to the interest of the commerce of the Mississippi Valley that that commerce may be extended to the

Atlantic seaboard by water communication, thus connecting the Mississippi river with the great lakes to the Northwest, and consequently with the commerce of the Atlantic seaboard. Now, sir, I want to know whether this Convention desires it to go forth to the country that they are opposed to the connection of the Mississippi Valley with the great commerce which lies along the great lakes of the great Northwest. I don't believe, gentlemen of the Convention, that that is the sentiment of the Convention, and hence it is I move a reconsideration of that vote, in order that we may take deliberate action upon it, and not act in the hasty manner we did yesterday, when a vote was registered against it, just on the eve of the adjournment of the Convention."

Mr. Murphy, of Iowa. "I second the motion of the gentleman from Louisiana. It seems to me, Mr. President, that if we would consider carefully and prudently not only the primary objects of this Convention, but the scope and exact meaning of that resolution, we would have no hesitation as to our action. As I understand it, this Convention is called primarily in the interest of cheap transportation; for it is cheap transportation or not cheap transportation. That is the question in which we are all interested. We, sir, are not, in Iowa, wedded to any particular route. If the market of New Orleans, by the establishment of barge lines, furnishes, in the competition for trade, a better market for the products of Iowa and the Northwest, she will obtain them; but if it does not, she will not; and it is due to this Convention to state this, speaking for myself individually, and I believe I reflect the sentiment of Iowa, that if the question before this Convention was whether the Mississippi river should be improved, or not, we would favor the improvement of the Mississippi river, and retire all other projects. [Cheers.] That is the way we feel; but, sir, we do not think that because we ask— mark you, only an expression of this Convention in favor of a water route upon the Northern Mississippi, indicating no particular route, but saying that it is in the interest of the commerce of the Northwest—that we shall have a choice of routes to the seaboard, and that is all we ask. We think that we are not antagonizing an interest—either the primary interest, for which this Convention was called, or any other. Now, it is a well-known fact, as a part of the history of these conventions, Mr. President, that a convention was called at Davenport, in May last, for the purpose of considering a water route, connecting the Northern Mississippi with the Eastern seaboard, by way of the great lakes; and it is also a part of the history of that convention, that the people of the Mississippi Valley, south of the Des Moines rapids, came to that convention and earnestly pressed and asked for an expression in favor of the improvement of the Mississippi river. They were treated kindly; they were treated generously, and, although that convention was called for another and an express purpose, a resolution in favor of the improvement of the Mississippi river was entertained and passed unanimously. Now, while I do not desire to say anything to this Convention in the way of menace, or in the way of inducing, or using any means to induce, an opinion other than is perfectly legitimate and proper, permit me to say that the history of Congressional action in the past warrants me in making the statement that the friends of the Mississippi river had better poll every vote they possibly can, to the end they may secure a liberal appropriation in Congress. [Applause.] And it is a fact, not to be denied or disguised, that New York, Michigan, Ohio, Illinois, Minnesota, Wisconsin and Iowa are all directly interested in the principle asserted by the resolution. Those States are represented in Congress. New York and Chicago are today jealous of the trade that they believe legitimately belongs to them, that is drifting down the Mississippi river; and mark you, their representatives in Congress feel that jealousy, and perhaps it is well, here and now, for us to recognize they are an important factor in the improvement of the Mississippi river. [Cheers.] Mr. Chairman, I have detained you longer than I intended. I hope that this motion will prevail, that the vote will be reconsidered and the resolution passed."

Mr. Stanard of Missouri. "Mr. President and gentlemen of the Convention, I do not desire to detain you more than a moment, or but a very few moments. I believe, as was stated by the gentleman from Louisiana, that this resolution, reported from the Committee on Resolutions without recommendation, was not thoroughly understood by this Convention. I believe that I understood it; I voted for the resolution. I did not then know how the Missouri delegation would vote, and I do not now know how they will vote upon the question under consideration. But as for me, I propose to vote for the reconsideration of this resolution; and if it is reconsidered, then I propose to vote for it on its final passage; and I would like to give a reason or two why I do this. I appreciate the fact most highly, that has been suggested by my distinguished friend from Iowa (Mr. Murphy), that if adequate appropriations are secured for the improvement of the Mississippi river and its great tributaries, that we have got to have the votes of Western members in Congress, members who live in Michigan, members who live in Wisconsin, members who live in Iowa and Minnesota, who are more largely interested in the commerce of the lakes, by virtue of their location, than they will be in the commerce of the Mississippi river, through the Mississippi, and through the Jetties to the Gulf, and from thence to the markets of the world. Because we cannot expect,—while we may get the votes of many distinguished patriots of the East for the improvement of these great water-ways, there are many votes that we cannot get. My mind this moment recurs with pleasure to the conduct of the Davenport convention, which was referred to by my friend from Iowa (Mr. Murphy), a convention called for the purpose of facilitating the improvement of water-way communication between the lakes and the Mississippi river. I shall not forget their treatment there, and their unanimous votes in favor of a strong resolution for the improvement of the Mississippi river, and that these appropriations should stand for this purpose, separate and distinct, and upon their own merits, without any other appropriation tacked upon the bill. And when a voice rang out so clearly the other morning, from a back seat, stating he represented Michigan, I remembered how they voted; how the Representatives in Congress and Senators of that State were to the appropriation for the improvement of the mouth of the Mississippi river, by the Jetty system, in the Forty-third Congress. [Cheers]. I doubt whether that would ever have been passed—and I was there and know something of what I speak—had it not been for the co-operation of Senator Conger, Representatives Burroughs and Williams of Michigan, and of Williams of Wisconsin, and also of the earnest co-operation of now United States Senator, Sawyer, from Wisconsin; and it seems to me we cannot afford to do anything that would antagonize any of the people from the Northwest. Now what does this resolution ask? It does not ask that the Hennepin canal be constructed; it does not ask that the Michigan canal to the Illinois river shall be constructed, or that adequate improvements shall be made there, but it simply asks the people here in this central city, congregated in this Mississippi Valley, to recognize the fact that it will be for the interest of the people—for many of the people of this great Mississippi Valley—that there shall be communication between the Mississippi Valley and the lakes, and thence to tide-water. It seems to me there is nothing unreasonable in this. There may be said to be jealousy between the cities of St. Louis and Chicago. There is, but the rivalry has been a healthy one, and it has helped us, and I hope it has helped them also. I have none of that parsimonious feeling, so far as I am concerned; and if I had, and if you had, what difference would it make? The man who ascends the mountain, and struggles with all his might and attains the summit, has a right to view the beautiful scenery around about him, and expand his lungs, and take in the air, while the laggard who undertook to go with him rests beneath the shadow of some friendly rock. And the city that uses its greatest exertion, puts forth its best energy, and is worthiest of the emoluments coming from energy and patriotism, and fidelity to the public interests, has a right to the enjoyment of those facilities which come to it. I hope that the vote will be reconsidered."

Mr. Hitchcock, of Missouri. "I do not think it necessary to add in the way of persuasion anything to what has been said from the extremes of this continent, on the part of the North, and by my colleague, the chairman of the delegation from St. Louis. I desire the privilege of saying for myself,—and I know that I reflect also the sentiments of gentlemen who are representative men of the commercial interests of St. Louis, as the last speaker is,—that I hope this resolution will be reconsidered, and that it will be passed. I desire to call the attention of the Convention in addition to the reasons given by the last speaker, to the simple proposition that this resolution avoids that which we all felt might be a source of danger or objection—undue prominence to any particular plan or interest, and simply sets forth a general universal expression of a spirit which will be in strict accord with the spirit and action of this Convention to-day."

Mr. Benton, of Minnesota. "I am convinced that the Convention made a mistake yesterday afternoon. The record of the Convention will read as now,—' Resolved, that in the judgment of this Convention, Congress should not consider the question of water-way between the Mississippi river and the great lakes; it ought to overlook and disregard these questions.' Now, Mr. President, I don't believe that this is the record this Convention wants to make here. I don't believe that this Convention wants to put the West in hostility and antagonism to the East. If it had been simply the question of adoption of one particular route—the Hennepin canal, or any other scheme, I would not have been content; if it had been simply a question of rivalry between these two great cities, in view of the magnificent reception we have had here, I would have voted for St. Louis every time. But, Mr. President, this is not a special scheme ; it does not commit the Convention to any one scheme, or to any one project ; it simply asks that all these questions have a fair consideration. If there be objections, as I am told there are, to the Hennepin canal, or to any other improvement offered for consideration, they should be fairly considered. But the record of this Convention, as it stands now, is one of hostility ; and it is not wise, when you go to present the action of this Convention, to have to say that the deliberate resolution of the Convention was that we want to put ourselves in hostile relations towards the very men we need to help us. It is not only inexpedient, but it is not right ; we must not permit sectional jealousies ; we have had enough of that ; the time is past. Let us hope the West will never be put in hostile relations to the East. Many of us remember the East with pride ; it is the home of our boyhood ; we love it still ; we respect the men, we love the citizens of the East, and we hope we shall never be put in hostile relations to them. I hope the motion will prevail."

Mr. A. W. Slayback, of Missouri. "Mr. President, as a member of the St. Louis delegation not yet heard from, and whose own chairman don't know where he stands, I wish to say that I am in favor of the reconsideration of this resolution, and for its adoption when it is put to the vote. I would like to inquire, Mr. President, what this Convention is afraid of. They seem to be timid about asking for what they want. Are we afraid because other bills have been loaded down with appropriations for Goose creek or some other little unknown stream, that it will always be the case? Is there nothing to be expected of Congressmen? Shall we assume that they will not learn to progress and advance ; will they never learn what the people expect of them? They ought to know by this time that the Mississippi river is an arm of the sea, and has with great propriety been called an inland sea, and not only through the Jetties at the mouth, but through the fountain and source there shall be an outlet to Liverpool, and other markets of the world. We are not here to discuss the local advantages of the recommendations of this Convention. I have gone to Minnesota every summer for several years, and I find up at that end of the river there are interests growing every year, just as vast as those at the southern end, —vaster if possible in the future, because in that northwest region there is a class of men, vigorous, brave ; men of energy, pushing ahead, making fortunes, and opening up a country so vast and so rich that it almost makes the South ashamed to see the progress that has been made in the golden Northwest in the last decade, as compared with our own progress, considering the advantages of climate and soil. Now, those people are interested in this question. I would have you open a way from the sources of the river, through the lakes by the way of Chicago, if you please. I regard Chicago as a whole-souled young village that ought to have more commerce than it has had in the past. I regard the northern lakes as but feeders to Mississippi river commerce ; we want to have through that avenue to the ocean a greater volume of trade than we have had. This is not whether it would benefit one city or another. The cities are not the people to be heard from. The people of this magnificent valley—the agriculturists, the thinkers, the toilers, the farmers, founders, manufacturers, the men who are developing the resources of the field and forest—they are the men that want to speak through this Convention, because city men can speak almost any time through the town meeting or the newspaper.

But to speak through a Convention, it is expected that voices shall be heard from the whole of the interests represented in the Convention ; and I would not wish to sit in this Convention, if I thought we simply represented St. Louis or the southern portion of the Mississippi river. We are representatives here of a broader thought, of a wider idea, of a greater question: that is, shall we, inhabitants of this Mississippi Valley, act in the future as we have in the past, letting the eastern portion of this country outstrip us in wealth, and having their way about appropriations for harbors and other improvements? Is it not about time that we ought to have our way? If we are to have it, we must bring all the aid, all the help that is interested along with us, and obtain the necessary appropriations. Thankful for the patience with which I have been heard, I wish to call upon every gentleman of the delegation to which I belong, to widen himself out and come up to the emergency, by seeking upon this occasion to forget St. Louis for a minute, and remember the Mississippi Valley."

Mr. Parsons, of Michigan. "I want to say one word in connection with this matter. I represent the great State of Michigan. We owe no debt; we are rich in all that makes wealth of empire, and yet we know no State lines, no local lines. Whatever promotes the glory of the Mississippi Valley promotes the grandeur of Michigan. I know—and the allusion by Gov. Stanard struck my notice—he said Michigan acted intelligently on the subject. In a conversation with Mr. Conger a few days ago, he told me that for forty days and forty nights he sat by the side of Mr. Eads before he made up his mind to vote in favor of an appropriation for the improvement of the mouth of the Mississippi. Let me say simply, I have changed my sentiment in connection with Michigan's relation to this great subject. I said yesterday we had no immediate interest in the improvement of the Mississippi river. We have an interest. The whole western part of our State is interested. Twenty years ago the trade between Michigan and New Orleans was immense; it is nothing to-day. I voted against the resolution before us yesterday, and yet I was thankful it was projected upon this Convention. But I want nothing to stand between the improvement; I desire that this should not stand in the way of the resolution for the improvement of the Mississippi river; that was first and foremost; but this is appropriate, and it should be reconsidered and passed unanimously. It will interest the entire delegation of Michigan, who are a unit, I think, in favor of the improvement of the Mississippi river."

Mr. Thomas B. Taylor, of Alabama. "Alabama has not been heard. I come from Alabama, Montgomery county. I solicited an opportunity to come here as a member from the mayor of the city, under your invitation. I come here with the deep interest I have always had in the Mississippi Valley. I come not representing Alabama, but I come as an American citizen, representing the United States, and all concerned. When I traveled through Tennessee, I rejoiced to see it flourishing. I rejoice at everything I see progressing in St. Louis. I correspond with Mr. Eads. I am delighted to hear his name mentioned. I have been corresponding with Mr. Eads to bring about the state of improvement of the river which I have been considering for fifty years. I voted yesterday in favor of this proposition. I don't represent Alabama alone; I came here to consider the welfare of my country. I don't represent Alabama alone; I represent the interests of every man I see here. I believe there is a way by which the natural forces of the river can be utilized so as to manufacture all the cotton manufactured in the North, to grind all the wheat ground in the North, and to saw all the lumber necessary. I recognize the right every man has to his individual opinion. I think every man should act for himself, and not be intimidated by threats that if he don't go for such and such a section, they will not go for his section. The impulses which actuate me are the grandeur and welfare of my country. I recognize no other power; I am for the people at large. I said I represented all concerned. I scratch "all concerned" out; I wish to be here as a delegate representing the whole interests of this country. I have been in favor of that resolution which was offered yesterday, and I shall vote for it now without fear of intimidation; and when threats are made of what one section will do, I hope such considerations will never be entertained by this Convention."

Mr. Underwood, of Kentucky. "I want to express my exceeding gratification at the broad, liberal and statesmanlike views that have come from these gentlemen all over this floor this morning upon this question, and above all am I gratified with the sentiments that flowed from the hearts and judgments of these men from the city of St. Louis, and from Alabama, and from this whole valley. Their fraternity is so manifest, the purpose to do equal justice to all parts of this valley, and leave no part of it untouched, and to give every part of it a fair show, is a circumstance that I have great cause to congratulate myself and this Convention upon. It shows the purpose of this Convention; it shows the unanimity of purpose, the unanimity of feeling; it shows that we are beginning, throughout this valley, to comprehend the broad position we occupy in the valley of the Mississippi. Allow me, gentlemen, for one moment—although it is a subject, doubtless, which has been contemplated by every man here—to invite you to a consideration of the position of the Mississippi Valley in its relation to the balance of the United States. The proper boundaries of the Mississippi Basin are the lakes on the north, the gulf on the south, the Alleghanies and the Rocky mountains on the east and west; that is the natural topography and geography of the country. The condition of this valley, and the identity and unity peculiar to itself, are also related to other parts of this country. This great basin occupies a position, in reference to our whole country, as the body occupies to the limb; and so long as heart and lungs and vitality exists here in this great body, so long as we continue to be the great feeder, not only of our own country, but of the world, shall we continue to command the power to influence, and become the great seat of the empire of this region of the world. Now, to come back to the point in question, there is no reason why the counterpart of the Mississippi system—that of the lakes—should not be considered; why is it not part and parcel of the great nation whose interests we are considering to-day? Aside from the question that it is important to have the full vote and strength of the Illinois delegation, both upon this floor and in Congress; aside from that —for that is a question of expediency—there is every reason growing out of the material wants of our valley, and the whole country, why we should contemplate and consider the interest of a communication between the system of waters in what we call our Mississippi Valley, with our lake system. Aside from the consideration of the vastness of the commerce of the great lakes, as well as that going to the mouth of the Mississippi river, it is important to remember that there are national considerations. These considerations strike my mind with a great deal of force, why we should connect our great system of rivers with our lakes, and I want to present them in a few words. It is not at all impossible—I hope and pray it may never occur—that we should have another war with Great Britain— God forbid ; God grant that it may never occur. But I invite your consideration, gentlemen, to the fact of such a calamity both to us and to Great Britain alike. Great Britain is the owner of the other shore of the lake system ; it commands the mouth of the St. Lawrence ; with her vast marine power she could place a single man-of-war at the mouth of the lakes, and at the mouth of the St. Lawrence, and prevent any ingress or egress on the part of our vessels ; she could send another man-of-war to sweep the lakes, and drive all our marine from those waters. It is very possible, and it is plain to be seen, how vulnerable our whole lake-shore system would be under those circumstances. Though you might fortify Chicago and Milwaukee and Detroit with our guns stationary, it wouldn't be at all difficult, on the part of Great Britain, to send a single man-of-war, and being sustained from their base of supplies in their own country, to burn and devastate our entire lake shore. I am not general enough ; I am not prepared to pronounce upon the necessities of the thing as to military system, but it does strike me as common sense that the best possible plan of relief to operate from the lakes is through some canal, to send resources of this great valley, in the shape of gunboats and iron-clads and men-of-war, to the relief of our lake shore. Aside from all that again, may it not be possible that the idea of a reservoir system, much thought of in Minnesota, is very desirable; it is very much thought of by some high in the Engineer Corps, and though we do not know whether it may ever be demonstrated, it may be possible in the absence of sufficient water; if it becomes necessary, there may be sufficient elevation in these broad lake reservoirs to furnish water as feeders to this great river. It is a question worthy of consideration and examination. I thank you very kindly for the attention you have given me."

Cries of "Question!"

A delegate moved the previous question.

Mr. Rozier, of Missouri. " I do not desire to detain this Convention, and merely ask it to pause for a moment, and see what we are going to do in a national point of view. You may destroy all the action of this Convention. I have taken the broad ground, like we did over thirty-six years ago, taken by the ablest men of this country, that the Constitution of the United States does not permit the appropriation of public money for local matters. It is against every principle of our Government. The only question to be decided by this Convention—[Cries of " Question!"] I see the popular sentiment is so strong against any movement in this direction that they do not wish to listen to any argument in the case, in violation of everything. The honorable gentleman himself from the Chamber of Commerce presented just the very proposition I am going to maintain. The very committee of this Convention have reported a set of resolutions, and yet to-day, in violation, in the teeth of those very principles, they wish to adopt a principle that involves a local improvement. Gentlemen may flatter themselves that they may succeed. On the contrary, they may have the ability to carry a few members; but, in a national point of view, you will find in time that if you admit this principle of building a canal from the northern part of Illinois, you will have to admit it in South Carolina, and every State in the Union, and where will be the termination of this matter? We have but one great object, and I wish this Convention to pause. It is the improvement of a great national river that has brought you here, and I hope you will not weigh it down with other matters. I hope this Convention will not make this fatal error. It will be fatal; it will hinder you; it will not aid you."

The President. "The question is, shall the vote of yesterday, by which the supplementary report of the Committee on Resolutions was rejected, be reconsidered. Are you ready for the question? [Cries of "Question!"] As many as favor reconsideration will say 'aye.'"

The vote was then taken.

The President. "The 'ayes' have it by a large majority, and the motion prevails. The motion is now in order, and made, that the resolution as offered be adopted. That is the question before the Convention."

Mr. George H. Shields, of Missouri. "I have listened to remarks made by gentlemen representing the extremes of this continent, and I am willing to say that I endorse every word that they have said. I believe that the improvement of the great Mississippi and its tributaries is of paramount importance to all other internal improvement schemes now before the people, or that ever have been before the people. I believe, sir, that the improvement of each of these rivers is absolutely necessary; but I believe that each and every one of those propositions ought to stand upon its own merits, to go before Congress asking appropriations for such schemes as meritorious, and for those only. I want it distinctly understood that I believe that the Hennepin canal, or any other canal that offers additional facilities for water transportation, and cheapens the rates to the great seaboard of this country, ought to be supported by Congress, and by the people all over the United States. I believe that every brick that is laid upon another in the city of Chicago redounds to the benefit of the city of New Orleans, as well as the city of New York. I believe that every acre of this country that is turned up by the plow, whether it is in the Southern States, or whether it is in the beautiful wheat fields of the Northwest, redounds to the general good of the whole nation, and this Convention ought to be broad enough to take into consideration any proposition that legitimately comes before it. But, sir, at the same time, I insist that all of these propositions ought to stand exclusively on their own merits. If this tide-water scheme referred to by Col. Slayback is of sufficient importance to attract the attention of Congress, I want Congress to make an appropriation for that improvement without being weighted with appropriations for the Missouri, Ohio, Red river, Arkansas river, or Mississippi river. I ask the gentleman from Illinois (Mr. Roberts), in view of the fact that this Convention has already laid down a proposition that these appropriations ought to be made separately; in view of the fact that this Convention was called to take into consideration the improvement of the Mississippi river and its navigable tributaries; in view of the fact that we have brought to bear all the talent of this Convention in that one direction, if he is not willing to accept an amendment to the resolution, amend by striking out the words ' in making the appropriations to improve the navigation of the Mississippi river and its tributaries?' If that was adopted the resolution would read:

"*Resolved*, That in the interest of cheap transportation, and to afford a choice of water routes to the seaboard, we regard connections between the navigable waters of the Upper Mississippi river and the great lakes as of great importance, and that Congress ought not to overlook or disregard the establishment of free water communication between the valley of the great river of the West, and the tide-water of the East.

" Now, Mr. Chairman, what is the reason we have not been able to get heretofore appropriations for the benefit of this great water system of the West? It is because those who were antagonistic to it have loaded it down with appropriations that never ought to have had anything to do with the bill; it is because they endeavored to so break the force of the public sentiment of this great valley; and I believe, that if the gentleman from Illinois will accept that amendment—Iowa—disconnecting it from the improvement of the Mississippi river, and letting it stand on its own merits, there will be one unanimous shout of approval in favor of it in this Convention. I offer this amendment."

The Secretary then read the amendment which had been offered by Mr. Shields.

Mr. Underwood, of Kentucky. "I wish to make an amendment to the amendment. It is to this effect:

"*Resolved*, That we invite the attention of Congress to all other practicable water routes connecting the Mississippi basin with the Atlantic seaboard."

The President. "Where would the gentleman have his amendment come in?"

Mr. Underwood. "I propose it as an amendment to the amendment; I wish to embrace not only seaboard connection with the lakes, but all other matters which, in the development of the great system, should be and will be made. Furthermore, upon the subject, I would like to say that we have invited here all members of Congress from this valley, and that the Hon. John T. White, from Kentucky, is present, and I would like him to be heard upon the subject of the amendment."

The President. "Mr. White is invited to speak to the amendment offered by the gentleman from Kentucky, if he desires to be heard upon that amendment."

Mr. Underwood. "I have the honor to introduce to you Hon. John T. White, the representative in Congress from the mountain district of Kentucky."

Mr. White said:

"I am exceedingly gratified at the compliment that has been paid to me by my friend from Kentucky, and by this Convention, and at the remarks that have been made this morning by gentlemen from all parts of the Union, but especially the liberality of the Missouri delegates. It occurred to us on yesterday, when this resolution was voted down, in which the Illinois delegation seemed to be divided in opinion, that it was an unkind thing in the Missouri delegation to refuse to call attention to a canal-way, connecting the waters of the Missouri with the great lake system, and I am happy, as I believe this Convention is happy, that this morning that seeming injustice,—that seeming disregard of the rights of another portion of this country,—should be recognized. This amendment to the resolution offered by the gentleman from Kentucky (Mr. Underwood), calls attention to a system of water-ways which you may remember was considered in 1868, in part; a canal-way connecting the Tennessee with the Atlantic seaboard, a canal-way connecting the Upper Ohio river with the Atlantic seaboard. At that time it was considered as not very important, but to-day we see the importance of considering more water-ways than one. The lake system will not answer, and this Mississippi river, when it is improved, will not supply the wants of the great valley any more than your bridge will now allow all freights to pass; we feel it necessary that St. Louis should have two or three bridges, and so this great Mississippi basin, with its wonderful resources, will, in a short time, feel the necessity of more water-ways than one. In the first place, the lakes are closed up in winter; that of itself is a condition to call attention to the Mississippi river, to say nothing of the great quantity of land that is annually submerged by overflow of the Lower Mississippi that has yet to be reclaimed, and the State of Louisiana be made an empire to feed this nation with productions now brought from abroad. These matters call for our greatest consideration of the Mississippi river. So are we to look for a route of transportation that will not freeze up, coming from the Mississippi river basin and connecting with the Atlantic seaboard, and the resolution presented by Judge Underwood of Kentucky looks to that point. I hold in my hand a statement from one of the foremost scientists of this country. I do not wish the Convention to think I am going to take up more than two or three minutes of its time. I don't propose to read all this pamphlet, but only one part. It is by Prof. Shaler, of Harvard College, but at that time Geologist of the State of Kentucky. He says:

"'After careful study of the route from the Kentucky river through Cumberland Gap, it is evident the project is entirely feasible, and likely to be of very great importance in developing the mineral resources of the State, as well as of East Tennessee; and, furthermore, that the cost of the water-way is likely to be exceedingly small when compared with the practical results likely to be obtained from this work.' And again: 'I believe this to be one of the most practical waterways from the central region of the Mississippi to the sea. It would have the advantage over the principal northern water routes of at least four months more navigation in the year.' Four months more navigation to St. Louis and to the great Northwest, and to the whole Mississippi Valley, is of incalculable moment to the deliberations of this Convention. I can remember, and other gentlemen on this floor can remember, when it was the policy of a great party in this country to make no appropriations for internal improvements; but the East has constantly gone on improving its rivers and harbors; the South and West, to a large extent, has fallen in with the idea that it is all wrong, and will not ask for any of these appropriations. Now, if the South changes its course, changes its base in this regard, the people of the South will have to instruct its members in Congress to vote for appropriations for Southern rivers, as well as to allow Eastern members to vote appropriations for Eastern harbors. And until the public are thoroughly aroused, your Convention will amount to nothing. What is the use of the Convention here adopting strong resolutions when members of Congress stand upon the doctrine that it is not right that Congress should make appropriations for internal improvements? I was happy to hear a letter read from a distinguished Senator from my own State yesterday, in which he said he regretted he could not be with this Convention, but that he would be heard in the National Senate this winter. It is only two years since that Senator came to this conclusion—one of the old landmarks of the Whig party. Judge Craddock, of Kentucky, wrote him a letter, in which he made this remark: 'I say to you, in all candor, in my opinion the Democratic party in Kentucky is only kept together by the utter abhorrence people have for the Republican party; but that for our hatred to it we would go to pieces in less than two years. No one who has observed the development of public sentiment can be mistaken as to the signs of the times.' The meaning of all this is, that we must be more practical in our policy, or else we will have to give way to others who are. That is what I call the attention of this Convention to; that when the voting for members of Congress takes place, when your Legislatures elect members of the Senate, let it be distinctly understood that they are going to vote five millions for the improvement of the Mississippi river—fifty millions, if necessary—for the removal of obstacles, and the perfecting of the river system; for this canal-way connecting the Tennessee with the Atlantic; for the improvement to connect Iowa with the Atlantic, and other improvements. In all cheap water-ways the State of Missouri is equally interested with the State of Kentucky, and this whole Mississippi river basin. We shall have to stand together as a unit, to bring to our aid all the support of the South, in Virginia, Alabama, from Pittsburg to the Rockies, from the lakes to the Jetties, if you want to carry your resolutions through Congress, and get a sufficient appropriation. I thank you."

Mr. Elliot, of Tennessee. "I rise to speak to the amendment to the amendment. If the amendment is added to the resolution before the Convention, then the adoption of the amendment proposed a little while ago by the honorable member from the city of St. Louis (Mr. Shields) will become of still greater importance, I wish to call the attention of the Convention simply to the phraseology of the resolution. It is evident that the great sentiment of this Convention is in favor of adopting the resolution which is proposed to be amended in some form. I don't propose to discuss its merits at all; I simply call the attention of the Convention to the phraseology of the resolution itself, and, as I take it, its scope is much more comprehensive than any of us seem to comprehend. Let us look at it for a moment. It is that Congress, in making appropriations to improve the navigation of the Mississippi river and its tributaries, 'ought not to overlook and disregard.' The time when, and the place where, Congress is expected to look, I suppose, to cheap transportation to the eastern seaboard, is clearly indicated here to be the time and place when appropriations are proposed to be made for the improvement of the Mississippi river and its tributaries, and it is in the making of that appropriation,—according to the plain meaning of this resolution,—that Congress is expected to mature and carry on a scheme for navigation to the eastern tide-waters. Now, if the Convention means that, and desires to couple these propositions together in this way, so that there shall be no appropriation made to improve the Mississippi river or its navigable tributaries, unless Congress shall mature a plan to extend navigation to eastern tide-water, and at the same time to be prepared to propose appropriations to carry out that plan, it does seem to me,—while I shall acquiesce in the judgment of the Convention as cheerfully as anybody,— that we shall have undone all the Convention has done up to this time; and instead of putting the improvement of the Mississippi river on its own bottom, to stand or fall on its merits, we have irrevocably connected with it a system of improvement to extend to the tide-waters of the East. If you adopt the amendment proposed by the gentleman from the city of St. Louis (Mr. Shields), and strike out these words, 'In making the appropriation to improve the navigation of the Mississippi river and its tributaries,' it does seem to me to give to the honorable gentleman from Iowa all he asks, certainly all he ought to ask."

Mr. Vandever, of Iowa. "In order to remove the objection made by my friend, I simply propose to strike out the words 'the Mississippi river and its navigable tributaries.' Then it will read that Congress in making appropriations should not overlook and disregard this connection with the lakes. I simply leave out 'the Mississippi river and its navigable tributaries.'"

Mr. Elliot, of Tennessee. "I don't think the amendment proposed by the gentleman meets the case. I will read it as it will stand according to the suggestion of the gentleman:

"'And that Congress in making appropriations ought not to overlook or disregard the establishment of free water communication,'" etc.

Mr. Vandever, of Iowa. "I suggest if that does not entirely disconnect it with appropriations for the Mississippi river?"

Mr. Elliot. "It does not; it couples the whole scheme together—the improvement of the Mississippi river and its navigable tributaries, and the extension of navigation—the opening of cheap communication with the tide-water of the East. It unites them in one proposition—that when appropriations are made for any of the objects,—'that Congress, in making appropriations!' In making appropriations for what? What is the object of the proceedings of this Convention? Isn't it for the improvement of the Mississippi river and its navigable tributaries? And in striking out the words 'Mississippi river and its navigable tributaries,' do you alter the sense of the resolution? No. There is no other object for which appropriations are contemplated in the proceedings of the Convention, but for the improvement of the Mississippi river and its navigable tributaries. When you say, Congress in making appropriations ought not to overlook or disregard this other scheme, you mean Congress shall not overlook it, and shall make appropriations for carrying it on. That is the platform the Convention will stand upon, if the resolution is adopted as it now stands."

Mr. Blakely, of Minnesota. "Any interest that seeks to improve the Mississippi river, from its source to its mouth, is the one object for consideration, and anything else except that is irrelevant. I appeal to you, in the interest of success, that we go back and simply recognize and stand where we did yesterday; that is, the endorsement and passage of the resolutions submitted to you by the Committee on Resolutions, and adjourn this Convention and go home."

Mr. Shields, of Missouri. "After consultation with the gentleman from Iowa, who offered the original resolution, I think we have arrived at a solution that will be satisfactory to all sides, and that is simply to strike out of this resolution these words: 'To improve the navigation of the Mississippi river and its tributaries.' That will leave the resolution to read:

"'That in the interests of cheap transportation, and to afford a choice of water routes to the seaboard, we regard connections between the navigable waters of the Upper Mississippi river and the great lakes as of great importance, and that Congress, in making appropriations, ought not to overlook or disregard the establishment of free water communication between the valley of the great river of the West and tide-waters of the East.'

"Now, the proposition, Mr. Chairman, is this: This Convention is in favor of any proposition that facilitates cheap transportation by water; and the reason the gentleman was not willing to accept my amendment was, it struck out the words: 'in making appropriations.' I immediately saw the force of the gentleman's suggestion, and am perfectly willing to modify my resolution to that effect, and so do."

The President. "The gentleman withdraws his first amendment?"

Mr. Shields. "Yes."

Mr. Vandever, of Iowa. "The amendment is accepted by the mover of the resolution."

Mr. J. P. Root, of Kansas. "I have been waiting patiently here; coming from a portion of territory which has not been heard from, representing a territory greater in extent—greater in land, greater in water,—than all the rest of the territory represented, and we have yet to be heard. It was my fortune to be on the Committee on Resolutions. We had almost everything presented to us yesterday before that committee that the Mississippi Valley demanded. The Missouri valley demanded certain things of that committee; the central portion represented in this committee opposed all that; St. Louis and the Mississippi river proper opposed it. I am very glad that they have come to their senses a little this morning; I am glad that the men who bitterly opposed everything that tended outside of a certain direction yesterday, to-day desire to open a little; and, therefore, I believe we shall be justified, if the amendment to the amendment is adopted, to also introduce some things we would like to have brought before this Convention. In the interest of harmony and peace, we made some concessions in the committee, and the original resolutions, as adopted here, were the result of long deliberations and some very sharp controversy. It was finally conceded that the object of this Convention should be attained by the original resolutions, without anything else. It was hoped by my constituency we would mention certain things in that Committee, which were entirely ignored. I think that we shall open a door through which may enter into this Convention things we cannot get rid of, if we adopt these amendments. I voted for the resolutions in the committee as a matter of compromise; every man from the Missouri valley voted for them, notwithstanding they felt they were aggrieved, and had just cause for complaint; and, sir, if this is pressed, they will introduce amendments and contend for them; but if you will let the original resolutions, as adopted unanimously, stand as the voice of this Convention, we will be with you; if not, we shall not be with you. That is all there is to it; that is all I have to say."

Cries of "Question!"

The President. "The previous question has been demanded. As many as are in favor of the previous question will say 'aye.'"

The question was put, and the previous question ordered.

The President. "The question is upon the adoption of the amendment offered by the gentleman from Missouri (Mr. Shields), which will now be read. The amendment to which the gentleman from Kentucky offered an amendment was withdrawn by the gentleman from Missouri (Mr. Shields), and he offered the amendment which is now pending before the Convention."

Mr. Underwood, of Kentucky. "Then I would like to know whether I could offer an amendment to the present amendment, offered by the gentleman from Missouri, covering my idea?"

The President. "Not now; the previous question is pending, and that will not now be in order."

The Secretary read the amendment, as follows:

"Amend the resolution by striking out all after the word 'appropriations,' to and including the word 'tributaries,' so that the resolution will read as follows:

"*Resolved*, That in the interest of cheap transportation, and to afford a choice of water routes to the seaboard, we regard connections between the navigable waters of the Upper Mississippi and the great lakes as of great importance, and that Congress, in making appropriations, ought not to overlook or disregard the establishment of free water communication between the valley of the great river of the West and tidewater of the East."

The President. "As many as favor the adoption of the amendment offered by the gentleman from Missouri will say 'aye.'"

A vote was taken by division.

The President: "The 'ayes' have it. It is evident more than two-thirds of the Convention have voted for the adoption of the amendment. The count will proceed if it is demanded. The amendment has been adopted, and the question is upon the adoption of the resolution as amended. As many as favor the adoption of the resolution, as amended, say 'aye.'"

A vote was taken, and 210 delegates voted in the affirmative, and 70 in the negative.

The President. "The resolution as amended has been adopted."

Mr. Walker, of Minnesota. "I wish to introduce for the consideration of the Convention, a resolution having a most important bearing upon the work, or execution of the work which has been laid out by this Convention. I wish, also, the privilege, very briefly to explain the motives and purposes for which this resolution was drawn, and the scope of the resolution."

The resolution was read as follows:

Resolved, That for the purpose of expediting the great work of improving 16,000 miles of water-way, comprising the Mississippi and its navigable tributaries, we do most earnestly insist and recommend that Congress make immediate provision for the rapid progress of the work, by adding to the Mississippi River Commission at least eight more members, five of whom shall be from the regular corps of engineers of the War Department of the United States, so that it may be susceptible of division into three working parties of five each, three of whom shall be United States Engineers.

Mr. Walker: "I may be permitted to say I represent a part of the Northwest, in part, which is not represented upon that map, which is visible; that if the curtain were just rolled up about ten feet we could see where there are golden fields of grain, more bright and beautiful than the beautiful gardens which adorn this great valley; 565 miles of navigable waters of the Mississippi river are now hid behind the curtain on that map; and I am the one man to talk for that 565 miles of navigable waters that remain of the Mississippi river; and, sir, I wish to call the attention of this Convention to a very important fact, that is, that we have—to put it in lumbermen's parlance—been biting off more than we can chew. We have been providing here, as the deliberate sense of the Convention, that the whole sixteen thousand miles of water-way of the Mississippi and its branches, shall be handed over to the care, custody, and control of the Mississippi River Commission. That Commission, gentlemen, is composed of the ablest men in this nation; they are peculiarly fitted and adapted to the work which has been assigned to them; we have endorsed their proceedings thus far; we have recommended that their sphere be enlarged, and forgetting all the time that the Commission was composed of seven men, four regular army engineers, and three other distinguished citizens from civil life; to whom we have handed over 16,000 miles of water-way, for them to adopt plans for their improvement; when the law under which they have been appointed requires that they shall also superintend the work which they lay out. It is well known to every gentleman in this Convention, that that Commission is now actively engaged in executing the grand work which they have devised, and that the work laid off already will require considerable time, and considerable money; and yet we, standing away out on the borders, have set down upon ourselves, by providing that the ways and methods to be devised yet for the improvement of our region and water-way outside, shall be in the hands of this Commission. Life is short, and our children will not live long enough to see the time when seven men of that Commission will be able to examine the sources of the Missouri river."

A delegate. "I rise to a point of order. The member who is now speaking is a member of our delegation, but the rule is that resolutions shall be submitted to the Committee on Resolutions without debate."

Mr. Walker, of Minnesota. "I ask permission of the

Convention that that rule will be suspended, and I be permitted to offer this resolution."

The President. "The gentleman was allowed to introduce the resolution without objection, and commenced his remarks. I would say to the gentleman from Minnesota that he has reached the limit of debate recognized by the Convention. I am aware that the rule was, that resolutions should go to the Committee on Resolutions without debate; but the committee has made its report, and the committee been discharged."

A delegate. "No, the committee has not been discharged."

Another delegate. "I move that the rule be suspended, and that the gentleman have time to elaborate the idea he is pregnant with."

The President. "The gentleman from Minnesota introduced a resolution quite late, the Chair confesses, in the business of this Convention; he was allowed to proceed without objection, and it seems to me that the gentleman should be allowed to complete the remarks which he had begun; and yet the Chair desires the gentleman from Minnesota to recognize the fact that this Convention does not desire long to listen to anything which he may have to say."

Mr. Walker, of Minnesota. "I had well-nigh concluded my remarks. In order to carry out the recommendations of this Convention, that this whole 16,000 miles of water-way should be relegated to the care and control of that Commission, it has been thought wise that the Commission itself, with extended jurisdiction, also be increased in number. At present this Commission has its hands full. If we have to have this work expedited, we must have a greater force at work on the Commission; and hence, I provide by this resolution, that with the increased work proposed by this Convention, there will also be provided a superior number on the Commission, and have them added to it. I submit this resolution for the consideration of this Convention. I hope that seven men will not be required to devise ways and methods for the improvement of the Alleghany, Monongahela, Kentucky, Tennessee, Cumberland, Ohio, the grand Missouri, and all its glorious tributaries, and to go up the Missouri and investigate what we need there. We want the work done quickly, and we intend that Congress shall make the necessary appropriations to carry it out quickly."

Mr. Hitchcock, of Missouri. "I wish to make a statement of fact, and the gentleman from Minnesota will, I think, see that his resolution is not needed, if he will look at the resolutions already adopted. He is mistaken in supposing that the Convention has adopted resolutions referring all this work to the Commission of seven. It has expressly declared that Congress should apply a complete system to all other rivers. In other words it has called for the very thing the gentleman wants. The Committee on Resolutions did not feel themselves justified, nor did they think it would be wise, to undertake in five minutes to dictate the extension of that Commission system."

The question was put on the adoption of the resolution, and it was not adopted.

Mr. McEnery, of Louisiana. "Mr. President, I understand there is present on the floor of this Convention one of Pennsylvania's ablest and most distinguished men, and now a member of Congress; I refer to the Hon. W. S. Shallenberger. I move that Mr. Shallenberger be invited to address this Convention from the stand." [Cheers.]

The motion was seconded and carried.

Mr. Shallenberger said:

MR. CHAIRMAN AND GENTLEMEN OF THE CONVENTION: I trust that I am not so little appreciative of the temper of a body like this as to trespass upon its time. Hence, if you will bear with me a moment, I shall just acknowledge the compliment you have paid to me, and to the great State of Pennsylvania, that appears here to-day to second what you have done, and to say that it, I pledge you, will appear on the floor of Congress with its twenty-seven votes. I hope [cheers] to give to the great Mississippi Valley that which you have said to-day she needs. I am here to speak for myself alone. When I say that I heartily endorse, not alone the specific action of this Convention, but in that broader, better sense, I endorse what I see in these intelligent faces to be the great outlying and underlying thought of the Mississippi Valley. [Cheers.] Because, gentlemen, you know, and I know, that resolutions sometimes express what we desire them to, and sometimes they do not. We sometimes get from a committee a dished-up resolution, that passes by common consent, neither binding upon those who desire to operate under it, nor upon those for whom it was intended.

But I take it, in accord with the sentiment of a distinguished member of the Commission, yesterday (Mr. Taylor), that the grand, central thought of this Convention must impress itself upon Congress and the country. It cannot be possible that delegates like those I see around me this morning, coming from all over the broad States bordering on the Mississippi and its tributaries, coming here from their business one thousand miles by rail and water, have come here for the simple purpose of enacting platitudes in the shape of eloquent resolutions. No! No! There is no language so eloquent or forcible as to convey properly the motive, the intellectual force, and the practical and powerful enforcement of what this Convention intends to convey. [Cheers.] I say, and say it with all the more pleasure because the Convention has recently adopted a resolution, which, while I didn't think it desirable to introduce,—while, indeed, I should have been glad if the Convention had left it out entirely,—I refer now to the resolution referring to the communication with the Atlantic seaboard,— I say while I should have hoped that this Convention, called for a specific purpose, having completed so fully, and as I think admirably, the purpose for which it was convened, should have adjourned, and allowed that specific effort, with all its force and cogency, to operate upon Congress; yet when that resolution was introduced I was exceedingly glad it was accepted, lest the impression should go out that we were against any competition by water, east or west, north or south. And I was glad that the recognition was made that there might possibly be other outlets for the Mississippi Valley than the great lakes of the North. Indeed, gentlemen, I think the time is coming when the United States will understand that engineering skill will give us from the Ohio a rapid, a free inter-communication with the Atlantic seaboard. And when you come to think that the Ohio has upon its bosom to-day more tonnage—together with the Monongahela, which I represent—more tonnage than all the railroads of the United States combined, then, gentlemen, you begin to understand why it is that we want the Mississippi river improved. We expect to send you millions upon millions of tons of freight that you need, and we want to sell coal by the hundred millions, that your manufacturing establishments south and southwest, your sugar mills and your cotton gins will use, and desire to have cheaper than you now get it. I say when you comprehend the fact, that the Ohio river alone sends upon its bosom to the Mississippi to-day more, perhaps, than all the Mississippi north of St. Louis, then you can understand why it is that Ohio has not made itself heard upon this floor, because she believes that the facts, the statistics, the power of her influence in Congress, will be felt in accord with the resolutions that have been adopted, and which I think so wisely framed to include these great tributaries.

And now, I say, Pennsylvania, at the headwaters of the Ohio, having there the tonnage which I have named, having there one hundred millions of bushels of coal coming through one lock in one year, to set aglow all your furnaces and forges, mills and manufactories—I say we come here to-day to emphasize our demand with yours for the rapid, scientific, and complete improvement of the Mississippi. [Cheers.] I congratulate the Convention upon the grand success which I think has attended its session. I sincerely congratulate you, gentlemen, that, in the language of our eloquent friend yesterday (Mr. Taylor), it has not formed a delta, but has spoken through one throat, and I shall hail the day as an auspicious one for this country when the great steamers of the Gulf shall ply between St. Louis and New Orleans, as an active, busy shuttle and web, knitting together in one common interest, one common destiny, one common prosperity, steaming along the great wharves from the headwaters to the Gulf, and through all its great tributaries, east and west, knitting them together in a bond that shall never sunder. [Cheers.]

Mr. Graves, of Iowa. "I offer the following resolution:

"*Resolved*, That our grateful acknowledgment is hereby made to the Merchants' Exchange of St. Louis, and to the several committees, for the generous hospitality extended, and the uniform kindness which has greeted us on every hand."

The resolution was adopted unanimously.

Mr. Michael McEnnis, of Missouri. "As chairman of the Executive Committee, I desire to say, that in our official call and other things, there are several words in there which rather reflect on the tardiness of members of Congress, and throw out some hints that we are very much displeased with them. But their action in reference to the appropriations that were final, and in establishing the Commission, places us under heavy obligations, and to give expression to this, I desire to offer the following resolution:

"*Resolved*, That this Convention fully appreciates the action of the friends of river improvement in Congress, who have advocated and sustained by their votes the granting of such needed appropriations as have been necessary to carry on the work already commenced for the improvement of our Western water-ways, and trust that their endeavors in promoting the interests of commerce will finally be crowned with success."

The resolution was adopted unanimously.

Mr. Chase, of Nebraska, offered the following resolution, which was adopted.

Resolved, That the thanks of this Convention be tendered to the Western Union Telegraph Company for courtesies extended to the members of this Convention, through Mrs. Hall, general manager of the telegraph office at the Southern hotel.

Mr. McEnery, of Louisiana, offered the following resolution, which was adopted unanimously by a rising vote:

Resolved, That the thanks of this Convention are hereby tendered to the Hon. M. H. Dunnell, President of this Convention, for the able and impartial manner in which he has discharged the difficult duties of his position; and also to the Secretaries, George L. Wright, Frank Gaiennie, N. M. Bell, and other officers of the Convention, for the very able and efficient discharge of their various duties.

Mr. Bain, of Missouri. "As chairman of the Committee on Reception, I desire to inform the gentlemen that as soon as the Convention adjourns, we shall have the Arsenal band, and will march down to the steamboat and barges that are to take us down the river. There will be a lunch, and probably something to drink on the boat [laughter], and every gentleman who has not had an opportunity to speak will have all the opportunity he wants there."

A delegate moved that the Convention listen to some remarks from Congressman Willis, of Kentucky.

The motion was carried.

Mr. Willis said:

MR. PRESIDENT AND GENTLEMEN: Although not as old a politician as my friend (the delegate just referred to), I am old enough, and am experienced enough in discussing questions before bodies like this, to know that there are two things against which no man can speak, and those two are a brass band and a prospective lunch. It is true, as my friend from Illinois, Mr. Springer, who is a gross sinner in regard to river and harbor appropriations [laughter], and whom you ought to call to the bar and ask for works meet unto repentance, and not me. I say— [A delegate. "What bar?"] A gentleman enquires what bar. When he is presented at the bar of that boat, he will speak for himself. [Laughter.] But there is another bar, before which he and I, and every member of Congress, has to appear, and that bar is represented by the intelligence of the enthusiastic gentlemen whom I see before me—it is the great bar of public opinion. And, fellow-citizens, allow me to say that there is cause for congratulation on the part of friends of Mississippi river improvement, not only in the presence here of a thousand delegates, called together from all parts of the country, and who have issued what I will call a second Declaration of Independence—independence of railroad monopolies [cheers]; independence of those who would change the course of what God intended should go down these great streams. I say, independent of that, you have, in the condition of the public treasury, great cause for congratulation.

These great cities of the Mississippi Valley have poured their wealth into the treasury of the United States, and now, for the first time in twenty-five years, we have more money than we know what to do with. It has been suggested by some that we have a high protective tariff; but we in this Convention, have a better suggestion than that, and that is that the money gathered from the taxes on whisky and tobacco be appropriated to the improvement of this majestic, this grand system of water-ways, and then we can hope for a return to the country of some of the money that has been expended on internal improvements. And, without detaining you, because I can almost smell afar off the battle I know there will be on the boat, there is another consideration that has not been alluded to from year to year, and we have not regretted it: we have witnessed the expenditure of millions of dollars for lighthouses, for harbors, and, if my friend from New York (Mr. Osborne) were not present, I would make a casual remark that, near the city of New York, there have been expended millions of money in removing obstructions at what is called "Hell Gate," and, doubtless, it was necessary to have that gate open there. [Laughter.] The amount of money expended at Hell Gate alone is greater than the whole Mississippi river has received in a decade. I say that, while we do not regret it, we can now look forward to an unexpected and irresistible ally to Mississippi river improvement, and that, fellow-citizens, is the census of 1880. You know—because the figures, which do not lie, are before us—that only a short time hence she will see the sceptre of power, that has so long been held in the hands of the East, will drop from its nerveless hand and enfeebled grasp, to be seized by the lusty, vigorous young child of the West; and that when Congress makes the new apportionments, based on the last census, you will have upon the floor of Congress an increased number of representatives, and a sufficient number of votes to demand and secure the proper and just improvement of your great river. [Cheers.] But, fellow-citizens, I have now detained you longer than I thought I would; as I said before, there are other gentlemen here whom I would like to see committed on this question. I was glad to hear such a good report from Mr. Cannon: I was glad to hear him say, as a member of Congress, that he would be found active in the support of these measures. What you want, what we need, is not resolutions, but votes, votes, and those votes come through the power of public opinion, molded, and shaped, and wisely guided by representative conventions such as this. I need not say that our own city and State delegations will ever be found ready to further, second, and promote these appropriations; and in the name of the city of Louisville, which I have the honor to represent, a city connected by twelve thousand miles of navigable rivers, I congratulate you upon the favorable surroundings that now present themselves, and I wish you and the friends of the Mississippi improvement a God-speed in the accomplishment of your fullest and wisest purposes in this direction. [Loud cheers.]

Mr. Underwood, of Kentucky. "I offer the following resolution:

"*Resolved*, That this Convention is not unmindful of the great loss the country has sustained in the untimely death of James A. Garfield, whose name is inseparably connected with the proposed improvement of the Mississippi river system, and we extend our profound sympathies to the bereaved family.

"Mr. President, I have no comments to make; I know the expression of feeling and sentiment from this body is more eloquent and powerful than any words I could utter; I would like, however, sir, if it be not inappropriate now, to call attention of the Convention to one other fact or consideration: We have heard from all quarters of this valley; there is, however, one important body of men who have not been heard from, and that is practical steamboatmen. There is a man in this audience, who is a representative of that body of men, from the city of New Orleans—Capt. Leather. I think this audience would like to hear from him at an appropriate time."

The President. "As many as favor the adoption of the resolution read by the gentleman from Kentucky, will so vote by standing."

The whole Convention rose and the resolution was unanimously adopted.

Mr. Cole, of Missouri. "I want the Convention to listen to Mr. Springer for a few minutes."

The President. "The chair will be glad, with the gentlemen of the Convention, to listen to the gentleman from Illinois, Hon. Wm. M. Springer."

Mr. Springer said:

" If there is anything more pleasing than another to the average American citizen, it is a brass band and a procession of American citizens stepping to music. Such a thing being in contemplation the idea of stopping to listen to a speech is out of the question. We are all very much interested in the improvement of our river system, and we propose to take our places on the boats and barges that go down to a place in the river which has received some of the benefits from the appropriations made by Congress, and we are now about to depart for that purpose. As you have finished the work you had in hand it may be proper for me to say, by way of recapitulation, that you have, as I understand it, agreed to two things, and agreed to them unanimously: The first is, that in future appropriations for the Mississippi river you will pursue the plan which has been adopted by the Commission of the United States, in pursuance of law. That plan has been explained to this Convention. It is understood now by all the people in the valley, that all future efforts in the direction of improving the navigation of the Mississippi river and its tributaries, are to be upon that plan. I congratulate the people of the Mississippi Valley that we have arrived at that stage of the question which gives the whole voice of the valley to one idea, and which directs all of our efforts to one system of improving this great river. So much, then, is understood. The next proposition which I believe was agreed upon by this Convention, is that this great question is of sufficient importance to make it a question by itself, to stand on its own merits. The difficulty with the improvement of the Mississippi river and its tributaries heretofore has been that every little stream in the country has recognized this question as one upon which to ride upon, therefore the Mississippi river has not been placed, owing to this condition of things, before Congress upon its own merits. But henceforth the stand to be taken upon it is that this is a national question, demanding recognition upon its own merits, and that this great river shall have appropriations to make it what it is by Nature—the highway from all this valley to the Gulf of Mexico. I congratulate you that we have reached this advanced stage in this great work, and it is well for representatives to have met here to consider this question at this early time. You have had statistics of the resources of this wonderful valley. If you will travel over the great territory between this point and the base of the Rocky Mountains, and see what there is lying still untouched and undeveloped by the hand of industry, you will see that our present resources are as nothing compared with what twenty-five years will bring to the Mississippi Valley of the products beyond the valley. It is time we should begin to put up our warehouses in order, and get our great river ready for the teeming products of the valley of the Mississippi. I congratulate you upon having done your work well; your voice will be heard not only in the Mississippi Valley, but will be heard across the Alleghanies; and Pennsylvania and New York will join hands with you, and recognize that the great problem of the future is the improvement of the Mississippi river and its tributaries." [Cheers.]

Mr. D. P. Rowland, of Missouri, offered the following resolution:

Resolved, That the thanks of this Convention be tendered to the proprietors of the Grand Opera-house for the use of their beautiful building for the deliberations of this Convention.

The resolution was adopted with acclamation.

The President. "The chair wishes to make a statement. Yesterday the Convention adopted a resolution, making it the duty of the President of this Convention to appoint a committee of twenty-one. The duty is a difficult one to perform, and the Chair will be pleased to have information communicated from the different delegations, so this committee may be made up happily and fortunately for the Convention."

Mr. Slayback, of Missouri, then moved that the Convention adjourn *sine die*.

The motion was put and carried, and the Convention adjourned *sine die*.

After the Convention adjourned the delegates and guests, headed by the Arsenal band, took up the line of march for the foot of Elm street, where the steamer " Future City " and five barges awaited them.

The following description of the excursion given to the Convention is taken from the *Globe-Democrat* of October 29th :

The most potent argument that could be adduced in favor of improving the Mississippi was presented yesterday afternoon, in the practical illustration of the river transportation, as exhibited in the make-up of the barge excursion down the river. The sight was a novelty of unquestionable attraction to numbers of delegates hailing from interior constituencies who had never had the satisfaction of inspecting or viewing a fleet of barges, which is an institution peculiar to the Mississippi river. Those from the North were surprised at the economical application of power, obtained by placing the motor in rear of the tow, instead of moving it from the van by a connecting cable. The capacious barges, each of them capable of receiving and carrying 60,000 bushels of grain, excited wonderment and amazement among gentlemen of an inquiring turn of mind, who enhanced their store of knowledge by investigating the means afforded by the Transportation Company for conveying the products of the West to the seaboard.

The engine-room of the steamer presented the appearance of a reception-room, as the delegates filed in on the starboard quarter and retreated on the port-side after minutely inspecting the ponderous machinery as it revolved in obedience to the signals from the wheel-house. The engineers and officers of the craft were most attentive in supplying intelligence relative to dimensions, power, capacity, pressure, etc., of the engines and boilers, and the facts thus tersely placed before the visitors proved a revelation in scientific engineering to many gentlemen who have hitherto plumed themselves on the acquaintance with all topics connected with navigation.

Entering on the main deck the arrivals were confronted by long rows of richly-laden tables, decorated with fine glassware and various specimens of the culinary art that it is unnecessary to mention. Stage planks were laid in position to connect the four boats and the tow-boat, and, to all intents and purposes, the accommodations were on a parallel with the largest steamers afloat. Greater liberty was afforded for circulation, and with the visitors a promenade around the fleet became a favorite feature of the trip. The upper decks were gained by improvised stairways opening out through the elevator hatches, and those who preferred the invigorating breeze to the confined atmosphere between the decks, had no occasion to complain.

The " Future City " was relegated to the ladies and their escorts, who found in her handsome saloon facilities for diversion that are not generally apparent on any other class of vessels than the palatial packets that ply between St. Louis and New Orleans.

On the bow of the "Future City" a canvas screen was erected, bearing the following scroll:

"Steamer 'Future City,' built in 1873, W. A. Goll, master, has completed ninety-five round trips between St. Louis and New Orleans. Average number of days to each trip, twenty-three. Has towed down stream 474 barges. Has transported down stream in cargoes 446,962 tons. Has towed up-stream 491 barges. Has transported in up-stream cargoes 41,677 tons. Has traveled 239,400 miles. If you tell this to Congress, be sure to add that with an improved channel this record of work could have been increased forty per cent. without any increase of expense. This means benefit to the producer."

Every one who read the statement was struck with astonishment at the magnitude of the figures, and Congressional delegates, whose conservative conduct in the deliberations of the Convention was the subject of remark, exclaimed, "Why, this is the greatest speech that has been brought before the Convention." Between the statistical information, presented in such a concise form, and the actual demonstration of the barge and tow-boat system, the last remnant of prejudice disappeared, and they were won over by "moral suasion" to be staunch adherents of the doctrines which they had thought to oppose.

At 1:30 P. M. the last bell sounded, and, under the direction of Capt. Goll, lines were cast loose and the throbbings of the giant engines were perceptible in the advancement of the fleet. The prows of the boats were pointed to the bridge, but once in midstream a turn of the wheel changed their direction down stream. A parting salute was given from the whistles, and the signal was caught up along the line until the air resounded with the piercing shrieks of a score of whistles of every abominable sound. A salvo of artillery from above the bridge on the Missouri side further emphasized the departure, and with flying colors and under brilliant auspices the trip was undertaken.

The process of turning the fleet down stream was obviously a cumbersome operation, but once under headway the steamer was run up to full speed, and the boats sped through their element with a velocity that caused the foam to fly from the forward barges. The water front of the city sped quickly by, and as Carondelet was saluted, dinner was announced, and a general stampede occurred to the lower decks, where the edibles and refreshments were spread in inviting array, tempting the appetite to do justice to the viands.

After the substantial meats had disappeared and other auxiliaries brought into view, George Bain debouched from concealment, and, in his role of master of ceremonies, called the assembly to a semblance of order to hear a toast from John Hogan, who proposed the health of Mr. McEnnis, President of the Executive Committee.

The toast was received with cheers, and Mr. McEnnis was

compelled to respond. He thanked the gentlemen for their courtesy and their kindly co-operation at the Convention, and after making a hasty review of the organization of the Convention, he expressed a hope that none would have reason to forget the hospitality of St. Louis.

Hon. M. H. Dunnell, of Minnesota, the Chairman of the Convention, was next induced to mount the rostrum.

He apologized for not having an elaborate address to deliver, but being called upon for some remarks, he would confine his attention to several features that had been overlooked at the opera-house. This was his first visit to St. Louis, for although residing within a comparatively short distance, and having many friends here, it had never been his privilege to stop in the city for any length of time sufficient to admire its beauties and advantages as a commercial center. He had lived in the Mississippi Valley for twenty years, and had to regret that he had never availed himself of opportunities to sojourn among the citizens of St. Louis, but would return home firmly impressed with the kindly reception. He promised that on returning to Congress he should do all in his power to recognize the importance of the Mississippi river and its connection with the growing commerce of St. Louis. He paid a flattering testimonial to the Convention, and designated the gathering as one that would do honor and reflect credit to any section of the country. The members were characterized as men of culture, education and practical knowledge, that combined could only result in distinguishing the cities of the Mississippi Valley as the foremost in the Union. The constant agitation of river improvements would be a great educator in cultivating the opinions of members from other sections, and he stated that before many years every Congressman would vote for all the improvements they required. He gave his experience as a member of the Committee on Commerce, as having heard of barges a hundred and a thousand times, and had taken action concerning them, yet all the time he never knew what a barge meant until he put his foot on the boat that day. Hereafter he was prepared to vote any sum of money for barges, or any river improvements of whatever nature or magnitude suggested by the Convention.

Many valued citizens—citizens of the State of Missouri—had almost taken possession of some of the beautiful lakes that lay without the confines of the cities of Minneapolis and St. Paul. During the summer months hundreds and thousands of the citizens of St. Louis visited the lakes of Minnesota, and he assured his hearers, that at all times and upon all occasions, they would be welcomed to the hospitalities of his State, and welcome to the privileges of its beautiful atmosphere and to the homes of its people.

SECTION 4.

The following are some of the letters received from members of the Senate and House of Representatives, and which were not read before the Convention:

DES MOINES, Iowa, October 17, 1881.
HENRY LOUREY, ESQ., *Chairman, St. Louis.*

SIR: In acknowledging your invitation to be present at the Mississippi River Improvement Convention at St. Louis, on the 25th instant, I deeply regret that my engagements require me to be in Washington at that date. The movement commends itself to my judgment. The trunk line of waterway takes precedence of its branches, in order of time and improvement, because the utility of the latter is largely dependent on the former. This is to be done, and the other not left undone. I hope that your Convention will present for the consideration of Congress more facts than speeches, more specific engineering plans and careful estimates than *hallelujahs.* The Western representatives will be greatly assisted in the solid work to be done by a plain presentation of facts and conscientious figures.

I am, gentlemen, the friend of your movement, and
    Your obedient servant,
                        JOHN A. KASSON,
            M. C., Seventh District, Iowa.

HOT SPRINGS, Ark., October 20, 1881..
GEO. L. WRIGHT, ESQ., *Corresponding Secretary, St. Louis.*

DEAR SIR: Your kind invitation of the 13th ultimo found me ill, at my home in Charlotte, Mich., and a few days later I passed through your city *en route* for this place, where I have since remained, your invitation still unanswered, because I was still hoping that my physician would consent to my leaving here early enough to meet with you on the 26th inst. But I am obliged at last to decline, owing to continued ill health. I regret this the more for the reason that I am very deeply interested in this question of transportation, in all its phases, and could not willingly absent myself from a Convention where the whole subject is to be so thoroughly, ably and opportunely discussed.

Very respectfully,
E. S. LACEY.

UNITED STATES SENATE CHAMBER,
WASHINGTON, Oct. 16th, 1881.

GEO. L. WRIGHT, ESQ., *Corresponding Secretary, Southern Hotel, St. Louis.*

DEAR SIR: Your postal card received. I did not respond to your invitation because I was waiting to see if I could attend. Now I find I will not be able to get away from here in time to do so, and I regret it very much.

Truly yours,
A. H. GARLAND.
United States Senator, Arkansas.

UNITED STATES SENATE,
WASHINGTON, D. C., Oct. 15, 1881.

GEORGE L. WRIGHT, ESQ., *Corresponding Secretary Mississippi River Improvement Convention, St. Louis, Mo.*

DEAR SIR: Replying to your postal card of the 13th instant, and also former invitation of September last, I regret to say that official business will prevent my attending the Improvement Convention on the 26th inst.

Trusting the Convention will be successful, and result in much good to the whole country, I am,

Yours, very truly,
T. W. FERRY.

DETROIT, September 21, 1881.

HON. GEO. L. WRIGHT, *Corresponding Secretary Mississippi River Improvement Convention, St. Louis.*

DEAR SIR: I thank you for the invitation of your committee to be present at the Convention on the 26th prox. It would give me great pleasure to be present if practicable, but I fear not.

I beg, however, to assure you, and the Convention, that I shall not be found inactive in the promotion of any well-ordered scheme for the improvement of our great inland water-ways, believing that they should be developed to the full capacity needed, and that they may be depended upon in competition with our great railway system, and by their reciprocal action upon each other to keep the rate of transportation within easy reach of the manufacturing and agricultural interests.

I am your very obedient servant,

HENRY W. LORD.
M. C., First District, Michigan.

WASHINGTON, D. C., Oct. 25, 1881.
To the President of the River Improvement Convention.

I resort to telegraph, having misplaced letter for your secretary. Am with you heart and soul. Efforts to open and improve Western rivers for free and consequently cheap transportation, are among the grandest and most beneficent enterprises inviting the present generation to ask specially for an appropriation for improving the Missouri which drains the future Egypt of the United States, already densely peopled, and laden with plenty. Our surplus must float to the sea upon our steamers, if railroads wont carry it at living prices.

ALVIN SAUNDERS.
U. S. Senator, Nebraska.

STATE OF IOWA,
EXECUTIVE DEPARTMENT,
DES MOINES, Sept. 19, 1881.

HENRY LOUREY, ESQ., *Chairman Committee on Invitation, Mississippi River Improvement Convention, St. Louis, Mo.*

DEAR SIR: I have the honor to acknowledge the receipt of your favor of the 13th inst., inviting me to be present at the Mississippi River Improvement Convention, to be holden at St. Louis on October 26th prox.

My views as to the much-needed improvement of the Mississippi river and its tributaries are well known. Suffice it to say that I am in full sympathy with the objects of your Convention.

That the improvement of this great natural highway and

its tributaries is an immediate necessity, is proven by the established fact that, at this date, with the very limited improvement which has been made in this system of waters, the produce of the States lying on the river is being daily shipped to the great markets of the world on these streams at a less cost for transportation than prevails on the all-rail routes. If this can be done with the meager improvement already accomplished, what may we not expect when the river is improved on a broad and permanent system?

In my opinion the time has come when the people of the West should make common cause in favor of this and kindred improvements, and unitedly demand of Congress appropriations to improve the Mississippi at once. The improvement of the river once made, with artificial water-ways to connect it with the lakes constructed, will insure to the grain and provision raisers of this great valley the least possible rate on the transportation of their crops. When it is considered that the exports of our agricultural products amount to more than fifty per cent. in value of all our exports, as was the case during the year ended June 30, 1881, it is time for the people of the Mississippi Valley, who furnish nearly all of this great amount of produce, to institute concerted action in favor of cheap transportation.

I much regret that official engagements will prevent my accepting your invitation. In accordance with your request, I have appointed ten delegates, a list of whom I have the honor to enclose you herewith.

Earnestly hoping that the action of your Convention will have effect in giving tone to public sentiment in such a manner as will best promote the object to be attained, I am,

Yours truly,

JNO. H. GEAR,
Governor of Iowa.

LOUISVILLE, KY., Oct. 17, 1881.

DEAR SIR: I regret very much that, as present advised, I will be unable to attend your Convention. The objects you have in view have my hearty approval, and, at the proper time, will receive my cordial support.

Yours truly,

ALBERT S. WILLIS.

On Board Steamer "J. M. White,"
October 21st, 1881.

Mr. George L. Wright, *Secretary Mississippi River Improvement Convention, St. Louis, Mo.:*

My Dear Sir: I have the pleasure to acknowledge receipt of invitation to attend the Convention to assemble in your city on the 26th of this month. I hoped certainly to be present with you, but my engagements in Mississippi may prevent, and I therefore write to express my thanks to your committee for their courtesy.

My interest in the subject-matter which will engage the Convention is unabated, and I never gaze on the great river without feeling regret that the vast commercial interests which line its banks and tributaries have so long met the almost studied neglect of the Federal Government. Becoming, as it has, the great water channel, through which the immense food crops of twenty-four States and six Territories flow into the Gulf of Mexico, it rises to a dignity and importance which will not suffer it longer to be neglected. All that is required is a perfect union of all the interests that belong to the river and its tributaries; and I hope this Convention may form this union, and present their claims in such simple and direct manner that the Federal Congress can no longer ignore them.

Hoping still to be with you, but fearing I may not, I write these few lines as I pass to Natchez, where I speak to-night. With best wishes for your health and prosperity,

Very truly, your friend and fellow-citizen,

Chas. E. Hooker.

U. S. Senate, Washington, October 17, 1881.

Geo. L. Wright, Esq., *Corresponding Secretary, St. Louis.*

Dear Sir: I have been away from home much of the fall, and did not receive the invitation to be present at the River Convention until late. I should be very glad to be present, for I take an interest in the movement, but my engagements are such that I cannot come. I hope the Convention will be all that its friends desire and expect.

Yours very truly,

Eugene Hale,
U. S. Senator from Maine.

WHEELER, ALABAMA, October 18, 1881.
HON. GEO. L. WRIGHT:

MY DEAR SIR: It affords me pleasure to acknowledge the receipt of your valued favor, extending to me an invitation to be present at the Mississippi River Improvement Convention. As I feel a great interest in a matter which is so intimately connected with the prosperity of more than half of the United States, I regret exceedingly that I will be unable to accept your kind invitation; but, I assure you, I shall take great interest in the deliberation of a body of such distinguised and practical gentlemen as will compose the Convention.

Again thanking you for your kind attention, believe me, with great respect, Your friend,
JOS. WHEELER,
M. C., Eighth District, Alabama.

HANNIBAL, Mo., October 8th, 1881.
HENRY LOUREY, ESQ., *Chairman.*

SIR: I have the honor to acknowledge receipt of your favor of 13th ult.; inviting me to be present and participate in the deliberations of the Mississippi River Improvement Convention, to be held in St. Louis, Oct. 26th, 1881.

Cordially endorsing the objects and purposes of the Convention, as set forth in the "Official Call," I accept your invitation with much pleasure.

Very respectfully, your obedient servant,
W. H. HATCH.

CHICAGO, October 15, 1881.
GEO. L. WRIGHT, ESQ., *Corresponding Secretary Mississippi River Improvement Convention, St. Louis, Mo.:*

DEAR SIR: I return thanks for the invitation to attend the Mississippi River Improvement Convention. It now looks very doubtful of my ability to be present, though should be pleased to do so. The vast importance of the business of the Convention will, I trust, draw out the wisest councils, and result in great good to your city and the whole West. With great respect, I am

Your obedient servant,
WM. ALDRICH.

Mt. Carroll, Ill., Sept. 21, 1881.

Henry Lourey, Esq., *Chairman Committee of Invitation, St. Louis, Mo.*

Gentlemen; Your favor of 13th inst., extending an invitation to be present at a Convention to be held in your city on the 26th prox., and to participate in its deliberations, is duly received. I regret that I have already engaged to be away from home during the whole of the month of October, and shall, therefore, be unable to attend your Convention. I desire to state, however, at this time, that I most heartily favor a judicious expenditure, by the National Government, of a sufficient sum to properly improve the great natural and national highway. I am heartily in favor of any carefully guarded expenditure of the public money, that has for its object the cheapening of transportation to the producers of the great Northwest. Many abuses must of necessity creep into any vast system of internal improvement on the part of the General Government, hence every precaution should be taken, and every point thoroughly discussed that bears upon the intelligent and economical prosecution of the contemplated work. You have my most cordial sympathy and support in any well-guarded plan for the improvement of our great river. With great respect, I am,

Very truly, etc.,

R. M. A. Hawk.
M. C. Fifth District.

Knoxville, Ill., October 15, 1881.

Geo. L. Wright, *Corresponding Secretary Mississippi River Improvement Convention, St. Louis, Mo.:*

Dear Sir: Yours of the 13th duly received and contents noted, and in reply would say, while I would be much pleased to be present on the 26th, my arrangements are such as to make it impracticable.

I hope the Convention will be full and enthusiastic. Cheap transportation is the one thing most desirable, at this time, to the producer and manufacturer, and every possible avenue leading in that direction should be sought out and opened. Many thanks to your committee for their kindly offers.

I am, truly yours,

J. H. Lewis.

VALPARAISO, IND., Sept. 22, 1881.
GEO. L. WRIGHT, *Corresponding Secretary.*

DEAR SIR: In answer to your invitation to be present at the Mississippi River Improvement Convention, to be held at St. Louis, Oct. 26, 1881, I will say, that if not prevented by circumstances, not now existing, I will be present on that occasion. I am, sir,

Yours truly,

MARK L. DEMOTTE.

WASHINGTON, D. C., October 17, 1881.
GEO. L. WRIGHT, ESQ., *Secretary Mississippi River Improvement Convention, St. Louis, Mo.:*

SIR: In reply to your postal, I have to inform you that I did not receive the invitation you speak of, and to express my regret at being unable to be present, owing to a press of business that I must attend to. Thanking you for your courtesy, I am, very respectfully,

Your obedient servant,

GEO. W. STEELE.

SHAWNEETOWN, ILL., Oct. 15, 1881.
MR. GEO. L. WRIGHT, *Corresponding Secretary Mississippi River Improvement Convention, St. Lovis, Mo.*

DEAR SIR: I am in sympathy with any movement which has for its aim cheapening the means of transportation of the products of the Mississippi Valley to the ocean and the markets of the world.

In proportion as the cost of transportation is lessened, the value of grain and other products in enhanced to our producers, and the material wealth of this region is increased.

I am convinced that the surest way to accomplish this great object is by the improvement of our navigable water lines of transportation, thereby providing a competition with the railways for freights, which will serve as an effectual protection from extortion by the legerdemain of railway pools and combinations.

The Mississippi is a grand, free highway, marked out by the finger of God for the commerce of the West and South;

one on which no tribute can be levied, no monopoly can be established—as free as the air for all.

Without now consuming time to assign reasons, I may say that I believe Congress possesses the power, and it is its duty to provide reasonable means for the necessary improvement of the Mississippi and its navigable tributaries.

I hope, however, that the friends of this improvement will place it upon its merits, and not permit the jobbers and schemers to couple with Federal appropriations for this work the expenditure of the people's money on streams and objects not of a national character, and which are not and cannot be made of value to the commerce of the country, and thereby prevent many conscientious members of Congress from voting in favor of the appropriation of reasonable and necessary sums for the systematic improvement of the Mississippi river and its tributaries.

I fear I shall not be able to attend the Convention on the 26th inst.

Very respectfully,
R. W. TOWNSHEND,
M. C. Nineteenth District.

BELVIDERE, N. J., Oct. 19th, 1881.

GEO. L. WRIGHT, *Corresponding Secretary, St. Louis, Mo.*

DEAR SIR: I regret to say that pressing business engagements will prevent my attendance at the River Convention on October 26th, instant.

I shall watch its proceedings with interest, as I heartily sympathize with its objects, as I understand them.

With thanks for the invitation to be present, I am,

Very truly yours,
HENRY S. HARRIS.

UNITED STATES SENATE CHAMBER,
WASHINGTON, October 16, 1881.

GEO. L. WRIGHT, ESQ.

DEAR SIR: I regret that my public engagements forbid me to accept your kind invitation to the interesting and important Convention to be held at St. Louis on the 26th.

Very respectfully,
H. B. ANTHONY,
United States Senator.

UNITED STATES SENATE CHAMBER,
WASHINGTON, October 24, 1881.
MESSRS. HENRY LOUREY, *Chairman*, NATHAN COLE, CHARLES
PARSONS, E. W. GOULD AND FRANK GAIENNIE, *Committee
of Invitation.*

GENTLEMEN: Please accept my thanks for the honor of your very kind invitation to be present and participate in the deliberations of the Mississippi River Improvement Convention, to be held in the City of St. Louis on the 26th day of October, 1881. I regret exceedingly that the present session of the Senate, which cannot complete its labors before the 25th or 26th inst., will keep me here and prevent my acceptance of your invitation and participation in your proceedings. I trust the Convention will be harmonious and its proceedings result in greatly increasing the general interest in and urgent demand for the rapid improvement of our great river and its navigable tributaries. The efforts to secure the improvement of the Mississippi river have, in the past, received, and shall in the future receive my unqualified and hearty approval. I have labored most earnestly and faithfully to secure, by Congressional legislation, the adoption of a matured plan and system for the correction, permanent location and deepening of the channel of the river and the improvement of its navigability.

By act of Congress, approved June 28, 1879, the "Mississippi River Commission" was provided; was afterward appointed and has made its report to Congress and submitted a plan and system of works, which has received the approval of Congress in appropriations of money to construct the proposed works according to the plan.

I believe the plan and system proposed is the only true one. The appropriations already made are entirely insufficient. It is absolutely necessary that a sufficient sum of money shall be appropriated annually by Congress to prosecute these works according to the plan during the entire period of each year when work can be done, and also at each of the wide places in the river, where the water is necessarily shallow.

I trust the Convention may be able to excite such influences as will convince Congress of the importance and necessity of appropriating sufficient sums of money to secure at the very earliest practicable time the completion of the proposed works, according to the system and plan already adopted.

Be assured that, as in the past, so in the future, I shall do all in my power to secure the improvement of the navigability of the Mississippi river and of all its navigable tributaries, which, when done, will settle the question of cheap transportation and forever thereafter regulate all freight charges and hold them down to the lowest rates.

I have the honor to be your obedient servant,

F. M. COCKRELL.

WARREN, PA., October 21, 1881.

HON. GEO. L. WRIGHT, *Corresponding Secretary of the Mississippi River Improvement Convention, St. Louis, Mo.*

DEAR SIR: The invitation to be present at your Convention on the 26th inst., came duly to hand. I regret that my engagements are such as will prevent my attendance and deprive me of the pleasure of participating in your deliberations on that occasion.

Yours, truly,

L. F. WATSON,
Member of Congress.

HON. HENRY LOUREY, *Chairman Executive Committee of the Mississippi River Improvement Convention, St. Louis, Mo.*

DEAR SIR: I have the honor to acknowledge the receipt of your letter of invitation to attend the Mississippi River Improvement Convention, to meet at St. Louis on the 26th day of October (prox.), and to participate in its deliberations.

It is to me a matter of sincere regret that engagements made previous to the receipt of your letter will deny me the opportunity to attend the Convention, and I beg to assure you that the regret I feel is greatly enhanced by the fact that I am in full and hearty sympathy with what I understand to be the object and purpose of the Convention, and yet debarred the privilege of sharing in its deliberations.

I do not fail to recognize the importance of cheap transportation in its bearing on all the industrial pursuits and interests of the country, nor am I indifferent to the fact that cheap transportation can only be permanently assured by competition among carriers, and that the most effectual of all competition is that which is or may be established between our interior water-ways and railways.

Hoping that the deliberations of the Convention may aid in the further development and material advancement of the "Great Mississippi Valley," upon which the future prosperity of the whole country so much depends, and thanking you and your committee for the invitation to attend its sittings, I am, very respectfully, your obedient servant,

J. J. FINLEY,
M. C. Second District, Florida.

MANSFIELD, Ohio, September 27, 1881.

HON. HENRY LOUREY, *Chairman, St. Louis, Mo.*

MY DEAR SIR: Your letter of the 13th, inviting me to attend the proposed Convention to be held at St. Louis, on the 26th of October, to advance the commercial, agricultural and financial interests of the Mississippi Valley, has been received. Nothing would give me greater pleasure than to join in such a conference, and contribute in any way in my power to the objects proposed by your Committee. I have given the subject great attention, not only from the interest felt by my constituents, but from the personal examination I have been called upon to make as a member of the Transportation Committee of the Senate. I have no doubt but that a concerted movement by the leading commercial citizens of the Mississippi Valley would give a proper direction to the interests you represent. I will not, however, be able to attend the Convention, as the Senate has a called session that will probably continue during the session of your Convention.

Very truly yours,

JOHN SHERMAN,
U. S. Senator from Ohio.

MONTICELLO, IOWA, October 17, 1881.

GEO. L. WRIGHT, ESQ., *St. Louis, Mo.:*

DEAR SIR: I am in receipt of your invitation to be present at the Mississippi River Improvement Convention, Oct. 26th. Please accept thanks for the same. My engagements are such it will be impossible for me to attend; but I assure you I am heartily in favor of the objects for which the Convention is called. Please send me a copy of the proceedings, if they are published in pamphlet form.

Very truly yours,

L. S. FARWELL.

UNITED STATES SENATE CHAMBER, }
WASHINGTON, October 15, 1881. }

GEO. L. WRIGHT, ESQ., *Corresponding Secretary, St. Louis, Missouri.*

DEAR SIR: I have received your invitation to attend the Mississippi River Improvement Convention, to be held at St. Louis, October 26th. I am very much interested in the subjects which will be before the Convention for consideration, but I regret to inform you that it will be impossible for me to attend as requested.

Very truly, yours,
BENJ. HARRISON.

UNITED STATES SENATE CHAMBER, }
WASHINGTON, October 17, 1881. }

Chairman of Committee of Arrangements, Mississippi River Convention.

SIR: I regret that my public duties will probably render it impossible for me to be present at the Convention, which meets on the 26th inst. I appreciate the importance of the object you have in view, and shall give my aid to whatever expenditure may be necessary or useful to the permanent improvement of the Mississippi River and all of its affluents.

Should my engagements permit me to be present I will notify you before the Convention meets.

Yours,
WILKINSON CALL.

WASHINGTON, D. C., October 4, 1881.

HENRY LOUREY, ESQ., *and others, Committee of Invitation.*

GENTLEMEN: Your letter of invitation to attend the Mississippi River Improvement Convention at St. Louis, October 26, 1881, was received. My engagements are such that it will not be possible for me to accept your courteous invitation, but allow me to add, that I sincerely trust that this meeting may result in calling the attention of the people to the paramount importance of developing and improving this noble water-way furnished by nature for carrying to the ocean the marvelous productions of the central plain of North America.

Very truly yours,
W. HUTCHINS.

MARTINSBURG, W. VA., September 20, 1881.
GEO. L. WRIGHT, ESQ., *Corresponding Secretary.*

DEAR SIR: I acknowledge, with thanks, the receipt of an invitation to attend the Mississippi River Improvement Convention, to be held in St. Louis on the 26th of October.

I cannot promise myself, with any certainty, that I can accept this invitation, as I do not know what my engagements will be at that time. If in my power, however, I shall most gladly avail myself of the opportunity to learn so much from representative men of the Mississippi Valley touching the improvement of the great river and its tributaries, and the means of effecting that great result.

With entire sympathy with the objects of the Convention, I have the honor to be, very respectfully, your obedient servant,

JOHN BLAIR HOGE,
M. C. Second District, West Virginia.

OSAGE, Iowa, October 8, 1881.
GEO. L. WRIGHT, ESQ., *Corresponding Secretary, St. Louis.*

DEAR SIR: In reply to your letter of 13th ultimo, I regret to say that business engagements will require my presence in Iowa, and prevent attendance at the Mississippi River Improvement Convention on the 26th instant. I am cordially in sympathy with the views you express and the objects of the Convention, and hope the meeting and interchange of opinions will be productive of good results.

I am, very respectfully, etc.,

N. C. DEERING,
Member Congress, Fourth District, Iowa.

WASHINGTON, D. C., October 22, 1881.
GEO. L. WRIGHT, ESQ., *Corresponding Secretary Mississippi River Improvement Convention.*

DEAR SIR: Your courteous invitation to attend the Convention as honorary guest is highly appreciated, but pressing official duties prevent acceptance. I appreciate the magnitude and importance of the work you are engaged in, and cordially wish you success.
B. K. BRUCE.

WASHINGTON, ARK., September 28, 1881.

MESSRS. HENRY LOUREY, *Chairman*, NATHAN COLE, CHARLES PARSONS, and others, *Committee*.

GENTLEMEN: Upon my arrival at home to-day I find your favor, inviting me to be present and participate in the deliberations of the Mississippi River Improvement Convention.

I regret very much that my engagements are such as to render it impossible for me to be present, but I assure you that in spirit I am heart and soul in favor of the great work.

It is one of so much importance that we cannot afford to make mistakes, and I therefore hope that the best talent of the country may be present, and that you may be able to give the cause such an impetus as will render early and triumphant success certain.

Again expressing my deep regret that I cannot attend, I am, very truly,

JAMES K. JONES.

MORGAN CITY, LA., Oct. 20, 1881.

GEO. L. WRIGHT, *Secretary Mississippi River Improvement Convention.*

SIR: I have received your invitation to attend the Mississippi River Convention, to be held in your city the 26th, and have hoped to be able to attend, but the press of my private business will prevent my doing so.

I am glad to see such a convention held, and it can only have good results.

With its objects I am in entire sympathy, as my course in Congress in the past will show. Regretting my inability to attend in person, I beg to subscribe myself,

Very respectfully, etc.,

C. B. DARRELL.

COLUMBIA, TENN., October 18, 1881.

GEO. L. WRIGHT, *Secretary.*

SIR: Acknowledging receipt of your invitation "to be present at the River Convention to be held in St. Louis, October 26th," for which I thank you, I have to regret that I cannot be present, as I have cordial sympathy with the main purpose of the Convention.

I am respectfully yours, W. C. WHITTHORNE.

WASHINGTON, October 16, 1881.

MR. GEO. L. WRIGHT:

DEAR SIR: The present session of the Senate is not likely to terminate in time to admit of my attending the River Convention on the 26th inst. I could scarcely express with too much intensity the interest I feel in this great subject, and my hope that in "the multitude of counsel" we may find the true solution of the problem of the improvement of this great highway of the people of the United States, and the security of the agricultural interest along the course of the Mississippi river. I believe that the Congress is only waiting for the development of the best plan, to take hold of this work with the vigor that is characteristic of this age of our progress. What should be done above all else is to ascertain what is the best plan. It would be a sad misfortune in every way should we make any serious mistake in starting this work on a plan that would prove impracticable or seriously defective. In the hope that careful research and impartial judgment may control in the important deliberations of the River Convention, I have the honor to remain, your obedient servant,

JOHN T. MORGAN,
United States Senator from Alabama.

MEMPHIS, October 16, 1881.

MR. GEO. L. WRIGHT, *Corresponding Secretary, St. Louis, Missouri.*

DEAR SIR: In reply to your postal of inquiry, etc., dated 13th inst., I have the honor to express my earnest regret that other engagements will prevent my acceptance of your prized invitation to attend the "Mississippi River Improvement Convention," to be assembled in your great city on the 26th inst.

There are, in my judgment, few questions of the present day so important to the interests of this giant young nation, as that of the unobstructed and continuous navigability of the Mississippi river from St. Paul to the Gulf of Mexico; and the judicious and early expenditure by the General Government of even a very large sum of money, under proper safeguards, to effect this grand purpose, would, I am firmly persuaded, prove to be an act of the greatest national wisdom.

I have the honor to remain, very respectfully, your obedient servant, WM. B. MOORE,
Member of Congress.

PHILADELPHIA, October 18, 1881.
GEO. L. WRIGHT, ESQ., *St. Louis.*

MY DEAR SIR: Acknowledging the receipt of your favor, with enclosure of invitation to be present at the Mississippi River Improvement Convention (received during my absence from home), I beg to advise you that it will be impossible for me to attend. I have always favored the improvement of the Mississippi river, and shall continue to co-operate and vote with the gentlemen who so ably represent your interests in Congress. Although absent, count me as present in all that may be calculated to promote the prosperity and welfare of your section of our country.

Very respectfully,
Your obedient servant,
A. C. HARMER, *M. C.*

BRATTLEBORO, VERMONT, Oct. 17, 1881.
GEO. L. WRIGHT, ESQ.

SIR: I have been absent from home during the past month much of the time, and your card of invitation was overlooked. I regret that my business engagements will prevent my acceptance of the invitation. I beg leave to assure you of my interest in all that looks to the improvement of that great water-way, the Mississippi river, and that I should have great pleasure in attending the Convention, did my engagements permit.

Yours, respectfully,
JAMES M. TYLER,
M. C. Second District.

MOBILE, Oct. 15, 1881.

DEAR SIR: Other engagements will prevent me from attending the Mississippi River Improvement Convention on the 26th inst. Hoping the Convention may promote the great object in view, I am,

Very respectfully,
THOS. H. HERNDON,
M. C., Alabama.

WHITE SULPHUR SPRINGS, VA.,
September 22, 1881.

HON. HENRY LOUREY, *Chairman.*

DEAR SIR: I am in receipt of the invitation from the Executive Committee of the Mississippi River Improvement Convention, of which you are chairman, to attend the Convention on October the 26th.

Accept my thanks, and unless prevented by a session of the Senate, or some overruling necessity, I shall certainly be present. As your address states, the time has come for a full interchange of opinion on this great question, and we of the West and South must assert our right to be heard and felt in the righteous claim for improvement of the great river. Sooner or later we will obtain all we ask.

Truly,

G. D. VEST.

COMMONWEALTH OF MASSACHUSETTS,
EXECUTIVE DEPARTMENT,
BOSTON, September 17, 1881.

GEO. L. WRIGHT, ESQ., *Secretary Mississippi River Improvement Convention, St. Louis, Mo.*

DEAR SIR: Will you kindly extend to the Mississippi River Improvement Convention my acknowledgment of the courtesy of an invitation to participate in its deliberations. My engagements will not permit me to be present, but I desire to express my interest in the occasion, and send to it my best wishes.

Very truly yours,

JOHN D. LONG.

NEW BEDFORD, MASS., October 20, 1881.

GEO. L. WRIGHT, ESQ., *Corresponding Secretary, St. Louis.*

MY DEAR SIR: My engagements do not permit my attendance of the Mississippi River Improvement Convention, which is to be held on the 26th inst. I am glad to learn that the number of delegates present will be large, and I hope the question of cheap transportation, which is involved in the improvement of the Mississippi, will have thorough and enlightened discussion, and that the Convention will be able to present such well-considered and practical plans for the improvement of the river as will aid Congress, the majority of whose members are really desirous of promoting the work.

Yours, truly,

WM. W. CRAPO,
Member of Congress.

NEW ORLEANS, October 31, 1881.

TO FRANK GAIENNIE, ESQ. :

Resolved, That the members of this Exchange hereby endorse the action of the River Convention, recently held at St. Louis, and we hereby pledge ourselves to work and talk in behalf of the improvement of the navigation of the Mississippi river, until the nation shall accord it as the just due, not only of the Valley States, but of the commercial interests of the entire country.

Resolved, That the thanks of this Exchange are due to Mr. Frank Gaiennie, of St. Louis, for his efficient services in behalf of the Convention, and for his uniform courtesy and consideration extended to our delegates in said Convention.

WM. M. SMALLWOOD,
Secretary New Orleans Produce Exchange.

PITTSBURG, November 9, 1881.

MERCHANTS' EXCHANGE, *St. Louis, Mo.:*

GENTLEMEN : I have been instructed to forward you the the following extract from minutes of a meeting of the Board of Directors of this Association, held on the 7th inst. On report of committee in attendance at Mississippi River Improvement Convention, held at St. Louis, on 26th October, 1881, they say, and which was unanimously adopted :

"Your committee sincerely think that the thanks of this "Chamber, and of all sections represented in the Mississippi "River Improvement Convention, are due to the Merchants' "Exchange of St Louis for the inauguration of the same, as "well as for the promised results which are certain to follow, "if the recommendations of the Convention are properly "brought before Congress."

Very respectfully yours,

G. FOLLANSBEE,
Superintendent.

The following interesting letter was received from Forstall, Ross & Clayton, of New Orleans, contractors for ocean tonnage, in regard to tonnage from that city in connection with the shipments from the Mississippi Valley.

NEW ORLEANS, Oct. 24, 1881.

GEORGE L. WRIGHT, ESQ., *Corresponding Secretary Mississippi River Improvement Convention, St Louis, Mo.:*

DEAR SIR: In addressing you on the subject of the probable results to be obtained from the improvement of the Mississippi river, which your approaching Convention aims to secure, we shall refer especially to the past and present facilities for ocean transportation to and from New Orleans, the causes that are now operating against a greater increase of these facilities, and the certain effect which a permanently navigable channel in the river would exercise, in procuring for New Orleans a constant supply of ocean tonnage, equal to the utmost requirements of the great Mississippi Valley.

It is almost needless to say that, during the past ten or fifteen years, the employment of steamers in place of sailing-ships has increased at a marvelous rate, until now there are few trades in which steam has not distanced sail, and every year sees fresh encroachments made by steamers on grounds that were recently supposed to be entirely beyond their reach.

The supply of steamers increased so rapidly, and competition among them became so keen, that the rates of freight obtainable were materially reduced, and every measure has been, and is still resorted to, in order to secure the greatest possible economy in working. One of the principal means employed to this end, especially in the Atlantic trades, was the construction of steamers of greatly increased carrying capacity, which could be worked at comparatively little more cost and earn much more money at less rates than smaller boats. Another great point aimed at is to avoid any unnecessary detention, and to have steamers handled with the quickest possible dispatch; to have cargoes always prepared in advance, and to secure the best appliances for loading and discharging goods with maximum speed and at a minimum cost.

Until the opening of the South Pass by Capt. Eads, New Orleans was almost inaccessible to such vessels, and her export trade was carried on, we may say, entirely by sailing-ships. Little was known of the port by the majority of English steamship owners, and especially by those on the east coast of England, where a large proportion of the general trading steamers are built and owned. To such an exent was this the case, that, in 1877, the latest English Amiralty Charts obtainable in the East Coast seaports, showed a depth of only eight to ten feet of water in South Pass, and thirteen to fifteen feet in Southwest Pass.

This, together with the very unenviable reputation that New Orleans possessed as an unhealthy and expensive port, made it very difficult to persuade steamship owners to send their vessels to load there, which was accomplished only by merchants guaranteeing high rates and quick dispatch.

The perfectly favorable condition of the South Pass for heavy drafted vessels soon became known to owners, however, as also the satisfactory results of the voyages made in the season of '77-'78, and as it was expected that the grain exports in '78-'79 would be greater than those of the preceding year, while the demand of cotton shippers for steam room kept increasing, owners who had already sent steamers to New Orleans, and many who had not, made up their minds that they had struck a new bonanza, and each one determined to be on hand when the cotton shipping season of 1878 commenced.

Some New Orleans firms taking the same view, entered into speculative engagements to load steamers at comparatively high rates of freight.

As is too well known, the unhappy epidemic of yellow fever upset all calculations. After the city was clear of the scourge, cotton came in but slowly, and the river was so low that it was for a time utterly impossible to move grain down at all. Owners had, therefore, the mortification of seeing their steamers detained for days, weeks, and, in some cases, over a month, waiting for cargoes which they finally obtained at very low rates.

They not only concluded in consequence that New Orleans was not such a bonanza as they had anticipated, but they went to the opposite extreme, and made up their minds that it was a delusion and a snare, and a place to be avoided by all steamers, unless provided with iron-clad charters, guaranteeing high rates of freight, heavy payments in case of detention in loading, and, in fact, entire immunity from all the risks that they usually take from other seaports.

In the summer of 1879, considerable quantities of grain were sold in Europe, for shipment from New Orleans, in the months of August, September and October. The sellers, in order to obtain ocean tonnage, guaranteed high rates of freights and quick loading. They purchased the grain in St. Louis, made the necessary arrangements to ship it, so as to meet the steamers, and all calculations showed a handsome profit on the transactions. But they had again reckoned without the river, which got so low that grain could not be moved down; while the steamers were on hand at the proper time, the cargoes were wanting, and penalties had to be paid both to the steamship owners, for failure to load, and to the buyers of the grain for failure to deliver.

In 1878 the owners suffered; in 1879 the New Orleans merchants took their turn, and the experiences of both years tended to make New Orleans anything but a favorite resort for steamers. In fact, the regular liners running to Liverpool, and depending principally on cotton for cargo, were almost the only steamers that frequented the port without a solid and certain inducement in the way of a guarantee of freight. While New York, Boston, Philadelphia and other Atlantic ports were kept well supplied with steamers, prepared to take their chances of the freight markets there, New Orleans could obtain tonnage only by guaranteeing rates of freight from 30 to 40 per cent. higher than those current in the Northern ports; and, although the expenses of loading grain at New Orleans were then much less than in the North, even this was not considered by many owners sufficient to cover the risk of sending boats there, only to find that the cargoes intended for them were fast aground six or seven hundred miles up the Mississippi. So strong did this feeling become, that when grain operations were resumed from New Orleans in the spring of 1880, several exporters got severely caught through their inability to procure ocean tonnage, although they had the cargoes in New Orleans ready to put on board steamers, for which they offered almost any price, so that they might implement their shipping contracts.

The summer and fall of 1880 saw the same state of affairs —high prices paid to secure steamers, and continued trouble in arranging for shipments to meet them, on account of delays to tows from a low stage of water in the river.

During the winter of 1880, large quantities of iron and steel were imported by New Orleans and other Gulf ports, on which liberal rates of freight were paid outwards, drawing many steamers towards our port, prepared to accept moderate rates of freight for return cargoes. Unfortunately, the ice blockade between St. Louis and Cairo cut off the supplies of grain for a considerable time, and, in consequence, many of the steamers proceeded to Havana, and loaded sugar for New York, Boston, etc.; others proceeded to these ports in ballast, and the balance accepted charters at low rates from New Orleans, rather than incur the cost of shifting ports. The majority of these last met with vexatious and costly delay in loading; and although, when navigation in the river was reopened, very liberal rates of freight were paid for some little time, and a few owners secured remunerative business, the general experience of last winter and summer certainly intensified the feeling that New Orleans is a most uncertain port for steamers to frequent.

Exporters of grain, also, have found the business so difficult to conduct, and so full of risk, that many have abandoned it entirely, and firms anxious to take it up have decided to abstain from it entirely, until these obstacles shall be removed.

The consequence of this state of affairs is, that New Orleans has regular steam communication only with Liverpool, Havre and Bremen, the trade to these ports being to a very great extent in cotton, while London, Glasgow, Antwerp, Hamburg and other European ports, that continually receive immense quantities of Western produce from New York, etc., are accessible from New Orleans only at rare intervals, except to firms in a position to supply full cargoes of grain, etc., for which they charter entire vessels. If uninterrupted navigation on the river were assured, there would be little difficulty in establishing regular steam services between New Orleans and the principal grain and provision receiving points in Europe, with which we have now only spasmodic connection; but as long as the supplies of cargo are subject to being cut off, as at present, we cannot expect to increase our means of communication with these places to any great extent.

A great deal has been said and written against the Jetties at South Pass, and it has been, and is still, asserted that heavy vessels cannot pass through the channel. We have loaded many steamers in New Orleans, drawing all the way from seventeen to twenty-five feet of water, and any that failed to go out without grounding, did so through some accident, or through defective steering on the part of the pilot or helmsman; but such accidents have been rare. We have had a steamer drawing twenty-two feet of water get aground by going out of the proper channel, and a few hours later, another steamer drawing twenty-three feet of water keep the proper channel, and go to sea without touching anything; still, the grounding of the twenty-two-foot steamer was cited as a proof that the Jetties are a failure! As a matter of fact, we do not now consider a vessel's draft of water of any importance whatever in engaging cargo or loading her; whereas, previous to the days of the Jetties, it was a question of the gravest importance. It is also a fact that the poorest channel is not in the Jetties proper, but in South Pass itself, where no provision has been made for improvements.

Capt. Francis, probably the most experienced of our bar pilots, says that far from the South Pass showing any signs of filling up, there are about two and one-half feet more water there now than at any previous time. Last spring we had the pleasure of conducting one of the largest and most experienced steamship owners in the world to Port Eads, where he inspected all the works and expressed himself to the effect that New Orleans possessed an entrance to her harbor superior in very many respects to the entrance to New York harbor.

At the same time we would ask your careful attention to the fact, that all experienced seafaring men are unanimous in saying that an accident in the channel of the South Pass, might at any moment cause the entire obstruction of navigation for a considerable time. The channel is narrow, the current is swift, and the chances of collision of incoming and outgoing vessels, with each other, or with vessels at anchor in the Pass are great. [See evidence in the collision case of the Steamship "Altonower" with bark "Ontario," in South Pass last February, where, by good fortune, neither vessel was sunk.] Besides, the single outlet would probably not be sufficient to accommodate the increased movement of tonnage that would follow any thorough improvement of the upper river, and we think no plan of improvement would be complete that did not include the deepening of Southwest Pass, and making it passable for vessels of the heaviest draft.

The cry of "hot corn by the river route" has been raised so often, that it has become comparatively ineffectual in creating any excitement. No doubt some years ago large quantities of corn shipped at New Orleans did get heated on the voyage across the ocean, and in some instances became quite rotten. But this corn was never in a condition to be shipped at all. Northern exporters would not have shipped it by fast steamers from New York to Liverpool, far less by sailing-ships, or by steamers that lay a week or two in New Orleans stowing cotton on top of the corn.

In 1877 and 1878 one firm here shipped some forty or fifty cargoes, full and part, of corn to Europe, and did not have one complaint as to the condition in which the grain was delivered; but all this corn was thoroughly sound when it was shipped at St. Louis, and was carefully handled and transferred at New Orleans.

We handled the parcel of 30,000 bushels of wheat shipped at St. Paul by barges, in the early part of last June, destined for Glasgow, Scotland. The wheat arrived in New Orleans in the latter part of the same month, during the hottest period of a very hot summer. On transferring it to the ocean steamer, it was found to be in perfectly good condition, and was received at Glasgow in the same state, having stood a severer test during its passage of 2,000 miles down the Mississippi, than grain would be subject to in any ordinary year.

From all the information we have received, as well as from our own experience, we know that any grain leaving St. Louis or other points on the river, thoroughly sound and dry, will take no harm whatever from climatic influence in the transit to Europe, via New Orleans.

The barges are thoroughly well ventilated, and are not, like railroad cars, exposed to the full heat of the sun, but are in great part kept cool by the surrounding water and ventilation obtained from the interior lining or cargo boxes, and the grain is not handled and rehandled, losing in weight each time, but is generally transferred direct from the barge to the ocean vessel, by floating elevators fitted with all the cleansing and blowing appliances in use in Northern ports.

It will be evident from the foregoing that since the opening of the South Pass, and the commencement of the grain exports from New Orleans on an extended scale by ocean steamers, there has been a series of obstacles, real and alleged, to the development of the trade, that have proved vexatious and costly to both shippers and carriers; the principal of these obstacles have been caused by the frequent stoppages to navigation on the river, through the want of an adequate stage of water.

The same causes and effects have been perceptible in the import trade via New Orleans. Merchants abroad and in this country have not been disposed to risk sending valuable goods by a route that held out no reasonable certainty of prompt delivery, and in consequence large shipments of imported merchandise come via New York, and other Atlantic ports, to points in the West, that ought naturally to draw their supplies via New Orleans.

But in face of all these obstacles and discouraging surroundings, let us look at the effect the opening up of the river to large carrying vessels by the South Pass Jetties, and the extension of the barge lines have had on the export and import trade via New Orleans.

As you state, in your letter of the 13th of September, to Mr. Horatio Seymour, Jr., the export trade in grain by the Mississippi route was merely nominal in 1875, while in 1879 there were exported 6,164,838 bushels, and in 1880, 15,762,664 bushels, showing an infinitely larger percentage of yearly increase than any other port in the United States.

When vessels were liable to lie aground at the mouth of the river, for weeks at a time, until the action of the current cuts them out, they were obliged to charge excessively high rates of freight on everything they carried, to cover this risk, and thirty, thirty-five, and forty cents per bushel was paid as freight on parcels of grain to Liverpool.

Now that the risk of detention from grounding has been reduced to the chances of an accident or mistake of the pilot, twenty cents per bushel has come to be considered a very high rate, and twelve to fourteen cents may be looked on as a full average rate, while grain has been carried to Liverpool as low as four and five cents per bushel.

The opening of the Jetties then may be said to have already effected a saving of from fifteen to twenty cents per bushel in the cost of carrying grain from New Orleans to Liverpool, in spite of the difficulties in the way of procuring free supplies of ocean tonnage, and the uncertainty of the arrival of cargo, owing to the interruption of river navigation, while the cost of carrying cotton, flour, oil-cake, and other goods has been reduced to a similar extent.

While other seaports, on which vast sums of money have been lavished to provide the best facilities for receiving and handling goods of all kinds, have been making little advance in the quantities of merchandise that passed through them,

New Orleans, with her imperfect system of communication with points abroad, and with her defective and interrupted means of communication with points in the interior, has been steadily increasing her importance, until she now stands very high in the list of seaports in the United States.

That a greatly increased export and import movement would immediately follow the establishment of a deep water channel in the Mississippi river, permitting barges to load to their full capacity, and to make their trips without interruption all the year round, is very evident.

Owners of ocean vessels would accept low rates of freight for bringing goods out to New Orleans, satisfied that on arriving there, they would certainly secure return cargoes without delay, at rates of freight on a parity with those current from other ports.

Importers would order their goods to be sent by the cheap water route, confident that they could reckon on receiving them within a reasonable time.

Exporters would patronize the route, satisfied that their goods would get through in less time than via the railroads and Atlantic ports, and that they would avoid the trouble and annoyance caused by the breaking of invoice marks and numbers, so often met with in shipments by rail through the divisions of trains.

(As an instance of what can be done in the way of rapid transit with a good stage of water, we may cite a shipment of 20,000 bushels wheat, 40,000 bushels corn, and 2,500 sacks of flour by Mr. George Bain, of the Atlantic Milling Company, of St. Louis, that left that place on the 26th day of February, 1881, by the Mississippi Valley barges, and was loaded by us on board the sailing-ship Siberia, in New Orleans, the vessel going to sea on the 11th of March, thirteen days after her cargo left St. Louis.)

Barges would be kept constantly moving, with full cargoes, both up and down stream, and could afford in consequence to carry grain and goods cheaper than they do now.

The saving in the cost of transportation would enable the Western producers to still better compete with all rivals in foreign markets, the volume of trade along the Mississippi Valley would be wonderfully swelled, new employment provided for thousands of laborers, and the whole Western country benefited to an incalculable degree.

When we see the immense expenditures on river improvements and canal construction undertaken by England, France, Germany, and even Holland, it appears impossible, in a country so full of resources, energy, and talent as the United States, that the greatest river, in the most fertile valley of the world, should be allowed to remain in such a condition that traffic over it between great and wealthy cities, is often almost impossible, even for the lightest-drafted vessels.

We confidently hope that the efforts of your Convention will result in removing this reflection on the enterprise, engineering skill, and public spirit of this great country, and that the Mississippi river will soon be transformed from an erratic and uncontrolled stream, into a new coast line—the Mediterranean of America—and the vast extent of lands now lying useless along its course, be brought under cultivation, enabling the great West to fulfil the role destined for her by Nature, and making her in reality the "Granary of the World."

Yours truly,

FORSTALL, ROSS & CLAYTON.

NOTE.—An interesting statement of vessels entered and cleared at the port of New Orleans from January, 1877, to December, 1880, compiled by Forstall Ross & Clayton, will be found on page 239.

SECTION 5—PRESS COMMENTS.

Detroit Free Press, November 2.

The great Mississippi River Convention was dissolved October 28. There were of record 656 delegates from the sources of the great river (the object of discussion) on the north, to the Crescent City on the south. I question whether in its *personnel* a more representative assembly was before convened in this country. It was composed almost entirely of men of gray hairs, yet men of energy, of note and influence in localities whence they came, drawn together for one purpose, from which they would not be swerved. The first day was consumed before reaching an organization. The real work was not touched until Thursday, when the Committee on Resolutions reported. There seemed prolixity in the resolutions, but most of the Convention knew just what was wanted, and if enlightenment was needed by any, the clear-cut thoughts of Judge Taylor, of the United States Commission, based on experience, observation, and the most exhaustive examination and study of the character and caprices of the great river, made all as clear as crystal. Therefore the schemes of interested localities, though pressed with the greatest power of eloquence and art, struck like ocean waves against a rocky, iron-bound coast; amendments and additional resolutions, though ably supported, were all voted down. The improvement of the Mississippi was the one great thought and aim; all else was of little account until that important matter was settled. Finally, under the influence of the previous question, the main resolutions were put, reaching a unanimous affirmative conclusion in the midst of a storm of cheers and congratulations. The first object of the assembly secured, an adjournment followed till 10 o'clock on Friday, the evening being devoted by nearly the entire delegation to an entertainment furnished by the merchants of St. Louis at the Opera-House, in listening to McCullough in his masterpiece of "Virginius." He was eminently successful, being inspired by the distinguished character of his audience.

At 10 Friday morning the Convention came together with fewer numbers, but no less enthusiasm, and abundant opportunity for discussion. The resolution ruled out Thursday was reconsidered. The gist of it was, in fact, the deepening of the Illinois canal and river by the National Government, so as to connect the waters of the lakes with the Mississippi river by a channel admitting the passage of steamers or barges from the inland seas of the North to New Orleans, with the same facility as from St. Louis, thereby securing cheap transportation for the lake region, and a great highway from the North to the extreme South, in case of military necessity. One of the finest speeches made on the resolution was by Congressman Shallenberger, from Pennsylvania. It was brilliant in thought and eloquent in manner. Springer and Thomas, of Illinois, and Willis, of Kentucky, members of Congress, committed themselves to this resolution by most acceptable and enthusiastic addresses, as did numerous other gentlemen present. As you may infer, the resolution was unanimously passed.

This concluded the work, but not the pleasure of the Convention. Headed by a brass band under the guidance of McEnnis, President of the St. Louis Board of Trade, who has been most untiring in his devotion to the comfort and pleasure of strangers, more than 1,000 persons made their way to the river for a practical illustration of river transportation as exhibited in the make-up of the barge excursion. There were five barges of a capacity of 60,000 bushels each, three abreast forward, with two in the rear, between which was the steamer "Future City," 200 feet long, 36 feet beam, 6 feet hold, with two engines, 28 inches diameter of cylinder by 8 feet stroke, with stern-wheel 28 feet in diameter, 27 feet 6 inches length of buckets, seven boilers, two flues 38 inches diameter by 28 feet length. This powerful steamer pushed us down the river to Jefferson Barracks, twelve miles, passing continuous evidence the entire distance of immense wealth in manufacturing establishments, in one hour, and against a strong current on our return in two hours and a half. More than an acre of surface with the capacity indicated moved with such facility, with an improved Mississippi, solves the question of cheap transportation and thereby cheap food to the consumer, and will forever hold in check the cost of railway transit. The steamer which moved our excursion has completed, since 1873, ninety-five round trips between St. Louis and New Orleans; has towed down stream 474 barges; has transported in down-stream cargoes, 446,962 tons; up, 491 barges, 41,667 tons; has traveled 239,400 miles; average number of days for each trip, twenty-three. With an improved channel this record of work could be increased 40 per cent. without any increase of expense. This means benefit to the farmer as well as consumer. Reduced to railway capacity the freight of corn in one of these barge tows would require fifty trains of cars; twenty cars for each train. A barge tow costs, for the steamer, $75,000, four barges $12,000 each, or with five in a tow $60,000, a total of $135,000, and the average consumption of coal for a trip is 25,000 bushels. With a full channel and ample freights, four cents per bushel would pay a fair profit, at which cargoes are often made up. This company has thirteen steamers and 100 barges of the first class, but in consequence of the failure of crops three-fourths of this fleet is laid up and will not be required until another harvest.

The system of loading and transfer is very simple and inexpensive, the barge while receiving freight being moored to an enormous wharf-boat, upon which teams are driven with their immense loads of rolling freight—grain being taken from elevators. There is a perfect system of interior ventilation as well as exterior, which protects the grain in transit from damage by heating. It is in reality a boat within a boat, the interior boat being accessible from all directions. Down and up cargoes on deck are handled with neatness, reaching their destination as clean as when delivered on board.

Another important end is attained in this mode of transit. Bulky produce, like hay and straw, which have heretofore been almost impossible of movement to distant points on account of cost and risk of fire, are now transported with profit to producer and consumer.

Without instructions from my Governor, and in accordance with my own conviction, I have advocated and voted for the improvement of the Mississippi as a national measure. It is beyond the power of private enterprise or State combination, and even could the States bordering the river combine, their financial position would prevent for a long period to come. The work, in my judgment, is as thoroughly national as the improvement of harbors or the construction of lighthouses.

Beautiful allusion was made to the nation's calamity in the death of the lamented Garfield, and South and North fraternized with far more sympathy and friendliness than in ante-war days. The arrangements by the Board of Trade were on a magnificent scale, costing $25,000, and not a circumstance occurred to mar the harmony of the proceedings.

St. Paul Daily Dispatch, November 7, 1881.

J. W. McClung presented the following report from the delegation which attended the St. Louis Convention:

To the President and Directors of the Chamber of Commerce:

The St. Paul Chamber of Commerce, through its committee of ten on the Mississippi river, having had the honor to call the River Improvement Convention, which met at St. Louis on the 26th of October, it seems appropriate that the same committee should make some report concerning the success of that Convention.

About twenty States and Territories were represented by some six hundred delegates, including the State of New York from the remote East, and the Territory of New Mexico from the extreme Southwest. The Convention was the largest river convention which has yet been held, and was composed of more distinguished and representative men. Minnesota was represented by over twenty delegates, and was honored by being tendered the Presidency of the Convention.

The large number of delegates sent from our city and State helped to swell the number of delegates to the Convention, which made it the imposing assemblage it was, and gave to it the influence and the power for good which will clothe its recommendations with the sanction of public opinion, and give to it its best passport to the favor of Congress. So that, in the language of Col. Taylor, of the River Commission, in his address to the Convention, "This great Convention will be sensibly felt in the legislation of Congress, and in this great work of improvement. The Convention itself speaks louder than any words it can utter. The presence in this city of this vast body of representative men is the great mountain in the landscape, which affects by the breadth of its base and the sublimity of its height; and you might go home and say nothing, feeling assured that your presence here has not been in vain."

The great benefits expected to result from this Convention are the education of a public opinion upon the improvement of our water-ways, and the creation of a sentiment among the masses of the people which will operate as an outside pressure upon Congress which they cannot resist. Each convention which has heretofore been held has proved to be the thin end of the wedge which has been driven home to the attention of Congress, by subsequent memorials and subsequent conventions, resulting in larger appropriations at each session of Congress, and promising soon to clear a highway through the bed of the great river to the markets of the world. The fact that only $25,000,000 have been appropriated for the Mississippi river and its tributaries, while about $100,000,000 in cash and $200,000,000 in lands have been appropriated for the Union Pacific and other railroads, shows how great was the need of agitating this subject among the people and through these conventions to arouse the public sentiment of the country, and secure the attention of our representatives in Congress.

Congress will only move as it is moved upon. Our Representatives are only beginning to learn that there is a Mississippi river. The appropriations voted for its improvement have been given in scanty measures and in a grudging spirit, as presents to a step-child; while more than double the amount has been voted in our own State and the State of Wisconsin for schemes of merely local importance and for canals of a chimerical character, over the amounts voted for the Upper Mississippi river from Rock Island to St. Paul.

The State is losing over four millions of dollars annually by this neglect of our Representatives to understand their duty to the people of the State.

The action of our Chamber of Commerce for the past four years, in inaugurating the first convention which recognized the Upper Mississippi river, and following up the work which resulted in subsequent conventions which have been the means of obtaining largely increased appropriations, illustrates the good which may be done in the primary assemblages of the people in rousing attention to this subject, and opening the hearts of our Congressmen and the purse of the nation. It also indicates the wisdom of the organization of such local bodies as our Chamber of Commerce, and should encourage their organization and co-operation until this great work, now barely commenced, shall have been pushed forward to complete success.

There are other Conventions which must yet be held, and

other fields yet to conquer, before Minnesota, and St. Paul, her great metropolis, will reap the full fruits of the improvement of the Mississippi river. Congress and the people of the United States must be further educated, and made to understand that this is not the small end of the river. They must be taught that for 1,500 miles northwest there spreads out like a fan a vast and fertile area of tillable land almost unlimited in extent, and destined to be the granary of the continent,—the Egypt where the children of all nations are even now coming for corn and the staff of life; and when they have fully comprehended this idea, they must be further taught that when millions are appropriated for the southern end of the river, thousands will not answer for the northern end.

Congratulaling the Chamber upon the work so far accomplished, and upon the quiet but efficient part which we have been able to bear in it, this report is respectfully submitted.

J. W. McCLUNG,
Chairman Committee on Mississippi River.

Louisville Courier-Journal.

The St. Louis River Improvement Convention decides "that it is the manifest and imperative duty of the Government of the United States to cause to be made such improvements of the Mississippi river and its navigable tributaries as shall permanently secure the safe and easy navigation thereof, thereby cheapening freights, reducing insurance," etc., etc. The mode of keeping up the agitation is to be commended, and the resolutions in their entirety are good. This Convention is a strong one. It is composed of strictly representative men, who mean business, and who are determined that Congress shall understand the length and breadth of the forces at work in the great interior of the country, which figures in such a potential manner in the agricultural products of the country and in the aggregate exports of the United States. The people of the fourteen States and Territories directly interested in the improvement of the Mississippi and Missouri rivers alone number nearly seventeen millions, fully one-third the population of the United States. The twelve States interested have twenty-four Senators and ninety-two Representatives in Congress, and with this leverage the reasonable demands of the people should be complied with.

From the Globe-Democrat, September 7.

In discussing the improvement of the Mississippi river, the New York *Times* advances some singular propositions. It admits the value of the great stream as an outlet for the products of the Mississippi Valley, but has serious doubts as to whether the work is one which the whole nation should be called upon to pay for. It says: "There is no question that the Western cities and States are entitled to all the benefits which the natural advantages of their rivers afford." This is gracious. It might be inferred that there was a serious proposition advanced to take some of these natural advantages away. The *Times* continues: "But it may be questioned whether they are entitled to have these supplemented by artificial improvements at the expense, in a large part, of other sections which have their own advantages and disadvantages to deal with." Since when has the United States adopted the policy of making those locally benefited improve their own rivers and harbors? How much national money has been expended on the rivers and harbors of the Atlantic coast since the foundation of the Government? Can the largest river in the world, draining half a continent, immediately situated in the midst of the greatest national production, embracing, with its tributaries, more than twenty States and Territories, be considered a work of sectional importance? What other work of improvement in this country could possibly demand the attention and aid of Congress more justly than this? What other work could possibly possess so much national significance?

The *Times'* argument is that the Atlantic coast and cities would not be, in any way, benefited by the improvement of the Mississippi; on the contrary, that they would be injured by it. Since when has Congress adopted the policy that natural advantages shall not be utilized and improved in one part of the country because such improvement would interfere with localities possessing less natural advantages? The *Times* argues also that the Mississippi improvement might result disadvantageously to some railroad interests. This is about as puerile a plea as could be advanced. It involves the proposition that the people should be denied the benefit of a competition which would reduce the general cost of transportation, for the sake of subserving the interests of a few corporations. If there is any one great responsibility resting upon the National Government, it is to consider the good of the whole people and to act for the common welfare. This is the principle which underlies the theory of the river and harbor improvements. It was this which led to the donations of public land and credit to the Pacific and other railroad companies. It is not the time to depart from this principle just at the juncture when the matter of the systematic treatment of river navigation in the heart of the country presses itself upon Congress. The East, having secured its share of national money, is not in the position to call a halt in the general policy without shamefacedness.

It is surely not necessary to dwell on the fact that the competition of water routes has a most salutary effect upon the railroad rates of transportation. This is the much-used argument of these Eastern journals, among which the *Times* is chief, for the enlargement of the Erie canal. It is true that they do not ask for Congressional aid in this matter, for the canal lies wholly in the State of New York, and is a very different thing from a national water-course extending from the northern boundary of the nation to the southern, and, through its tributaries, from the Rocky Mountains to the Alleghanies. The *Times* sees much wisdom in the improvement of Hell Gate at the general expense, and doubtless endorses the important decision of the Supreme Court establishing the principle that navigable rivers are national highways. A little exhibition of magnanimity and justice in this particular would vastly become the people of the Atlantic coast. The center of population at present lies west of Cincinnati, and is rapidly gravitating toward the Mississippi. The representation of the Mississippi Valley in Congress is strong enough to take care of its interests, but anything like an organized sectional opposition on the part of Eastern members would be greatly to be deplored. The subject calls for broad and liberal statesmanship, and it ought to receive it from all sides.

The *Times* mentions other projects for improved water communication, and classes them with the Mississippi scheme. One is the cutting of a canal through the State of Michigan, from Lake Michigan to Lake Erie; another is the Hennepin and Illinois River canal, and still another is the enlargement of the Erie canal. "All this work," it says, "is as much entitled to Government aid as the improvement of the Mississippi river." This kind of talk answers itself. It loses all reference to the sense of proportion, and places wholly artificial water-ways on the same plane as a natural one of great magnitude. It alludes to St. Louis and New Orleans as being the main beneficiaries from the proposed improvement, and endeavors to raise an issue between them and the Eastern cities. St. Louis and New Orleans certainly will be benefited by anything which adds to the prosperity of the twenty-five millions of people in this garden of the world, but such a narrow view of the matter is playing with the subject. St. Louis and New Orleans certainly do not claim any business which must come to them at the expense of the great economic interests of the country. The *Times* represents the spirit which would lay the whole population under tribute to support an artificial prosperity in New York City.

The policy which the *Times* advocates is thus expressed: "It will be easier, more equitable and more economical for each local jurisdiction to furnish its several links in the great system of transportation, than for the nation, as a whole, to undertake at general expense to make it complete." Considering all the circumstances of the case, and the money which the Government has already expended upon existing improvements, this is an exhibition of concentrated hoggishness which, it is to be hoped, for the credit of American citizenship, will not be extensively endorsed even in the East.

St. Louis Advance (Colored).

THE NEGRO AND THE MISSISSIPPI IMPROVEMENT.—The issue in the West is not the success of any political party, but the improvement of the Mississippi river. The river is our only natural outlet to the sea. It is Nature's great highway of inter-State commerce. In its basin live 3,000,000 negroes, who subsist upon its products, and help to load its waters with commerce for all the world. Its alluvial plains extend from St. Louis to the Gulf. Under the system of slave labor large plantations upon the bottom of these plains were opened in the dense forests which covered them. Vast tracts of unsurpassed fertility are yet covered with canebrakes, cypress and cottonwood. These bottoms are subject to inundations which, while they bring annual enrichment, destroy the usefulness of many millions of acres of the most fertile land on the globe. Upon this land the colored man lives in large numbers, and he derives from its soil the means of sustenance. Whatever will increase the area of arable and habitable land, and make the commerce of this stream greater and more lucrative, is in a large and particular sense the interest of nearly 3,000,000 colored people. We want to deepen the channel and redeem the swamps from St. Louis to the Gulf. The negro of the bottoms is interested in the proposed improvement. It means millions for his labor and tens of millions for the products of his toil, which in some way will return to the promotion of his comfort and prosperity. The negro must partake of the prosperity of the South. Increased facilities of commerce means increased wages for his labor. The improvement of the Mississippi means business and not politics. If the Government can give 50,000,000 acres of land to a railroad, on the proposed line for which there is neither population nor commerce, it can more wisely appropriate $100,000,000 to improve a highway that would save 50,000,000 acres of land from annual destruction, and increase the comfort and wealth of the region by many hundred millions of dollars. The Mississippi drains a region nearly as large as half of Europe, and the products of its banks are more valuable than the gold and silver of California and Nevada. Millions of colored people toil upon its bottoms, and handle the staples of commerce upon its banks, and hence become directly interested in the great question of its improvement, and in that interest we shall look forward with great expectations to the coming Convention, which shall meet in this city during October, for the improvement of the mighty stream.

St. Louis Post-Dispatch, October 29.

Our River Convention was a great success. It was well managed throughout, and its influence will certainly be felt when Congress meets. Our visitors will carry away pleasant recollections of St. Louis, and we have an idea that the river already begins to feel better.

St. Louis Globe-Democrat, October 30, 1881.

Gone, but not forgotten—the River Convention. It has left behind a fragrant memory of deeds well done. Now for the memorial to Congress, which should fire the solid shot of facts with the good powder of argument. The committee must not fail to take accurate aim. It cannot fail when aided by the telescopic sight of the 125 representatives from the Valley States.

St. Louis Post-Dispatch, December 15, 1881.

The memorial prepared by the committee of twenty-one, appointed by the Mississippi River Improvement Convention to bring the matter before Congress, is an able and wise document. There were a great many dangers against which the memorialists might have wrecked the whole work of the Convention, and these have been skillfully avoided by the masterly piloting of the St. Louis members of the committee. The tendency to divide the demand and ask appropriations for the Ohio and Missouri was very strong, and there were gentlemen who did not abandon the hope of getting these two words into the memorial at the last moment. Had they succeeded, behind them were the friends of the Arkansas, the Red river, the Tennessee, the Cumberland, and so on down in a diminishing ratio, each ready to seize any precedent for including their own stream in the omnibus. The fight was fought out over the Ohio, and ended there. As a result the whole Mississippi Valley goes before Congress united in one single simple demand—Mississippi improvement. Injudicious friends to the great river are already demanding many millions at once for improvement. This is a mistake on the other side. We do not want twenty millions. What we do ask and what this memorial very plainly demands of Congress is the yearly appropriation requested by the Mississippi River Commission. The matter and the manner of improvement are left in the hands of the experienced and able engineers selected by Congress itself for the task, and the Valley unites sensibly and practically upon the one platform of giving these engineers the money necessary to do their work.

St. Louis Republican, October 28.

THE CONCLUSIONS OF THE CONVENTION.—More than half the States and two of the Territories of the Union, represented in the Convention in this city, yesterday declared:

"That it is the manifest and imperative duty of the Government of the United States to cause to be made such improvement of the Mississippi river, and its navigable tributaries, as shall permanently secure the safe and easy navigation thereof, thereby cheapen freights, reducing insurance and other burdens and expenses; promoting the vast inland commerce of the nation, and creating new avenues of foreign trade, and thus not only inviting increased production and population, but assuring greater prosperity to the whole people."

This declaration was emphasized by citing the pertinent and important fact that the Government, for the purpose of protecting commerce and enhancing the public welfare, by the construction of railroads, the property of individuals and corporations, had granted them 200,000,000 acres of the public domain, and given $100,000,000 out of the Treasury. While this has been done for the construction of artificial highways, less than $25,000,000 had been bestowed on the improvement of more than 15,000 miles of natural water-ways. This mode of dealing with this great and vital subject is made to appear in a light strikingly illogical, and, upon any reasonable ground, indefensible.

The act of Congress creating a Mississippi River Commission was strongly commended, and the course of that Commission and its recommendations in pursuance of its duties warmly approved.

The Convention, after full and careful deliberation, adopted the wise and significant language of "the Mississippi river and its navigable tributaries," in indicating the scope of the work which the Government is asked to undertake. The *Republican* regards this as eminently just and judicious. It embraces all that could be safely asked, and does not omit such auxiliaries as are essential in making an effective struggle against the inertia or positive opposition which has hitherto thwarted or delayed Congressional action.

The work of the Convention has been well done. Its proceedings have been absorbingly interesting. There is not the slightest room to doubt that the movement for the improvement of the natural water-ways of the country has received an impetus which, from this time forward, will gather momentum till it will be found irresistible. The subject has never before been so brought before the country as to make it a present positive issue, which will not and cannot be put aside. Henceforward this is the paramount public consideration with the people of the largest half of this Union.

The Nautical Gazette, New York, Nov. 5, 1881.

The Mississippi River Improvement Convention, which was held at St. Louis, Mo., Oct. 26, 27 and 28, was doubtless the largest and most influential gathering of gentlemen interested in water transportation ever held in the United States, and there can be no question that its influence will be felt throughout the entire length and breadth of the land, and no amount of petty sectional jealousy can belittle its importance. The Convention was called for a specific purpose, and despite the varied interests represented, it kept to its work, and within the scope of its official call, which was to devise some concerted action for the improvement of the Mississippi and its natural tributaries. We know that some of our Eastern cotemporaries looked upon this movement as one which threatened to absorb all future appropriations for the improvement of channels of transportation by natural water conveyance in the great West.

We watched in vain for an evidence of sectional feeling which betokened a desire on the part of Western men to exclude the East from the blessings of Federal aid in honest improvement of natural navigable waters; while, on the other hand, there was an unanimous sentiment expressed that for the future no section must hope for indiscriminate appropriations to benefit those who sought to enrich themselves on the improvements (?) to mill-streams, mud-puddles, oyster-boat harbors, and all sorts of imaginary water-courses; and to a man the Convention proclaimed its detestation of such practices as were openly urged and passed at the last session of Congress.

We look upon the judicious and thorough improvement of the Mississippi river and its natural tributaries as of vital national importance. It will create a demand for tonnage, and of American tonnage, not only in the river service, but in the coastwise trade, and in the early future, as a natural consequence, in tonnage for Transatlantic trade.

The safer the navigation of these great river highways are made, the cheaper will become the rate of transportation, and to a greater extent will be the demand for tonnage to move the necessary products of that rich and fertile valley. More money will then be available for investment in vessels of all classes, and in due season capitalists will see that in vessel property there is an excellent investment. We do not despair of seeing Western capital largely interested in sea-going tonnage, and at no distant date. The East lost her opportunity when she allowed the Atlas line, and other foreign lines, to secure such a large share of the West Indian and Central American trade, direct from American ports, and no one can blame the South and the Southwest if she should step in and secure the benefits which can be had by supplying the west coast of South and Central America with her products, both of soil and manufacture; and, mark our words, she will do it sooner or later.

The far-seeing men of the West, and the progressive men of the South, are alive to the importance of securing this great trade, now almost wholly monopolized by the English and Germans; and we see no reason why, with the proper business tact, cheap freights, and shorter and less expensive water routes, that a golden harvest may not be reaped in a field but sparsely occupied by our people. There need be no sectional jealousies in the development of such a grand and practical scheme, which in its results would be a national blessing, as well as an enrichment of the people at large.

All the "cold water" thrown upon the Mississippi River Convention by a few Eastern journals, has been instigated by the same influence which for years has attempted the repeal of our navigation laws, so that British ships, under the American flag, might swallow up American commerce. The men of the West must learn that England is her bitterest foe; that she is playing quietly a lone hand, and that she has been working for years to get the whip-hand of Americans. It was England that was the prime mover in the war of the Rebellion, seeking to cripple the South and destroy the power of the North so that she might control the manufactures as well as the commerce of the world. Her efforts bore their fruits. The South was left impoverished; the North, which owned the major portion of the sea-going tonnage of this country, was crippled; but the great West grew strong, as she was the granary of the world. She now turns her attention thitherward, and year after year she has been flooding the agricultural districts of that section with her pernicious free-trade doctrines, set forth in glibly and insidiously-prepared pamphlets, and has succeeded in indoctrinating leading newspaper writers into the teachings of the Cobden Club, whose emissaries—some of them men of power and influence—were on the floor of the St. Louis Convention as delegates; but none of whom had the opportunity of speaking forth their sophistries, so closely did the delegates confine themselves to the true purpose of the call.

The East has no reason to be jealous of the West in its action at St. Louis; and if our leading men had been there, as the writer was, and could have seen and heard, as we did, they would dismiss this foolish fear from their minds and thoughts. Unity, harmony, and a determination to ask for nothing but what was honorable, just, and for the nation's good, was the prominent and universal sentiment expressed. Sectarianism was absent in all the resolutions, debates and discussions, while the Eastern delegates were as welcome as if to the manor born, and they of the Great Lakes received that courteous, warm reception due to their commanding importance and close relationship, and even those from distant localities met with a cordiality as honest as it was sincere. The Convention was a most marked success in every particular.

St. Louis Post-Dispatch, October 26.

The work cut out for the Mississippi River Improvement Convention is clearly and unmistakably put in the call which brings the delegates together. Its mission is to secure the improvement of the Mississippi and its navigable tributaries. The day of Goose Neck run and Cross Timbers branch has gone by, and the people of the Valley have at last come together as a unit to demand the real bettering of the great national water-way to the Gulf. Heretofore money has been spent in the interior, not to improve the streams, but to bring money into the country. This Convention more logically will ask Congress for appropriations for the great river which must float out the wealth of the whole Valley. The money is not to be spent that Hooppole county or Crackerbox corners may have plenty of cash, but that we may have a nine-foot channel to the ocean. The late revolution in the carrying trade by which the barge system has restored the economy of transportation to the river was really the call for this Convention. Practically unaided by the General Government, private enterprise has proved to the world that the grain of the great Mississippi region can be sent from St. Louis to Liverpool by New Orleans two cents a bushel cheaper than by way of New York, despite all the drawbacks of insufficient water and unimproved navigation. The principle demonstrated thus finds one more expression in the Convention which met to-day. The body of gentlemen now sitting in the Opera-House represent the commerce of the Valley, and that commerce says to the General Government: We have shown that the river route already saves millions yearly to the trade of this country, and we demand that this saving shall be multiplied and increased by the proper improvement of the stream. The whole argument can be stated thus: That the saving on every bushel of wheat now going out by the river route is two cents; with an improved river that saving will be four cents,—and Congress *must* improve the river.

ECHOES FROM THE CONVENTION.—The Louisville *Courier-Journal*, after quoting from the New York *Herald's* article on the River Convention, remarks:

"To turn that argument on yourself, we would ask why the merchants and capitalists of New York go begging to Congress for millions of dollars to improve their harbor, blow up masses of rock at Hell Gate, widen and reconstruct Harlem river and do numerous other jobs for the convenience of New Yorkers? The people of the West and South do not ask the Government to build a canal to the Gulf. The highway is already there. It is the Government's water-way, and it needs deepening for the purpose of a business which embodies four-fifths of our exports. It is the duty of the Government to repair its own highway. As for the rivalry, the railroads and canals eastward are not equal to the demands of shippers; the freights are higher than they should be; millions can be saved in freights. Both the Eastern and Southern outlet are needed. There is abundant business for them both. On seaboard freights the Southern outlet will be a competing route, preventing the exactions of railroads and giving justice to shippers. The position of the New York *Herald* is grossly illogical."

The same paper justly remarks further:

"The mode of keeping up the agitation is to be commended, and the resolutions in their entirety are good. This Convention is a strong one. It is composed of strictly representative men, who mean business, and who are determined that Congress shall understand the length and breadth of the forces at work in the great interior of the country, which figure in such a potential manner in the agricultural products of the country, and in the aggregate exports of the United States. The people of the fourteen States and Territories directly interested in the improvement of the Mississippi and

Missouri rivers alone number nearly seventeen millions, fully one-third the population of the United States. The twelve States interested have twenty-four Senators and ninety-two Representatives in Congress, and with this leverage the reaonable demands of the people should be complied with."

The Spectator, St. Louis, October 1, 1881.

The advancement of St. Louis may not have been as rapid as some of her sister cities moving under the impulse of immediate advantage, but it has been sure and steadfast, and each step has been the herald of a grander advance. Fine churches, commodious hotels, and elegant theatres have sprung up like magic during the last two years, and these are the best indications of a city's progress. Some people find in the enlargement of our export trade by river the sole reason for these results. There seem to be reasons to justify, to some extent, this opinion. The investment of three and one-half million dollars in elevators, and of three millions in barge tonnage, the receipts of fifty-two million bushels of grain, and foreign shipments by river during 1880 of fifteen and a half millions, are important factors in the development of the materials which characterize the growth of our city. That this belief has taken hold of the people is evident by the manner in which they are responding to the call for the coming river convention. Letters are pouring in from men of high national reputation as well as representatives of communities, and all breathe the same tone—the necessity for the improvement of the river. The convention now bids fair to be the largest ever held in the Mississippi Valley, and will be composed of men of the highest intelligence. The success of the project will be largely due to the thorough manner in which it has been organized. The "Official Call" was a model document, and has attracted the general notice of the press. The style and formation of the letters of invitation were works of art, and displayed commendable taste. There has been no bungling or mistakes. The whole management has been thorough, and distinguished by the exercise of sound judgment and commanding ability, which reflects great credit upon the Executive Committee and upon the city of St. Louis. The Convention, composed, as it will be, of the representative men of all the States in the Valley, and from the various societies of those States, will have necessarily a potent influence. Its action may accomplish the stupendous purpose of solving the problem of cheap transportation for this interior empire, by improving the water-ways. It is possible that results of such magnitude may be accomplished that will mark a new era in our city's history, and the progress which commerce brings and the unity which trade engenders may hereafter be measured for this valley from the time of the great Convention.

St. Louis Republican.

THE RIVER CONVENTION.—The difficulty in the way of conventions hitherto held in regard to the matter of river improvement has been the lack of popular representation, and consequently the want of popular sympathy. The conventions have been composed of representative men, to be sure, but they have represented only immediate transportation and trade interests. They have spoken for the State, with always potential voice, and for commercial bodies which act at great commercial centres.

The river convention which will assemble in this city on the 26th of October comprehends not only the line of representation heretofore adopted, but makes a new and most important departure. It has not only invited the co-operation of the States, boards of trade, and other commercial bodies largely interested in the business of transportation, but it has appealed most successfully to the larger representation which lies outside of, and yet subsidary to these controlling influences.

The Governors of the States and commercial bodies in the great valley have responded with the usual able representatives, but outside of and beyond these there are the responses of nearly four hundred incorporated cities in the valley, the mayors of which have forwarded the list of delegates. One can comprehend the extent of these responses when we mention that they come from Wyoming in the far West, to South Carolina on the Atlantic coast, from Colorado to West Virginia, scarce an incorporated town of any magnitude in that broad area being omitted.

When it is remembered that these cities and towns of the interior are the heads of communities most interested in the question of cheap transportation, the gathering centres of the active thought that reaches and swells the greater cities, and when, as the correspondence shows, these cities and towns have clothed their best citizens with the power of representation, we may well conclude that the River Convention will embody a power of representation such as has never been witnessed in our past commercial history.

It is the interior cities and towns, away from the rush of great trade activities, that public sentiment on this, as upon all other great questions, is created. The great wealth-producers are around and in them, and their representatives must of necessity voice the wishes and interests of these important classes. So the convention will be more largely popular in its character. It will be more than ever before the people speaking for themselves and for their immediate interests, and the expression of their desires will reach with more effect the ears of their servants in Congress and the Legislatures.

It is pleasant to record, and creditable to all those connected with the important movement, to say that in every step taken thus far it has been handled with great judgment, and that the preliminary arrangements have been wisely planned.

President McEnnis, of the Merchants' Exchange, and who is also President of the Executive Committee, has been unwearied in efforts to make the Convention a success. He has shown from the beginning a soundness of wisdom and judgment and liberality of views in administration which will largely account for the glowing promises of success. His aim from the beginning has been to make the Convention reach the great end proposed as a commercial movement, and redounding to the honor of the city of St. Louis and the State of Missouri. He has been ably seconded by the Executive Committee and the efficient secretaries, and there can be no question that the River Convention will be a great success.

N. O. Picayune, October 18, 1881.

How Shall we Accomplish our Purpose.—The New York *Times* thinks that there is no question that Western cities and States "are entitled to all the benefit which the natural advantages of the rivers afford," but assumes that it may be questioned whether those cities and States are entitled to have "their natural advantages" "supplemented by artificial improvements at the expense, in large part, of other sections which have their own advantages and disadvantages to deal with." The *Times*, no doubt, possesses sufficient logical acumen to enable it to see that its position does away with the whole question of internal improvements. It will scarcely undertake to say that any city whatever is not "entitled to the benefits which the natural advantages" of its situation afford. It will not assert that any measure of internal improvement under Government auspices can be carried out except " at the expense, in large part, of other sections which have their own advantages and disadvantages to deal with." But it will not have the candor to state these conclusions from its own logic, because it will not have the audacity to proclaim in New York's face that New York's "Hell Gate" is not entitled to "artificial improvements at the expense, in large part, of other sections."

The original estimate for the reefs at Hell Gate, and Diamond and Coenties reefs was $5,189,120. Gen. John Newton's report for the fiscal year ending June 30, 1869, stated the amount expended at $1,621,699.99, the amount expended during that year at $198,577, and the amount estimated to complete "the existing project" at $3,213,278.55. How much has been expended since, we do not know, but it is a large sum. That it has been well expended is certain. Gen. Newton is one of our best engineers, and the improvements are necessary, and ought to be completed. Neither do we know how much New York needs for the improvement of Harlem river and Spuyten Duyvil creek, also requisite for the advancement of the commercial well-being of our greatest entrepot. New York State had received for the improvement of rivers and harbors from the General Government during the years 1789-1878 no less a sum than $8,355,716, while Louisiana had received $2,855,190. We do not think that New York has received too much; but if the New York *Times* is correct, New York's commercial interests have been subserved at the expense, in a great part, of other sections.

If the theory of internal improvements at national charge were new; if it were a question of establishing principles upon which to conduct the Government, there would be a greater show of reason in the position of the *Times*. But the principle has been settled by use, and the practice of the country has become fixed. It is not a question of the propriety of the Government undertaking internal improvements at the public expense, but merely a question of distribution of the money that can be reasonably spared from the Treasury for such purposes. And right here the meanness of the *Times* creeps out. Having obtained a very large disproportion of established facts, its left hand is behind its back open to receive the next appropriation for New York, and its right hand is gesticulating to the West in opposition to any Western demand for "artificial improvements at the expense, in large part, of other sections."

The theory of internal improvements having been made a part of our governmental system, the question of distribution naturally falls into the very simple category of the greatest good to the greatest number. The improvement of the Mississippi river is of interest to one-half the people of this country, and appeals for aid with greater force than a lake harbor which subserves the wants of a single county. The Mississippi river and its tributaries have not received relatively so large a proportion of public aid as the Atlantic coast. If this partiality is corrected, by giving to the Mississippi what is needed to make it the great thoroughfare of the nations, the *Times* sees that New York will suffer.

If we reflect a moment on the greatness of the undertaking, we shall not fail to see that an appropriation adequate to the worth and want of the Valley can scarcely be had at the hands of Congress. We must begin. We must content ourselves with beginning. We must begin somewhere. And we cannot begin at the headwaters, because they are too widely dispersed to permit of concentration, and we would probably not get a dollar. We therefore should begin at the chief concourses and join in the defense of the greatest volumes, which bear the largest shipping, and serve the whole of the territory.

It is on this principle that the appropriation for the Jetties was obtained. That so vast a navigation should have no exit to the ocean, that the commerce of the earth should have no inlet to the half of our country, was seen to be an evil concerning so many of our people that the obviation of it almost assumed a national aspect. The purchase of Louisiana was because Jefferson saw the impropriety of leaving the entrance to our interior navigation in foreign power. But if the entrance be choked up, what matter what power holds it? And if the channel be shoaled till it is worthless, what difference does it make whether there is a mouth or not? The argument began at the mouth, but it ascends the river.

It would be well to postpone minor schemes of improvement, and ask Congress to give us a reasonable channel as far as seems reasonable, say at first from the mouth to Cairo. If the entire West would forego its respective local wants, and unite in favor of its one general want, the end would be gained. There is no part of the West, not even the remote wheat fields of Nebraska or Dakota, which will not at once feel the weight of the want of a channel in the Mississippi river, if that river is closed against it. Take away from the trnsportation problem the constant pressure of river competition, and you know the consequences. Open the river to its fullest capacity, and the farmers of the West can see the result. The railroads carry water on their shoulders,—water in the shape of bonds, stocks, etc.,—and they don't need the water in the river. But the farmers need water under the keels of commerce.

From the Davenport Gazette.

At a meeting of citizens of Davenport to hear the report of the delegates to the Convention, Mr. Russell offered the following resolutions, which were unanimously adopted:

Resolved, That this meeting, representing the citizens of Davenport, desires to express its great satisfaction at the results reached by the River Improvement Convention at St. Louis, and its hearty approval of the resolutions adopted by that body.

Resolved, That we pledge an earnest and unremitting support to all efforts of the Executive Committee appointed by said Convention to press upon Congress at its next session and thereafter, the necessity for continuous and liberal appropriations for the prosecution of the work of internal improvements commended in the resolution of the Convention thus approved by this meeting.

SECTION 6.

LIST OF DELEGATES.

ARKANSAS.

W. H. Fulton, Little Rock.
R. Pritchard, Little Rock.
Logan H. Roots. Little Rock.
Wm. M. Fishback, Fort Smith,
C. V. Buckley, Fort Smith.
H. M. Grant, Helena.
G. W. Brown, Camden.
Jno. E. Bennett, Helena.
W. V. Johnson, Helena.
T. F. Sorrells, Warren.

D. W. Fellows, Warren.
J. F. Robinson, Arkansas City.
Albert Smith, Batesville.
H. Glitsch, Eureka Springs.
J. A. Newman, Eureka Springs.
Thomas Hardeman, Pocahontas.
W. B. Moore, Fayetteville.
J. V. Walker, Fayetteville.
J. B. Trullock, Pine Bluff.

ALABAMA.

Dr. Thomas B. Taylor, Montgomery.

COLORADO.

L. E. Sherman, Colorado Springs.

DAKOTA.

R. F. Pettigrew.

P. Donan.

ILLINOIS.

Edward Rutz, Springfield.
J. C. Willis, Metropolis.
W. O. Towle, Metropolis.
H. Fullerton, Havana.
Lewis Ihorn, Harrisonville.
J. P. M. Howard, Effingham.
W. H. Barlow, Effingham.
R. A. Wilbanks, Mt. Vernon.
Geo. H. Varnell, Mt. Vernon.
A. G. Henry, Greenville.
W. S. Smith, Greenville.

Geo. A. Boyle, Alton.
J. W. Koppinger, Alton.
H. G. McPike, Alton.
E. M. West, Edwardsville.
J. Gillespie, Edwardsville.
A. Keller, Edwardsville.
J. W. Ott, Virden.
H. W. Harrison, Belleville.
Samuel S. Page, Peoria.
Chas. D. Clark, Peoria.
P. D. Cheny, Jerseyville.

ILLINOIS—Continued.

T. M. Rogers, Quincy.
Wm. P. Halliday, Cairo.
C. F. Nellis, Cairo.
Chas. T. Ware, East St. Louis.
J. H. McCormick, Peoria.
Wm. L. Huse, Peoria.
John T. McBride, Chester.
C. C. Williams, Chester.
C. H. Seybt, Highland.
C. M. Wheeler, Kaskaskia.
J. G. Burch, Kaskaskia.
C. A. Roberts, Pekin.
E. F. Urland, Pekin.
J. Rickert, Waterloo.
H. O. Billings, Alton.
L. C. Washburn, Jerseyville.
J. Fouke, Vandalia.
R. T. Higgins, Vandalia.
F. M. Eckard, Vandalia.
E. S. Stoke, Centralia.
H. G. Weber, Belleville.
E. B. Buck, Charleston.
J. R. Cunningham, Charleston.
Chas A. Walker, Carlinville.
John I. Rinaker, Carlinville.
Walter S. Dray, Havana.
Samuel Bibens, Havana.
Anson Low, Havana.
N. B. Thistlewood, ——
W. T. Doudall, Peoria.
H. W. Clendin, Springfield.
W. W. Wallace, Newton.
Robt. W. Rees, Vandalia.
W. Y. Wetzell, Fulton.
G. A Henry, Louisville.
R. J. Burnes, Louisville.
Daniel Berry, Carmi.
J. A. Benner, Alton.

W. L. Huse, Peru.
Geo. W. Cox, Virdin.
H. S. Welton, Springfield.
J. J. McLean, East St. Louis.
D. Perrine, Newton.
F. J. Foster, Carmi.
B. L. Patrick, Carmi.
J. M. Crebs, Carmi.
J. W. Springer, Jacksonville.
J. F. Webb, Lebanon.
H. Leiter, Lebanon.
H. H. Horner, Lebanon.
S. P. Tufts, Centralia.
W. B. Grimsley, Springfield.
W. C. Bennett, Moline.
S. H. Velie, Moline.
Jas. H. Livingston, Alton.
R. H. Davis, Carrollton.
Orman Pierson, Carrollton.
J. Decker, Collinsville.
Jno. Higley, Collinsville.
J. G. Gerding, Collinsville.
W. R. Bush, Peoria.
Samuel Wilkinson, Peoria.
G. O. Webster, Salem.
H. C. Fellman, Salem.
J. S. Martin, Salem.
W. H. Allen, Grafton.
C. P. Stafford, Grafton.
L. Warnock, Columbia.
Jno. T. Angerer, Columbia.
D. H. Harez, Lincoln.
R. J. Hornsby, Bunker Hill.
H. N. Belt, Bunker Hill.
J. B. Bowman, East St. Louis.
Thos. C. Jennings, East St. Louis.
A. H. Gambrill, Alton.
J. B. Fahs, Olney.

QUINCY BOARD OF TRADE.

D. D. Meriam, Quincy.
H. R. Whitmore, Quincy.
Robt. E. Coxe, Quincy.

INDIANA.

Argus Dean, Otto.
Alfred Moore, Sr., Huntington.
M. M. Hurley, New Albany.
Jno. S. Hopkins, Evansville.
G. V. Menzies, Mount Vernon.
J. M. Reynolds, Lafayette.
A. D. Straight, Indianapolis.
Josiah Grim, New Albany.
R. S. Taylor, Fort Wayne.
C. A. Zollinger, Fort Wayne.
M. J. Hamilton, Fort Wayne.
A. C. Troutman, Fort Wayne.
Chas. F. Muhler, Fort Wayne.
J. J. Swuzich, Evansville.

Chas. T. Hinde, Evansville.
A. J. Branch, Evansville.
John Gilbert, Evansville.
J. A. Leincke, Evansville.
Jno. W. Bingham, Evansville.
Wm. Rahm, Jr., Evansville.
J. A. Forsythe, Seymour.
W. C. Fahrer, Mount Vernon.
A. Coleman, Logansport.
J. W. Talbott, Logansport.
Jno. W. Grubb, Richmond.
L. R. Wolcott, Mitchell.
W. E. Gibson, Aurora.
E. D. Langton, Aurora.

INDIANAPOLIS BOARD OF TRADE.

D. Blackmore, Indianapolis.

Jno. M. Shaw, Indianapolis.

IOWA.

Robert Donahue, Burlington.
John Thompson, Dubuque.
George H. French, Davenport.
Geo. W. Jones, Dubuque.
N. C. Ridenour, Clarinda.
E. H. Thayer, Clinton.
J. K. Graves, Dubuque.
Wm. Vandever, Dubuque.
J. H. Murphy, Davenport.
Edward Russell, Davenport.
P. G. Ballingall, Ottumwa.
Wm. L. Joy, Sioux City.
R. B. Tomlinson, Cedar Rapids.
H. Schierholz, Lansing.
Robt. Hufschmidt, Lansing.
H. H. Hemenway, Lansing.
J. W. Thomas, Lansing.
E. C. Herrick, Cherokee.
Robert Buchanan, Cherokee.
C. F. Myers, Rockford.
R. C. Mathews, Rockford.
A. C. Roberts, Fort Madison.

C. M. Primeau, Fort Madison.
J. P. Patrick, McGregor.
G. S. C. Scott, McGregor.
Wm. Butler, Clarinda.
W. E. Webster, Clarinda.
E. Van Houten, Pella.
S. A. Marine, Vinton.
J. Hageman, Keokuk.
J. H. Craig, Keokuk.
L. Bentley, Malvern.
Thos. Gernett, Mendon.
S. Casaday, Des Moines.
H. C. Colver, Des Moines.
L. Mott, Des Moines.
B. A. Lockwood, Des Moines.
J. J. Town, Des Moines.
E. C. Leach, Des Moines.
C. H. Toll, Clinton.
J. H. Flint, Clinton.
W. F. Coan, Clinton.
E. H. Odell, Council Bluffs.

BURLINGTON BOARD OF TRADE.

W. W. Baldwin, Burlington.

J. C. Osgood, Burlington.

KANSAS.

J. P. Root, Wyandotte.
C. M. Keller, Wichita.
D. G. Stockwell, Atchison.
J. M. Smith, Atchison.
J. H. Bonsall, Arkansas City.
W. H. Caldwell, Beloit.
Alfred Taylor, Gardner.
A. D. Brown, Gardner.
David Grimes, Burlington.
A. B. Jetmore, Topeka.
F. P. Baker, Topeka.
A. L. House, Topeka.
A. B. Lemon, Newton.
J. G. Stonecker, Topeka.
Dr. Cornell, Wyandotte.
V. J. Lane, Wyandotte.
N. A. Ocheltree, Olathe.
H. A. Taylor, Olathe.
S. Guerrier, Emporia.

KENTUCKY.

Frank Troutman, Eminence.
Eugene Underwood, Louisville.
W. W. Hite, Louisville.
Lucian Anderson, Mayfield.
B. C. Levi, Louisville.
Jno. A. Robertson, Bowling Green.
S. W. Combs, Bowling Green.
E. Farly, Paducah.
J. C. Cobb, Paducah.
J. H. Fowler, Paducah.

Thomas James, National Board of Steam Navigation, Louisville.

LOUISVILLE BOARD OF TRADE.

Chris. Busche, Louisville.
H. Verhoeff, Jr., Louisville.
Jos. O'Connor, Louisville.
Frank Carter, Louisville.
C. B. Robinton, Louisville.
W. B. Gray, Louisville.

LOUISIANA.

Duncan F. Kenner, New Orleans.
Dr. J. B. Wilkinson, Plaquemine.
Capt. Dick Sinnett, New Orleans.
Capt. Richard Frances, Port Eads.
Capt. John Roy, New Orleans.
Capt. B. D. Wood, New Orleans.
Capt. Thos. B. Leathers, New Orleans.
Capt. Jas. T. O. Pry, New Orleans.
Capt. A. Q. Kennett, New Orleans.
Jas. Lingau, New Orleans.
Wright Schaumburg, New Orleans.
Oscar J. Forstall, New Orleans.
G. L. Hall, New Orleans.
Geo. Foster, New Orleans.
A. Currie, Cotton Exchange, Shreveport.
J. M. Dowling, Steamboat Association, New Orleans.
C. J. Barrow, New Orleans.
H. C. Brown, Baton Rouge.

NEW ORLEANS PRODUCE EXCHANGE.

E. K. Converse, New Orleans.
Geo. E. Sears, New Orleans.
Geo. Maxent, New Orleans.
J. M. Frowenfeld, New Orleans.
C. F. Dillingham, New Orleans.
Thos. A. Clayton, New Orleans.
Ex-Gov. John McEnery, New Orleans.
S. P. Hill, New Orleans.

NEW ORLEANS COTTON EXCHANGE.

A. J. Gomila, New Orleans.
A. A. Lelong, New Orleans.

NEW ORLEANS CHAMBER OF COMMERCE.

F. J. Odendahl, New Orleans.
S. A. Trufant, New Orleans.
W. H. Bell, New Orleans.
J. D. Pelt, New Orleans.
M. F. Pinckard, New Orleans.

MISSISSIPPI.

H. F. Simrall, Vicksburg.
S. H. Parisot, Vicksburg.
C. E. Webb, Vicksburg.
Green Clay, Boliver Landing.

MISSOURI.

J. F. Philips, Sedalia.
James R. Shields, Carthage.
A. H. Livington, West Plains.
H. H. Mitchell, Bolivar.
C. B. McAfee, Springfield.
James R. Milner, Springfield.
J. H. Turner, Carrollton.
W. H. Phelps, Carthage.
Wm. S. Jewett, Crystal City.
Mepher Huy, Crystal City.
K. Coates, Kansas City.
C. W. Baker, Mexico.
A. E. Simpson, M. D., Charleston.
C. R. Combs, Memphis.
W. Dan Fowler, Memphis.
Geo. Myers, Glenwood.
H. H. Harding, Carthage.
Firmin A. Rozier, St. Genevieve.
John L. Bogy, Ste. Genevieve.
Charles C. Rozier, Mayor City of Ste. Genevieve.
Gustavus St. Gem, Ste. Genevieve.
O. Koshtitzky, New Madrid.
Dr. M. G. Hatcher, New Madrid.
Hon. Wm. Dawson, New Madrid.
Geo. B. Clark, Cape Girardeau.
M. A. Gilbert, Ste. Mary.
Louis Schaff, Ste. Mary.
J. H. Morse, Jefferson county.
J. H. Wheeling, Steelville.
Capt. O. T. Irons, Rolla.
L. I. Matthews, Carthage.
R. E. Lewis, Huntsville.
L. E. Cooley, St. Charles.
A. F. Jones, Maryville.

J. W. Chambers, Maryville.
S. Harris, Cape Girardeau.
G. C. Thilenius, Cape Girardeau.
A. B. Carroll, Cape Girardeau.
M. A. Bierwirth, Cape Girardeau.
Wm. Warner, Cape Girardeau.
Wm. V. Leech, Cape Girardeau.
W. Speed Stephens, Boonville.
John Porter, Boonville.
John Doniphan, St. Joseph.
James E. Payne, Independence.
Alexander Graydon, Carthage.
Waddy Thompson, Warrensburg.
O. P. Davis, Seliegman.
H. Eshbaugh, Hanover.
J. W. Boulware, Fulton.
J. B. Snell, Fulton.
Geo. Hubbard, Fulton.
Charles T. D. Eitzen, Hermann.
Thos. J. Johnston, Hermann.
R. Q. Roache, California.
Jno. E. Pearson, California.
J. P. H. Gray, California.
D. C. Basey, Brunswick.
Mack J. Leaming, Jefferson City.
J. H. Waugh, Columbia.
O. Gentae, Columbia.
Richard Gentry, Columbia.
C. H. Hardin, Mexico.
John F. Rucker, Sturgeon.
S. Phillips, Mexico.
John F. Williams, Macon.
F. B. Kercheval, St. Joseph.
Martin J. Hubble, Marshfield.
W. R. Samuel, Randolph Co.

MISSOURI —Continued.

J. Piner, St. Joseph.
J. W. Ringo, St. Joseph.
E. Wagner, St. Joseph.
R. Womark, St. Joseph.
F. B. Thompson, St. Joseph.
S. Geiger, St. Joseph.
A. Geiger, St. Joseph.
A. Saltzman, St. Joseph.
E. J. Crowther, St. Joseph.
M. J. McCabe, St. Joseph.
Dr. J. H. Stringfellow, Buchanan County.
E. W. Price, Brunswick.
W. H. Lusk, Jefferson City.
Wm. W. Wagner, Jefferson City.
W. H. Lee, Warrensburg.
C. H. Miller, Jefferson City.
Jno. A. Collins, Washington.
H. Wellenkamp, Washington.
Anton Reuter, Washington.
J. T. Childs, Richmond.
Jos. Hughes, Richmond.
Hermann Ferguson, Steelville.
G. F. Rothwell, Moberly.
J. J. Russell, Charleston.
Jos. M. Lowe. Plattsburgh.
Jos. H. Birch, Plattsburgh.
J. P. Norvell, Richmond.
D. A. Ball, Louisiana.
T. J. C. Fogg, Louisiana.
H. C. St. Clair, Independence.

J. H. Decker, Hannibal.
D. M. Delany, Hannibal.
W. A. Jacobs, Chillicothe.
C. H. Mansur, Chillicothe.
E. D. Graham, Mexico.
P. W. Harding, Mexico.
R. E. Lawder, Mexico.
Wm. Pollock, Mexico.
H. A. Ricketts, Mexico.
J. Schirmer, Jefferson City.
Robt. M. White, Mexico.
T. M. Gill, Mexico.
J. McD. Trimble, Mexico.
G. A. Burkhardt, California.
J. H. Burkholder, Moberly.
A. W. Lamb, Hannibal.
Thos. E. Day, Mexico.
J. B. Forbis, Jr., Independence.
Theodore Bruere, St. Charles.
W. A. Alexander, St. Charles.
A. H. Stonebraker, St. Charles.
E. G. Lunceford, Bolivar.
Charles Rosenbaum, Fayette.
D. S. Thomas, Carthage.
Champ. Clark, Bowling Green.
Henry McPherson, Boonville.
Jonas Clark, Carthage.
J. W. Wingo, Salem.
John R. Reddick, Salem.
Kossuth N. Webber, Farmington.
J. S. Rollins, Columbia.

ST. LOUIS MERCHANTS' EXCHANGE.

E. O. Stanard, St. Louis.
Julius S. Walsh, St. Louis.
Gerard B. Allen, St. Louis.
Nathan Cole, St. Louis.
Frank Gaiennie, St. Louis.
George L. Wright, St. Louis.
Chas. F. Orthwein, St. Louis.
E. W. Gould, St. Louis.
M. McEnnis, St. Louis.
H. Lourey, St. Louis.
P. D. Rowland, St. Louis.
Wayman Crow, St. Louis.

Marcus Bernheimer, St. Louis.
G. H. Shields, St. Louis.
A. Krieckhaus, St. Louis.
James E. Yeatman, St. Louis.
Robert B. Brown, St. Louis.
Thos. C. Reynolds, St. Louis.
Louis Fusz, St. Louis.
John Wahl, St. Louis.
J. G. Baker, St. Louis.
Web. M. Samuel, St. Louis.
Wm. J. Lemp, St. Louis.
E. F. Huppe, St. Louis.

ST. LOUIS MERCHANTS' EXCHANGE—Continued.

George Bain, St. Louis.
G. A. Madill, St. Louis.
J. O'Neil, St. Louis.
R. P. Tansey, St. Louis.
J. T. Davis, St. Louis.
W. H. Scudder, St. Louis.
J. M. Noble, St. Louis.
Conrad Fath, St. Louis.
D. P. Dyer, St. Louis.
A. H. Smith, St. Louis.
Erastus Wells, St. Louis.
B. W. Lewis, St. Lewis.
George Partridge, St. Louis.
Wm. L. Ewing, St. Louis.
John Hogan, St. Louis.
Pierre Chouteau, St. Louis.

Alex. Cochran, St. Louis.
A. T. Harlow, St. Louis.
Henry C. Haarstick, St. Louis.
Charles Parsons, St. Louis.
John Jackson, St. Louis.
S. M. Breckenridge, St. Louis.
Henry Hitchcock, St. Louis.
E. B. Kirby, St. Louis.
John M. Gilkeson, St. Louis.
Miles Sells, St. Louis.
C. E. Slayback, St. Louis.
Jerome Hill, St. Louis.
Given Campbell, St. Louis.
Waldo P. Johnson, St. Louis.
A. W. Slayback, St. Louis.
John R. Shipley, St. Louis.

ST. LOUIS COTTON EXCHANGE.

Theo. G. Meier, St. Louis.
A. W. Mitchell, St. Louis.
W. M. Senter, St. Louis.

James L. Sloss, St. Louis.
W. C. Madeira, St. Louis.
J. W. Paramore, St. Louis.

ST. LOUIS WOOL DEALERS' ASSOCIATION.

J. C. Love, St. Louis.

W. F. Warner, St. Louis.

SEDALIA BOARD OF TRADE.

A. A. Jaynes, Sedalia.
F. Houston, Sedalia.

Jno. T. Heard, Sedalia.

KANSAS CITY BOARD OF TRADE.

W. H. Miller, Kansas City.
R. T. Van Horn, Kansas City.

E. H. Allen, Kansas City.
T. B. Bullene, Kansas City.

ST. JOSEPH BOARD OF TRADE.

H. R. W. Hartwig, St. Joseph.
Col. Jno. Doniphan, St. Joseph.

Gen. James Craig, St. Joseph.
Abe Furst, St. Joseph.

MINNESOTA.

W. B. Lutz, Lake City.
J. O. Simmons, Little Falls.
Platt B. Walker, Minneapolis.
Fred. Driscoll, St. Paul.
M. G. Norton, Winona.
E. L. Baker, Red Wing.
E. W. Durant, Stillwater.

F. A. Fogg, St. Paul.
T. B. Casey, Minneapolis.
R. C. Leavitt, Minneapolis.
V. G. Hush, Minneapolis.
Mark H. Dunnell, Owatonna.
F. M. Thornton, Benson.

MINNEAPOLIS BOARD OF TRADE.

C. C. Sturtevant, Minneapolis.
O. C. Merrimon, Minneapolis.
Col. G. F. Brott, Minneapolis.
Col. R. H. Benton, Minneapolis.

ST. PAUL CHAMBER OF COMMERCE.

R. Blakely, St. Paul.
Wm. Leip, St. Paul.
I. W. Ingersoll, St. Paul.
W. F. Davidson, St. Paul.
Edmund Rice, St. Paul.
J. W. McClung, St. Paul.
G. W. Walsh, St. Paul.

WINONA BOARD OF TRADE.

Wm. F. Phelps. Secretary.
H. C. Bolcom.

MICHIGAN.

A. Sessions, Ionia.
Philo Parsons, Detroit.

NEBRASKA.

R. B. Windham, Plattsmouth.
J. Carson, Brownville.
C. C. Housel, Omaha.
Victor Vilquain, Lincoln.
O. P. Mason, Lincoln.
H. T. Clark, Bellevue.
J. Sterling Morton, Nebraska City.
Frank Martin, Falls City,
C. H. Rickards, Falls City.
W. W. Hackney, Brownville.
Henry Sheldon, Nebraska City.
Champion S. Chase, Omaha.
H. G. Clark, Omaha.
S. J. Faris, Nebraska City.
J. E. LaMaster, Nebraska City.

NEW YORK.

B. S. Osborne, Secretary National Board of Steam Navigation, New York.
A. H. Dugan, National Board of Steam Navigation, New York.

NEW MEXICO.

P. J. Kennedy.

OHIO.

John A. Townley, Cincinnati.
John Newton, Marietta.

CINCINNATI BOARD OF TRADE.

S. F. Covington, Cincinnati.
W. L. Perkins, Cincinnati.
Jos. Hargrave. Cincinnati.
W. W. Peabody, Cincinnati.
J. G. Stove, Cincinnati.
S. F. Dana, Cincinnati.
Jos. A. Scarlett, Cincinnati.

CINCINNATI CHAMBER OF COMMERCE.

E. C. Goshorn, Cincinnati.
Paris C. Brown, Cincinnati.
G. W. Neare, Cincinnati.
J. J. Raipe, Cincinnati.
Jas. K. Morrison, Cincinnati.

PENNSYLVANIA.

Capt. R. C. Gray, Pittsburg.
Hon. G. H. Anderson, Pittsburg.
Jas. G. Siebeneck, Pittsburg.
Capt. J. T. Stockdale, Pittsburg.
Hon. H. S. Shallenberger, Roches'r

Capt. John A. Wood, Pittsburg.
Charles Meyran, Pittsburg.
P. C. Knox, Pittsburgh.
J. H. Dunlap, Pittsburg.
John A. Keys, Pittsburg.

TENNESSEE.

Edward S. Jones, Nashville.
H. T. Ellett, Memphis.
R. J. Morgan, Memphis.
Smith Parks, Newburn.

W. O'Niel Perkins, Franklin.
J. B. Heiskell, Memphis.
S. H. Shock, Memphis.

TEXAS.

T. T. Gammage, Palestine.
W. H. Flippen, Dallas.

Geo. A. Wright, Palestine.
Thos. F. McEnnis, Dallas.

WEST VIRGINIA.

Alexander Campbell, Bethany.
John A. Gibney, Wheeling.
D. R. Wolfe, Wheeling.

F. O. Hearne, Wheeling.
John W. Good, Wheeling.

WISCONSIN.

E. Mariner, Milwaukee.
H. J. Rogers, Appleton.
Charles E. Mears, Osceola Mills.
W. T. Price, Block River Falls.
Wm. Wilson, Menomonee.
J. C. Gregory, Madison.

J. R. Berryman, Prairie Du Chien.
J. H. Foster, Oshkosh.
B. J. Stevens, Madison.
O. H. Ingram, Eau Claire.
D. A. McDonald, LaCrosse.
John C. Huggins, Racine.

USHERS.

J. W. M. Boyd, St. Louis.
Walter S. Bartley, St. Louis.

E. B. Grace, St. Louis.
E. B. Eno, St. Louis.

PAGES.

W. J. Lemp, Jr., St. Louis.
Edward McEnnis, St. Louis.
Thomas Booth, Jr., St. Louis.

Booth Alexander, St. Louis.
Ben Allen Samuel, St. Louis.
Michael McEnnis, Jr., St. Louis.

MEMORIAL TO CONGRESS.

To the Senate and House of Representatives of the United States, in General Assembly convened:

The Executive Committee of the Mississippi River Improvement Convention, held in the city of St. Louis, Missouri, in October last, under one of the resolutions unanimously adopted, were charged with the duty of preparing and presenting to the Congress of the United States, a Memorial embodying the action of the Convention, accompanied with such statistics and information as the Committee might deem expedient.

The Convention which committed this grave duty to your memorialists was one representing, in an unusual degree, the commercial and industrial power of the country. The highest order of talent, judgment, matured by careful thought and large experience of the great question so intimately connected with the progress and development of the imperial domain comprehended, met in council, and the important question was considered by men representing twenty States and three Territories, and half the population of the Union. Not less remarkable was the variety of interests gathered and given utterance to there. The farmers, the merchants, the bankers, the manufacturers, the professions, and the heads of great transportation lines by river and rail, with earnest zeal discussed, and with striking unanimity reached the conclusions embodied in the resolutions adopted by the Convention, and which it now becomes the duty of your memorialists to urge upon the National Legislature.

The Convention was no new move, and the presentation of its conclusions is but a repetition of a thrice-told tale.

For a half century, from the period when the now mighty West was but a wilderness, the people of the Valley have from time to time gathered to present the claims of the noble streams which intersect it, and to urge upon the General Government the necessity and the duty of so improving them that they would become the cheap and convenient highways for intercommunication between the producers of the upper and the lower valley. The grand culmination of these gatherings was presented when, on the 26th of last October, the last Mississippi River Convention assembled in the city of St. Louis. Meantime, the progress of trade, the development of industrial resources, the growth of population, have invested the movement with vaster importance. It is no longer a matter of local interests, but of national, in truth, of international importance, and as such we commend its action to your consideration.

The initial proposition is, that just in proportion as the rates of carriage have been diminished, the growth of the West can be traced, and that the question of cheap transportation is found underlying all progress and development.

Just in proportion that the aid of the Government has been given to render the water-ways safe and easy to navigation, just in that proportion have freights been cheapened, have the burdens and expenses upon capital and labor been removed, have disasters destructive to life and property been averted, and the beneficent results of commerce showered upon all the people of the country.

In view of such results, it may be deemed strange that the aid of the General Government has been accorded to the West, in a ratio so incommensurate with the whole benefit to be realized, while to artificial and expensive modes, money and credit to more than a hundred millions have been given, and the choicest public domain lavished with unstinted generosity, while scarcely a fourth of that princely sum has been bestowed upon the great water-ways, and the lands given for their improvement and safety were only made useful and valuable by the toil and the taxes of the people of the lower valley in the vain and unequal contest with the destroying floods. The losses in property for lack of the aid which the Government might have easily given, have in single years of disaster exceeded all that has ever been given to the improvement of the channel of the Mississippi river.

Your memorialists in presenting such facts would not be understood as challenging the acts of Congress in granting liberal aid to the system of artificial carriage. These systems have been grand and noble factors of the material career, the splendid co-workers of a progressive and vitalizing civilization. The combinations of the two systems have been required to give the complete development witnessed throughout the whole country. Neither, alone, could have wrought the results which, unitedly, they have achieved. We invite your careful attention to some of these results. In the area drained from north to south by navigable water-ways, and intersected from east to west by lines of railroads, are produced nearly three-fourths of the food and textile products of the whole country, while in manufacturing industries it is destined as the natural center of food and material to become in the near future the proper home of all productive industry. To this it would be vain and idle to deny that the artificial lines have largely contributed.

Yet we can but point to the fact that as the two systems have been developed, the natural and cheaper route has been the counter-check of the artificial and more expensive, has saved to the producer the profits of capital, labor and industry, and cheapened the necessities of life to the consumer.

Even as the water-ways now stand, with imperfect and obstructed channels, one-eighth of the export trade of the country goes to the sea at less than one-third the cost at which it could be transported by rail. The establishment of a deep outlet at the South Pass, through the genius of Eads, the signal-light service at the shoal and dangerous localities, and the channel improvement effected by a meager dole from the National

Treasury, have in one season doubled the tonnage from the port of St. Louis alone, and raised the through shipments of bulk grain from 6,164,838 bushels in 1879 to 15,762,664 bushels in 1880, while the savings of freight have added millions to the profits of capital and labor. So we say, that while it was well and wise for Congress by liberal aid to foster and encourage the splendid features of greatness found in the railway system, it has not been either wise or well to withhold from the cheaper, and therefore more important channel the aid which would make them equal to the needs of a gigantic trade. "These things ye ought to have done, and not to have left the other undone."

Without stopping to consider in full the capabilities of the great valley, the full development of which is only to be found in the needed improvements of the Mississippi and its navigable tributaries, we can only point to the fact that in this area is contributed the proportion of seventy per cent. of the internal revenue; and that if the progress now manifested is fostered and enlarged by the liberal action of Government on this line, the strengthening of the national credit is assured, and the generation now emerging into the fields of active life can record the extinguishment of the national debt without a strain upon either individual citizen, or the resources of the States or the Nation. Here, the internal commerce is more than half that of all the country besides, is twelve times greater than its foreign commerce, aggregating in values the commerce of the world. This interior commerce carefully preserved to our citizens and jealously guarded by our laws finds its grandest field of profitable exercise upon the inland seas that span the continent, floating in various modes all the commodities to the ocean, to be thence borne to all the people abroad. The fact has been pointed out that the fleets of steamers and barges leaving the wharves of St. Louis in a single day would have accomplished on their return an aggregate voyage of 13,000 miles, and St. Louis is only one of the ports sending fleets of proximate magnitude throughout the Valley.

Nor need we pause to discuss the constitutional right of the Government in this behalf. On this, parties and sections are agreed, for it has been recognized as not only sanctioned by the Constitution but demanded by the necessities of the people, that it is the imperative duty of the Government to so improve these great arteries of trade that they shall be equal to all business needs. No one of the twenty States and Territories lying along the 15,000 miles of navigable waters comprised in the river system has either the power or right to set about improving the channels. The work of one would be found detrimental to the other. The whole system of improvement is a legitimate charge upon the Government, in the common interests of all, by plans at once uniform, intelligent and homogeneous. To this, as the Convention viewed it, the Government is fully committed.

First. By liberal appropriations made at the mouth of the river, which, in facilitating the export trade, the bulk of which is furnished by the staples of the West and South, have returned to the people of the Valley ten, nay, an hundred fold in benefits to trade, advantages and profits to labor.

Second. By the action of your body on the 28th of June, 1879, in the creating of the River Commission, a body charged with the work of improving the great river throughout its entire extent, and by the appropriations subsequently made to carry on its magnificent work.

Your memorialists point with great satisfaction to the hearty and unanimous endorsement given by the Convention to the work of so important a body created by yourselves, and to the earlier proceedings of which you gave your deliberate and emphatic approval. The Convention recognized the Commission as a fair, just, and liberal tribute to the great ends to be accomplished through it, and which, upon well-placed convictions, it declared could only be accomplished according to the plans formulated and estimates made by the Commission.

The Convention felt deeply and expressed itself warmly to

the effect, that the legislation so wisely, and the work so auspiciously begun, should be carried forward according to these plans, by regular and separate appropriations from year to year, such as shall be deemed necessary, and under the supervision of the body which created it. For that end we now ask your approval, and to its accomplishment urge your co-operation.

There are economic and advantageous considerations involved which we deem proper to press upon your attention. The action of the Convention was a hearty and unanimous response to the action of Congress in creating the Commission, and it would be a retrogression in legislative action to stop short of the end proposed; distasteful, too, to an energetic race, whose motto, under the impulses of destiny, is ever "forward." Besides the profits alike to the producer and consumer, pointed out by deepening and rectifying the channels of the water-ways, the ulterior and practical purpose of the Commission, is, by its work, to confine the river, even at flood seasons, to its bed, and thus reclaim to habitation and productive industry the vast and fertile regions of the lower riparian States, which, under the calamities of an unhappy past, have been remanded to the desolation of the wilderness.

Such a result is eminently commended alike to the generosity and unselfish patriotism of the whole people, and will restore homes long since abandoned, to those on whom the hand of misfortune has been heavily laid, give to suffering States the return of a needed property, and cement anew the ties of fraternal sympathy between once alienated sections, now seeking to blot out forever the memories of unhappy and unnatural discord.

The aid now asked, and benefits sought to be received through the liberal action of the Government, is not alone for the present, nor for the near succeeding years, but stretches to the distant future—that eventful and busy future for which it is the duty and business of statesmanship to prepare. The Valley States and those in the farther West and Southwest, bound together by the chords of a common interest, are fast gaining the political power which will make them the grantors instead of the solicitors of favors through the instrumentality of the Government. A compliance now with their reasonable demands will be gratefully recognized, and will hereafter find reciprocal response. A refusal will breed an antagonism of sections which may lead to sectional issues.

The action of the Convention was not a thing done in a corner, in the interest of sections, or to carry out the objects of parties. It was broadly national in its call, in its representative membership, and in its declared objects. It was the result of matured policies, to which the executive and representative authorities of one half, and far from the least important part of the Union, gave the most unqualified approval. To this members in both your houses can bear testimony.

And now we ask, can there be a more propitious time for the National Legislature to recognize the value and importance of the work?

The products of the Mississippi Valley, carried cheaply by the river route (and through its influence less expensively by rail) to the outer markets, have thrown the balance of the world's trade grandly in our favor. Since this power and influence has been recognized, for the first time in our history we now have, among kindred commercial nations, the rank of creditor. The long-sought position has been obtained through the agency of cheap transportation from the interior to the sea; a policy we can only maintain by carrying the thought to the utmost conclusion.

The report of the Secretary of the Treasury, and favorably presented by President Arthur in his message, shows a surplus revenue of over $100,000,000 for the last fiscal year, and the question suggests itself, how can this accruing surplus be properly and most beneficially expended. Those for whom we speak do not complain of the burdens of taxation. They do not ask for the present reduction or speedy extinguishment of the national debt, but they do ask that this surplus shall in part be applied to their great and cheap thoroughfares, feeling that when this is done they can bear the burdens imposed by the Government in the form of taxes, much easier than those resulting from defective and crippled transportation. Now, in the days of our prosperity, they ask those to whom they have entrusted their rights, to lay aside local antagonisms and sectional jealousies, to compass the height of the argument and conclusions presented, and meet the action of the Convention by the exercise of a statesmanship as broad and comprehensive as that which marked its deliberations.

E. O. STANARD, *Chairman*, St. Louis.
DUNCAN F. KENNER, New Orleans.
J. F. STOCKDALE, Pittsburg.
WM. P. HALLIDAY, Cairo.
MICHAEL McENNIS, St. Louis.
GEO. H. FRENCH, Davenport.
E. P. BAKER, Topeka.
CHAS. A. ZOLLINGER, Fort Wayne.
ALEX. CAMPBELL, West Virginia.
S. F. COVINGTON, Cincinnati.
NATHAN COLE, St. Louis.
C. C. STURTEVANT, Minneapolis.
JAMES CRAIG, St. Joseph.
WM. F. PHELPS, Winona.
H. G. CLARK, Omaha.
LOGAN H. ROOTS, Little Rock.
EUGENE UNDERWOOD, Louisville.
H. F. SIMRALL, Vicksburg.
ED. T. JONES, Nashville.
WM. CROOKS, St. Paul.
B. J. STEVENS, Madison, Wis.
Committee of Twenty-one.

GEORGE L. WRIGHT, *Secretary*, St. Louis.

STATEMENT OF VESSELS ENTERED AND CLEARED AT THE PORT OF NEW ORLEANS FROM JANUARY, 1877, TO DECEMBER, 1880.

Entered from January 1, 1877, to January 1, 1878.

American vessels from foreign ports	255
Foreign vessels from foreign ports	500
American and foreign vessels entered coastwise	311
Total for 1877	**1,066**

Entered from January 1, 1878, to January 1, 1879.

American vessels from foreign ports	270
Foreign vessels from foreign ports	612
Foreign and American vessels entered coastwise	264
Total for 1878	**1,146**

Entered from January 1, 1879, to January 1, 1880.

American vessels from foreign ports	232
Foreign vessels from foreign ports	573
Foreign and American vessels entered coastwise	328
Total for 1879	**1,133**

Entered from January 1, 1880, to January 1, 1881.

American vessels from foreign ports	269
Foreign vessels from foreign ports	706
Foreign and American vessels entered coastwise	364
Total for 1880	**1,339**

Cleared from January 1, 1877, to January 1, 1878.

American vessels for foreign ports	217
Foreign vessels for foreign ports	535
American and foreign vessels cleared coastwise	383
Total for 1877	**1,135**

Cleared from January 1, 1878, to January 1, 1879.

American vessels for foreign ports	206
Foreign vessels for foreign ports	594
American and foreign vessels cleared coastwise	370
Total for 1878	**1,170**

Cleared from January 1, 1879, to January 1, 1880.

American vessels for foreign ports	193
Foreign vessels for foreign ports	637
American and foreign vessels cleared coastwise	411
Total for 1879	**1,241**

Cleared from January 1, 1880, to January 1, 1881.

American vessels for foreign ports	226
Foreign vessels for foreign ports	768
American and foreign vessels cleared coastwise	355
Total for 1880	**1,349**

INDEX.

Title page..	1
Preface...	3— 4

SECTION 1.—FIRST DAY.

Calling the Convention to order, by Michael McEnnis............	5
Reading the "Official Call".......................................	5— 8
Address of Michael McEnnis......................................	8— 10
Address of Welcome, by Hon. Henry Hitchcock...................	10— 23
Election of Gov. T. T. Crittenden, of Missouri, as Temporary Chairman...	23
Address of Governor Crittenden.................................	23— 25
Selection of Committee on Credentials...........................	26— 33
Chairmen of Delegations..	33— 34
Selection of Committees on Permanent Organization, Order of Business, and Resolutions.....................................	37— 43
Address of Gen. Jones, of Iowa.................................	45— 46

SECTION 2.—SECOND DAY.

Prayer by Rev. W. G. Eliot......................................	50— 51
Report of Committee on Order of Business......................	52
Report of Committee on Permanent Organization................	53
Address of Hon. Mark H. Dunnell...............................	54— 56
Communication from President of the Mississippi River Commission..	56— 60
Letter from Capt. James B. Eads................................	60
" " Hon. Randall L. Gibson............................	61— 63
" " Hon. James B. Beck................................	64
" " Hon. A. D. Gorman.................................	64
" " Hon. Abram S. Hewitt..............................	65
" " Hon. B. F. Jonas...................................	66
" " Hon. Thomas L. James.............................	66
" " Hon. George B. Loring.............................	66
" " Hon. Joseph R. Hawley............................	67
" " Hon. R. G. Horr....................................	67
" " Hon. Thomas Updegraff............................	67
Reception of Resolutions..	69— 89
Communication from Hon. James S. Rollins.....................	90— 95
Letter of Invitation, Hulsey C. Ives.............................	95

Letter of Invitation, John N. Dyer............................ 96
Reception of more Resolutions................................ 96— 98
Address of Judge R. S. Taylor................................ 99—105
Speech of Capt. McKenzie..................................... 107
"   " Hon. Joseph G. Cannon................................ 108—110
"   " Gen. Rozier... 111—112
Report of the Committee on Resolutions....................... 113—116
Debate on Supplemental Report................................ 118—130

SECTION 3.—THIRD DAY.

Telegram from Hon. James G. Blaine........................... 131
Renewal of Debate on Supplemental Report..................... 132
Speech upon it by Ex-Gov. McEnery, of La..................... 132
"   "   " Judge Murphy, of Iowa........................ 133—135
"   "   " Ex-Gov. E. O. Stanard, of Mo................ 135
"   "   " Hon. Henry Hitchcock, of Mo.................. 137
"   "   " Mr. Benton, of Minn.......................... 137
"   "   " Hon. A. W. Slayback, of Mo.................. 138—139
"   "   " Hon. Philo Parsons, of Mich................. 140
"   "   " Hon. T. B. Taylor, of Ala................... 141
"   "   " Hon. Eugene Underwood, of Ky................ 141—144
"   "   " Mr. Rozier, of Mo............................ 144
"   "   " Hon. Geo. H. Shields, of Mo................. 145—146
"   "   " Hon. John T. White, of Ky................... 147—150
"   "   " Hon. H. T. Elliot, Tenn..................... 150—152
"   "   " Dr. J. P. Root, Kas......................... 154
Debate on Resolution of Mr. P. B. Walker, of Minn............ 156—159
Address of Hon. W. S. Shallenberger, of Penn................. 159
Resolutions of Thanks.. 162
Speech of Congressman Willis, of Ky.......................... 162—164
"   "   Hon. Wm. M. Springer........................... 165—166
Adjournment.. 167
Excursion on the River....................................... 167—171

SECTION 4.—LETTERS.

Letter from Hon. John A. Kasson.............................. 172
"   "   Hon. E. C. Lacy.................................. 172
"   "   Hon. A. H. Garland............................... 173
"   "   Hon. T. W. Ferry................................ 173
"   "   Hon. H. W. Lord................................. 173
"   "   Hon. Alvin Saunders............................. 174
"   "   Hon. John H. Gear............................... 174—175
"   "   Hon. Albert S. Willis........................... 175
"   "   Hon. Chas. E. Hooker............................ 176
"   "   Hon. Eugene Hale................................ 176
"   "   Hon. James Wheeler.............................. 177
"   "   Hon. W. H. Hatch................................ 177

"	"	Hon. Wm. Aldrich...............................	177
"	"	Hon. R. M. A. Hawk............................	178
"	"	Hon. J. H. Lewis................................	178
"	"	Hon. Mark L. DeMotte..........................	179
"	"	Hon. Geo. W. Steele.............................	179
"	"	Hon. R. W. Townshend.........................	179—180
"	"	Hon. H. S. Harris...............................	180
"	"	Hon. H. B. Anthony.............................	180
"	"	Hon. F. M. Cockrell.............................	181
"	"	Hon. L. F. Watson..............................	182
"	"	Hon. J. J. Finley................................	182—183
"	"	Hon. John Sherman.............................	183
"	"	Hon. L. S. Farwell..............................	183
"	"	Hon. Benj. Harrison.............................	184
"	"	Hon. Wilkinson Call.............................	184
"	"	Hon. W. Hutchins...............................	184
"	"	Hon. J. B. Hoge.................................	185
"	"	Hon. N. C. Deering.............................	185
"	"	Hon. B. K. Bruce................................	185
"	"	Hon. J. K. Jones................................	186
"	"	Hon. C. B. Darrell..............................	186
"	"	Hon. W. C. Whitthorne.........................	186
"	"	Hon. John T. Morgan...........................	187
"	"	Hon. Wm. B. Moore.............................	187
"	"	Hon. A. C. Harmer..............................	188
"	"	Hon. Jas. M. Tyler..............................	188
"	"	Hon. Thos. H. Herndon.........................	188
"	"	Hon. G. G. Vest.................................	189
"	"	Hon. John D. Long..............................	189
"	"	Hon. Wm. W. Crapo.............................	190
"	"	New Orleans Produce Exchange..................	190
"	"	Pittsburg Chamber of Commerce.................	190
"	"	Forstall, Ross & Clayton........................	191—199

SECTION 5.—PRESS COMMENTS.

Detroit Free Press..	200—203
St. Paul Daily Dispatch...	203—205
Louisville Courier-Journal..	205
Globe-Democrat...	206—208
St. Louis Advance (Colored).....................................	208—209
St. Louis Post-Dispatch...	209
St. Louis Globe-Democrat..	209
Post-Dispatch...	210
St. Louis Republican..	210—211
The Nautical Gazette, N. Y......................................	211—214
St. Louis Post-Dispatch...	214
Louisville Courier-Journal..	215—216

The Spectator (St. Louis)	216
St. Louis Republican	217
New Orleans Picayune	218—221
Davenport Gazette	221

SECTION 6.

List of Delegates	222—230
Memorial to Congress	231—238
Statement of Vessels Entered and Cleared at New Orleans from January, 1877, to December, 1880	239

www.ingramcontent.com/pod-product-compliance
Lightning Source LLC
Chambersburg PA
CBHW031738230426
43669CB00007B/390